F 12-7-92

F 12-7-92

RECREATION LEADERSHIP TODAY

Richard G. Kraus
Temple University

SCOTT, FORESMAN AND COMPANY
Glenview, Illinois   London

Library of Congress Cataloging in Publication Data

Kraus, Richard G.
  Recreation leadership today.

  Includes index.
    1. Recreation leadership. 2. Recreation—Study and
teaching. 3. Recreation—Vocational guidance—United
States. I. Title
GV181.4.K72 1985   790'.023   85-1952
ISBN 0-673-18140-5

Portions of this book are based on *Recreation Today: Program Planning and Leadership*
by Richard G. Kraus. Copyright © 1977 Goodyear Publishing Co., Inc.

  2 3 4 5 6 7 - KPF - 90 89 88 87 86 85

PREFACE

The book, *Recreation Today: Program Planning and Leadership,* was first published in the mid-1960s and has been widely used in many college and university recreation, park, and leisure-services curricula since that time.

Recognizing that most such curricula today offer separate courses in program planning and leadership, it was decided to write two new specialized texts—one dealing with program planning and one with leadership. *Recreation Leadership Today* and its companion volume, *Recreation Program Planning Today,* are the obvious result. Although in many respects they are closely linked—just as are programs and leadership linked in professional practice—they are entirely independent publications in terms of purpose and content, and serve as distinctly separate learning resources.

Recreation Leadership Today presents an up-to-date analysis of the role of leisure-service professionals in terms of direct program involvement. It has many references drawn from the current literature, and from manuals, guidelines, and other materials submitted by recreation and park agencies throughout the United States and Canada which describe current leadership practices in the 1980s.

Beyond this, the book presents a contemporary view of leadership. In the past, leaders were thought of as individuals working primarily with children and youth in parks, playgrounds, and community centers. Today, it is recognized that the settings for organized recreation service have diversified greatly, and that any discussion of the role of leaders must include public, voluntary, commercial, therapeutic, corporate/employee, and other sponsors. Beyond this, it is also recognized that the term *leader* may not be as widely used in such departments as in public agencies; instead, practitioners may be called therapists, specialists, activity directors or coordinators, or may have other titles. A third important development reflected in the text is that many leisure-service agencies have shifted to "marketing" or "human-service" program models, and that leadership personnel in such agencies have assumed new and innovative functions based on these new models.

Recreation Leadership Today seeks to present this contemporary view of leadership as fully and realistically as possible. At the same time that it offers a conceptual analysis of leadership qualities and styles and of group dynamics, it also provides a practical selection of program activities and guidelines for presenting them effectively.

Part One, "Introduction to Recreation Leadership," defines leadership and presents an overview of the role of recreation leaders in modern society. It describes different types of sponsoring agencies, and summarizes current research on group dynamics and varying leadership styles. Based on a thorough review of the literature and on manuals and other printed materials published by numerous leisure-service agencies, it identifies the typical roles and functions of leaders and presents guidelines for their effective performance.

Part Two, "Activities for Recreation Leaders," describes several major categories of program activity from a leadership perspective, such as sports, games, and fitness activities, or music, drama, and dance. While this section of the text does not attempt to provide a comprehensive encyclopedia of program activities and events, it *does* offer a broad range of actual games, dances, arts and crafts projects, and similar pastimes which can be used to plan events and have in-class workshops in teaching and leading activities. Most of these activities represent familiar, "tried-and-true" program elements, and instructors and students should be encouraged to add other, newer activities to them, to reflect changing interests or current fads.

Part Three, "Specialized Functions and Career Development," includes a useful chapter dealing with problem-solving techniques based on small-group leadership methods and participative management approaches. It ends with two chapters dealing with the process of professional development and with the more personal concerns of students with respect to embarking on a career in this field, building a solid foundation of experience, and striving to become a better leader.

Each chapter throughout the text ends with a set of suggested readings or brief bibliography. In addition, each chapter also offers either a set of suggested questions for class discussion or several student projects. The projects involve practical tasks that may be carried out by individuals or groups of students, usually including presentations to be made before the class or leadership activities involving class members. Instructors are strongly urged to make use of these projects to help students sharpen and practice leadership skills, and to help make classes more interesting and challenging. However, instructors should involve students in planning such sessions within a framework of shared decision-making, rather than rely on an autocratic approach to class scheduling.

The purpose of this text is to provide faculty members and students with a comprehensive, systematic, and up-to-date collection of ideas and materials concerned with the process of recreation leadership. It is based on the conviction that recreation is a vital human experience and form of community service—and that leadership is the essential element that helps to make it successful.

Richard G. Kraus

ACKNOWLEDGMENTS ⎯⎯⎯⎯⎯⎯⎯⎯⎯⎯⎯

Numerous individuals and leisure-service agencies contributed significantly to the preparation of this text. Among the public recreation and park departments, for example, that have provided examples of their leadership manuals or annual reports, or that sent photographs or other useful materials, are: Oakland County, Michigan, Park and Recreation Commission; Bureau of Recreation, Reading, Pennsylvania; Portland, Oregon, Park Bureau; Department of Municipal Recreation and Adult Education, of the Milwaukee, Wisconsin, Public Schools; Essex County, New Jersey, Department of Parks, Recreation, and Cultural Affairs; and the Portsmouth, Virginia, Parks and Recreation Commission.

In Canada, public recreation and park agencies sending useful materials include: City of Nepean, Ontario, Recreation Department; Board of Parks and Recreation, Vancouver, British Columbia; and the Province of Saskatchewan Department of Culture and Recreation.

In the United States, numerous armed forces bases provided newsletters, manuals, and other reports of their programs and services, including: the Natural Resources Branch of the U.S. Army Corps of Engineers; the Naval Military Personnel Command; the Charleston, South Carolina, Air Force Base; the Naval Air Station in Leemore, California; and the Eighth Army Recreation Services Operation in Korea (EUSA ROK). A number of well-known commercial recreation sponsors and manufacturers sent useful materials, including: WaveTek Automated Swimpools, Inc., of Mansfield, Ohio; Sesame Place, Langhorne, Pennsylvania; GameTime, Fort Payne, Alabama; Busch Gardens of Williamsburg, Virginia, and the Busch Entertainment Group. The Wells Fargo Company provided descriptions of its National Fitness Campaign; and descriptive materials were also received from the Hershey National Track and Field Youth Program.

Numerous examples of leadership guidelines and program activities were received from agencies serving special populations, including: Special Olympics; Napa State Hospital, Imola, California; Moss Hospital, Philadelphia; Camp Confidence, the Minnesota Therapeutic Camp, Brainerd, Minnesota; Camp Courageous of Monticello, Iowa; the Patton, California, Developmental Center; the Children's Seashore House, Atlantic City, New Jersey; and the Recreation Center for the Handicapped in San Francisco. Canadian therapeutic recreation agencies include: Souris Valley Regional

Care Centre, Weyburn, Saskatchewan; the Penetanguishene, Ontario, Mental Health Centre; and the Ontario March of Dimes in Toronto.

Individuals who were particularly helpful in providing leadership materials in specific areas included: Anne Mattes, formerly of the Cigna Corporation, who assisted in the area of corporate/employee recreation; Pam Crespi, now of the Operations Division, Naval Material Command, of the Department of the Navy; and Kenneth Joswiak, coordinator of the Center for Individuals with Disabilities (CID), a joint program of the City, County, and Unified School District of San Bernardino, California.

Three reviewers, Charles Corbin and Randy Virden of Arizona State University and Linda Hook of Georgia Southern College, contributed perceptive reviews that were helpful in the revision of the manuscript. The author also wishes to thank Roger Holloway of Scott, Foresman and Company for his assistance and support in carrying out this project.

CONTENTS

PART 3
Specialized Functions and Career Development 224

CHAPTER 11
Leadership of Human-Service Activities 226

CHAPTER 12
Problem-Solving: Principles and Methods 236

CHAPTER 13
Professional Development in Recreation Leadership 253

PART 1

Introduction to Recreation Leadership

Recreation leadership takes many approaches. Here, disabled children in Oakland County, Michigan, take a bus trip while participants of all ages attend a band concert in Mt. Vernon, New York. Honeywell Corporation employees in Minneapolis plan their own recreational events, and Omaha day campers take part in flag-raising ceremonies. Reading, Pennsylvania, youngsters enjoy a nature tour, and Omaha campers compete in a play-day tug-of-war contest.

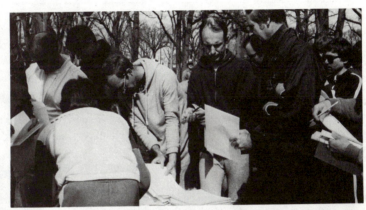

CHAPTER 1

Leadership in Recreation Service Today

Many young people who enter the recreation and park field today do so with an immense amount of enthusiasm, based on their own experiences in varied forms of leisure activity or as members of youth organizations.

However, often their understanding of the recreation field is limited. They are likely to think of leadership solely in terms of the playground or center leaders they encountered in their childhood, or the coaches and club leaders they encountered later in voluntary organizations. Typically, they will regard recreation programming as being concerned primarily with sports and games, arts and crafts, or similar group pastimes.

The purpose of this text is to broaden the background of such readers and to give them a fuller understanding of the roles of recreation leaders in many different types of community organizations. It presents a number of the key concepts that underlie successful leadership today, describes the goals and programs of several major types of recreation agencies, and analyzes leadership techniques in the most popular recreational activity areas.

IMPORTANCE OF LEADERSHIP

Organized recreation service has many essential elements, including the provision of adequate facilities and funding, and the administrative structure of sponsoring agencies. However, of all of these, the key component is *leadership!*

Leadership is absolutely essential in providing the expertise, enthusiasm, and varied skills needed to make recreation programs successful. It is the central theme of this book, and is presented here in both conceptual and practical terms. Essentially, it is the text's purpose to help the reader understand the dynamics of leadership in varied leisure-service settings, as it helps individuals of many types and backgrounds meet their needs for enriching and refreshing recreational involvement.

Any young man or woman who seeks to enter the recreation field should have a clear understanding of the nature of leadership and the skills and strategies it employs. Although such individuals may move rapidly to supervisory or managerial job responsibilities, it will always be necessary for them to be able to guide and direct other staff members who carry out important group leadership functions.

Before examining leadership itself, it is helpful to gain a clear understanding of the meaning of recreation, its role in contemporary society, and its values and outcomes.

MEANING OF RECREATION

Most people—including many leisure-service professionals—probably believe that they have a good understanding of the meaning of recreation. But, when they are asked to define it precisely, the results are likely to be hazy or inconsistent.

Traditional Views of Recreation

In simple terms, recreation is often defined as "what one does in one's free time for fun." Historically, the term was applied to those activities that provided relaxation after toil, and that helped workers restore their energies in order to be able to return to work again. Often, it was viewed as having no purpose beyond that of immediate enjoyment and relaxation. For example, two well-known sociologists, Martin and Esther Neumeyer, offered the following definition:

> Recreation is any activity, either individual or collective, pursued during one's leisure time. Being relatively free and pleasurable, it has its own appeal.[1]

Such definitions, which saw recreation chiefly as a form of fun or relaxation, without any sense of serious purpose or social outcome, made it difficult to view recreation as a matter of serious public concern. Further, they made it possible to include various morally questionable or self-destructive forms of play, like drug-taking, alcoholism, or compulsive gambling, as examples of recreational involvement.

Recreation as Goal-Oriented Behavior

Gradually, this concept of recreation has changed. Today, recreation and leisure scholars tend to regard recreation as a form of behavior that is goal-oriented, and that is designed to meet important personal and societal needs.

Particularly when it is sponsored by government or other publicly funded agencies, recreation should contribute significantly to the well-being of individual participants, and to society at large. This emphasis is crucial if organized recreation service is to be respected and adequately supported in modern society.

Obviously, people engage in many forms of play besides those that are offered by social agencies. These pursuits may be active or passive, simple or complicated, mechanical or creative, healthful or harmful. No one can control what others do for their private amusement—unless they are overtly breaking the law. In terms of organized *community recreation service,* however, values and social purpose must predominate, along with the very important goal of providing a high level of personal pleasure to participants.

RECREATION: A MODERN VIEW

Recreation is therefore defined in this text in the following terms:

Recreation consists of an activity or experience, usually chosen voluntarily by the participant, either because of the pleasure and satisfaction to be derived from it, or because it may yield other personal or social values.

It is carried on in leisure time, and has no work connotations, such as study for promotion in a job. It is usually enjoyable and, when it is carried on as part of organized community or agency services, it is designed to achieve socially acceptable goals of the individual participant, the group, and society at large.

In some situations, it may be necessary to modify this definition. For example, when recreation is prescribed or recommended for a psychiatric patient who may not be capable at the time of making sound, independent choices, the individual's participation may not be altogether voluntary. In other situations, the fact that activities have been selected and scheduled by a program director obviously reduces the degree to which participants may make voluntary choices.

Recreation as Emotional Experience

Usually, people think of recreation as activity—playing a game, singing a song, or going on a trip. However, some authorities suggest that it is not the activity itself that is recreation, but rather the experience that participants have while taking part in it. Gray and Greben write:

Recreation is an emotional condition within an individual human being that flows from a feeling of well-being and self-satisfaction. It is characterized by feelings of mastery, achievement, exhilaration, acceptance, success, personal worth, and pleasure. It reinforces a positive self-image. Recreation is a response to aesthetic experience, achievement of personal goals, or positive feedback from others. It is independent of activity, leisure, or social acceptance.[2]

Thus, an activity may or may not be recreation, depending on the motivations and expectations of those taking part in it. As a simple example, the Little League baseball player is engaging in recreation, while the highly paid big league professional is carrying out his job, although both are playing baseball.

ORGANIZED RECREATION IN MODERN SOCIETY

Apart from seeing recreation as a form of activity that people take part in or an emotional experience stemming from participation, recreation must also be viewed as a social institution. Clearly, there has been an immense expansion of participation in forms of organized leisure activity.

Throughout the United States and Canada, recreation has made a major contribution to the national economy. Hundreds of millions of visits are made each year to federal, state, and municipal parks, and spectators crowd into sports stadiums, theaters, art galleries, museums, concert halls, and race tracks.

Economic Impact of Recreation. Active sports like tennis, golf, racquetball, and varied forms of conditioning activities, along with outdoor pastimes like hunting and fishing have grown rapidly in popularity. Memberships in health spas and other fitness centers have boomed. Millions of families have purchased recreation vehicles or vacation homes for brief or protracted holidays.

Recreational fads sweep across the land, and billions of dollars are spent on the arts, personal hobbies, and other pastimes and cultural or self-enrichment pursuits. The purchase of many forms of recreational equipment and supplies, including stereo and electronic home-entertainment products, gardening, toys, crafts, and reading materials are all part of the diversified growth in leisure involvement.

To illustrate, according to *U.S. News and World Report,* consumer spending on selected aspects of recreation goods and services grew 321 percent from 1965 to 1981. In 1982, the leisure-service industry was reported to be in excess of $262 billion.[3]

Shift in Public Values. Supporting this dramatic expansion in leisure participation, there has been increased awareness of the value of recreation involvement. In the past, the work ethic dominated our thinking, and recreation was at first condemned and later tolerated only because it helped to restore individuals for renewed toil. Today, there is full awareness of the contribution recreation makes to the quality of life for all.

Americans and Canadians have become extremely health-conscious, and accept the importance of play in promoting both physical and emotional well-being. With the expansion of many forms of organized community recreation programs, leisure has come to be respected as a high-priority aspect of modern life. Today, it is recognized that it contributes significantly to community well-being and to the lives of all residents.

COMPLEXITY OF THE MODERN RECREATION MOVEMENT

Until recently, the organized recreation movement was thought of primarily in terms of programs sponsored by local public recreation and park departments. Although other types of organizations provided recreation facilities and activities, textbooks, courses, and professional societies all were concerned chiefly with local public leisure-service agencies.

Today it is recognized that the recreation movement is a complex phenomenon, with at least eight different types of sponsors that employ hundreds of thousands of professional staff members and serve many millions of participants. These agencies include *public, voluntary, private, commercial, armed forces, corporate/employee, campus,* and *therapeutic* recreation programs. In considering career opportunities, it is essential that students be fully aware of the wide range of employment possibilities offered by these different types of sponsors.

How did all this come to pass? What social factors led to the dramatic growth of the recreation movement and to the expansion of leisure service as a major form of career development for hundreds of thousands of young people?

Social Factors Promoting the Recreation Movement

While this text is primarily concerned with the development of recreation programs and leadership in the present era, it is helpful to understand the factors that contributed to the growth of recreation in modern society. These include the following:

1. *Expansion of Leisure.* Over the past century-and-a-half, there has been a dramatic expansion of leisure—defined here as ''free'' or ''discretionary'' time. Today, people on all socioeconomic levels have a considerable amount of such time, thanks to a shorter workweek, increased numbers of holidays and vacations, and longer periods of paid retirement for most workers. In addition, varied forms of labor-saving devices in the home have added to the free time generally available to all of us.

2. *Changing Social Values.* As indicated earlier, for centuries the Protestant work ethic dominated our thinking and both play and leisure were condemned. In recent decades, these values have shifted markedly. Work is no longer venerated, and growing numbers of people have come to regard recreation and leisure as an important part of their lives and as a vital means of self-actualization and healthy living.

3. *Awareness of ''Wellness'' Benefits.* Both research findings and the common-sense experience of people have contributed to public awareness of the ''wellness'' benefits of play. As later sections of this text will show, recreation is a vital element of physical, emotional, social, intellectual, and spiritual well-being. Taken altogether, it contributes to holistic health in an unmatched way. Particularly in an era marked by stress and burnout, and by the demands of urban living in a high-pres-

sure, complex culture, opportunities for creative and enriching leisure involvement have become all the more critical.

4. *Needs of Special Populations.* Since World War II, there has been a heightened concern about the needs of special populations—such as the physically or mentally disabled, or the economically disadvantaged. Increasingly, special recreation programs have been developed to serve such groups.

   Similarly, the rights of racial or ethnic minorities, the aging, or sexual minorities have been recognized, and recreational opportunities have been developed for such populations.

5. *Economic Impact.* Annual recreation spending in the United States has risen steadily over the past several decades. Today, leisure needs and services constitute a major industry that employs millions of workers on all levels, and helps provide a solid economic base for many regions, states or provinces, and communities.

   As a single illustration, it was reported in *Time* magazine in 1984 that more than 4.55 million people are employed in the tourism industry alone. Travel receipts make up over 6.5 percent of the gross national product and generate $18 billion in tax revenues to federal, state, and local governments.[4]

6. *Cultural Values.* With the increased number of individuals attending colleges and universities, the level of cultural taste and involvement in various forms of artistic pursuits has increased markedly. As a result, public attendance at theater, dance, and musical performances, and participation in the arts generally have become a major aspect of leisure in contemporary society.

7. *Environmental Concerns.* Since the 1960s, there has been increasing awareness of the critical problems of environmental pollution and the need to protect and preserve open space, as well as the nation's wildlife, waterways, and other great natural resources. Because of the close linkage between the park and recreation movements, major government programs have sought both to enact ecologically sound policies and to meet outdoor recreation needs in environmentally compatible ways.

8. *Professional Unity and Recognition.* The park and recreation movements, once separate areas of public concern and service, have become closely joined over the past two decades. Today, with hundreds of higher education curricula preparing skilled practitioners in these fields and with major national organizations such as the National Recreation and Park Association and the Canadian Parks/Recreation Association promoting their interests, the leisure-service professions have gained a new sense of unity and public visibility.

Thanks to all these factors, recreation and leisure have emerged as key aspects of national life in American and Canadian society. In so doing, they have become better understood and more sharply defined as forms of human experience and social processes. Increasingly, awareness of the positive values of recreation has grown.

BENEFITS OF RECREATION

These may be examined both in terms of the value of recreation for the personal well-being of participants and with respect to social needs in the modern community.

Psychological Benefits

A number of leading psychiatrists have subscribed to the value of recreational experience as an essential part of happy and well-balanced living. Dr. William Menninger stressed the great importance of hobbies, sports, and games, and group involvement in maintaining emotional health. He pointed out that recreation has been increasingly recognized as an important tool, not only in the prevention of illness, but also in the process of rehabilitation of mentally ill patients, in institutions, and in community settings after discharge.

Another well-known psychiatrist, Dr. Alexander Reid Martin, stressed the need to divest ourselves of the notion that work represents the only significant value in daily life. He urged that both work and leisure be recognized as enriching and self-actualizing forms of personal expression.

Psychologists today recognize that play is a vital ingredient in healthy childhood development. It provides the opportunity for exploring the environment, learning appropriate age-level physical and social skills, and joining with friends and other family members in rewarding and enjoyable leisure activity.[5]

The psychological implications of recreation include its use as a therapeutic technique for the mentally ill. However, it must also be recognized as essential to the healthy emotional development of *all* individuals. Two important examples today include the growing awareness of *stress,* which may often lead to psychosomatic illness or emotional breakdown, and *burnout,* which stems from pressure and lack of satisfaction and a sense of achievement on the job. In both cases, recreation may help to provide a sense of balance and relaxed creative involvement that helps prevent these problems from occurring.

Physical Benefits

Recreation in the form of sports, games, dance, outdoor pastimes, and exercise programs makes an important contribution to the physical well-being of all Americans and Canadians. Following World War II, we became uncomfortably aware that our children and youth ranked shockingly low in selected measures of physical fitness, compared to children in other nations. It was recognized that the sedentary, inactive, and overfed lives that too many young people led was responsible for this finding. As a consequence, many communities and school systems initiated new physical education and fitness programs.

In the late 1970s, there was a dramatic explosion of adult interest in running, jogging, racquet sports, and other fitness activities. Commercial health spas proliferated, and colleges, Y's, employee recreation programs, municipal recreation and park departments, and other agencies joined the bandwagon. It was recognized that physical exercise helped reduce cardiovascular illness and other health risks. Beyond this, many adults sought to improve their physical appearance and sense of youthful well-being.

Increasingly, evidence suggested that company-sponsored sports and fitness programs helped men and women employees improve productivity, cut down on illness and absenteeism, and function more effectively on the job. York Onnen, Director of Program Development for the President's Council on Physical Fitness and Sport, commented:

> . . . important paybacks of work-force fitness programs are such unquantifiables as higher morale, improved company loyalty, a better public image and an edge in the labor market for competitive, aggressive, into-life people—the kind companies want to lead them.[6]

The holistic nature of many of today's recreation programs is illustrated in employee fitness activities, which often are combined with smoking cessation, weight control, stress management, and nutrition and hypertension workshops and counseling. Rather than focus exclusively on exercise machines or weight-training, many of the most successful programs include jogging, basketball, skiing simulators, racquetball, saunas, whirlpools, and other enjoyable leisure-related activities and facilities.

Social Benefits

One of the most obvious values of recreation is that it provides the opportunity for enjoyable group experiences that meet the fundamental human need for social involvement.

At every age level, recreation contributes to healthy socialization. It provides an outstanding opportunity for children, youth, and adults to share enjoyable group pastimes with each other. In social clubs, sports teams, informal playground or community center groups, and similar settings, young people gain a sense of acceptance and close friendship with others.

For adults, recreation provides an indispensable means of gaining social satisfaction and avoiding isolation and boredom. For families, recreation offers an ideal means of promoting interaction, sharing interests, and strengthening the bonds of affection and respect, in an unpressured and relaxed way.

For retired adults in particular, leisure villages and other retirement communities or senior centers help meet the social needs of older people. Probably more than for any other age group, the elderly require social outlets and satisfactions that can best be met through recreation.

Other important outcomes of recreation experience include *intellectual* and *spiritual* values. Although it may frequently be thought of as primarily physical, recreation may also encompass numerous intellectual, linguistic, and cultural pursuits—ranging from reading or creative writing to dance, theater, and music. The very fact of being involved in regular forms of physical activity may help to improve the academic performance of students, as a number of research studies have shown.

From a spiritual point of view, many religious leaders have pointed out that leisure represents an arena in which positive and constructive values may dominate. Indeed, many religious organizations provide extensive recreation programs. On the other hand, however, negative or self-destructive uses of leisure may serve to corrupt the human spirit.

Negative Forms of Play. To illustrate, we have become increasingly aware of many of the self-destructive forms of play that many youth and adults pursue in their search for sensation and ''highs.''

As an example, *Time* Magazine describes the drug problem that has become a ''monkey'' on the nation's back, reaching into every region, every age group, every social class:

> The scourge of drugs, which for years has afflicted America's youth, is now so widespread among adults that it threatens to sap the nation's strength at a critical juncture in its history. Millions of Americans—from children in schoolyards to computer analysts in California's Silicon Valley and stockbrokers on Wall Street—are turning on to all kinds of pot, pills, and powders, giving the United States the highest rate of drug abuse of any developed country on the globe.[7]

Similarly, alcohol abuse has spread rapidly to the point that increasing numbers of children and youth—as young as the age of 12 or 13—are experimenting with liquor. Overall, there are over ten million individuals with serious drinking problems in American society, and the cost in both economic and human terms is staggering. Thanks to shifting moral standards and new permissive codes of sexual behavior, pornography, prostitution, and illegitimate pregnancy have spread rapidly. The steady growth of gambling, including racetrack and sports betting, the ''numbers racket'' and state-sponsored or legalized lotteries, casinos, video-poker, and other gambling machines, represents a multibillion dollar industry each year.

LEISURE: A SOCIAL CHALLENGE

Such activities all represent widely found forms of leisure involvement. In moderation, they may not be harmful; in excess, they can lead to the most serious consequences.

The basic point is that within modern society, recreation and leisure represent a choice and a social challenge. They offer potential participants the opportunity for positive and constructive social experiences that contribute to healthy development and self-enrichment. But, at the other end of the continuum, they represent social evils and outlets that pose serious threats to the well-being of those who participate in undesirable forms of play.

Over the past several decades, government and other community agencies which serve the public interest have accepted the responsibility for providing an extensive range of recreation and park facilities and programs designed to meet public leisure needs in positive and creative ways. They do so within a general framework of what might be described as a philosophy of community recreation.

PHILOSOPHY OF COMMUNITY RECREATION

It is widely accepted that government has a basic responsibility to serve the needs of community residents, within certain broad spheres of civic need—such as public safety, health, environmental protection, and education. One major responsibility which government has assumed in all modern, industrial societies is providing parks, playgrounds, community centers, and other facilities and programs designed to meet community needs for constructive and creative leisure activity.

While government has the chief responsibility in this field, it is not its obligation, or within its power, to meet all possible needs for leisure activity. Thus there is a place in community life for agencies that have specialized interests, or serve special populations with more advanced interests or unique needs. And, while government should provide basic facilities and programs without charge, particularly for low-income groups, it should be prepared to levy fees and charges for more expensive or elaborate programs and services.

The ultimate basis for providing recreation in modern, democratic society is the dual conviction that: (a) all human beings are worthy of respect, and must be given the fullest possible opportunity for achieving their maximum potential in life; and (b) recreation and leisure provide an important means of enriching personality and promoting personal growth, constructive social relationships, and positive participation in community life.

Specific Goals and Objectives

Translating these broad principles into action, recreation and park agencies are generally regarded as having the following specific goals and objectives: (1) enriching the quality of life for all community residents; (2) promoting the healthy growth of participants; (3) improving and beautifying the natural environment of communities; (4) reducing negative uses of leisure, and helping to prevent anti-social behavior and delinquency; (5) meeting the needs of special populations, such as the physically or mentally disabled; (6) strengthening community life, by promoting civic pride and morale; (7) improving intergroup relations; (8) stimulating the economic well-being of communities; (9) promoting community safety; (10) meeting the special needs of disadvantaged populations, particularly youth; (11) contributing to cultural development; (12) providing a release for tensions and hostility in crowded urban environments; (13) promoting a concern for nature; and (14) increasing public awareness of leisure values.[8]

Summing up these values, it is the purpose of recreation, park, and leisure-service agencies to enrich community life in many ways. Through the provision of varied recreation programs and activities, the lives of individuals are made fuller and happier and the relationships among different community groups are made more positive and constructive. In the fullest sense, leisure-service programming can help to contribute to a sense of celebration of life and to bring joy and self-fulfillment to community residents of many backgrounds.

CONTRASTING MODELS OF LEISURE SERVICE

Beyond these specific purposes of recreation and park agencies, it is apparent that many such organizations today have adopted differing models of priorities and service-delivery approaches. Three such models that may readily be identified today in public, voluntary, and other leisure-service organizations are: (1) *quality-of-life;* (2) *marketing;* and (3) *human-service* orientations.

Quality-of-Life Recreation Service Model

This approach to directing recreation and park programming and leadership views recreation as a socially desirable service which contributes significantly to the quality of life in the modern community. All of the values described earlier are recognized, and recreation itself is seen as an important focus of daily living. Physical, social, and creative expression are perceived as key elements in recreational involvement, and recreation is designed to meet the needs of population groups on various age levels.

In a sense, recreation service is seen as an ''amenity'' in that it helps to make life richer and more enjoyable and provides the opportunity for personal growth and pleasure. However, it is *not* regarded as a critical area of social service, comparable to police or fire protection, or to other municipal functions which relate to health or other life-related concerns.

At the same time, the quality-of-life model of recreation service holds that the community has an obligation to provide an adequate range of leisure opportunities to all citizens, at little or no cost. Both in terms of varied types of activities and with respect to providing parks and other scenic or historic areas and facilities, this traditional viewpoint assumes that the community should meet the basic leisure needs of all residents as part of its overall civic responsibility.

Marketing Recreation Service Model

This relatively new approach has become popular in many public agencies, which suffered significant cuts in funding in the late 1970s and early 1980s, and which came to rely heavily on their own fund-raising capabilities as a matter of survival.

Many public departments at this time raised their fees and charges for various programs or the use of facilities. They used business-based marketing procedures in identifying leisure needs and potential audiences, designing and pricing new services, and promoting and advertising them aggressively. In addition, a host of other innovative managerial techniques, including the use of concessions, contracting and leasing arrangements, gift catalogues, cosponsorship arrangements, fund-raising drives and foundations, and grants, emerged as part of the marketing process. In effect, as Howard and Crompton state, the public recreation and park agency came to be viewed as the following:

> [a] business which happens to operate in the public rather than a private sector. The agency is required to seek out scarce resources from a wide range of possible sources to ensure that the scarce resources acquired are used in such a way that they yield the maximum social and economic benefits possible. These are exactly the same requirements which are demanded of an entrepreneur, except that the entrepreneur's organization measures the benefits which emerge almost exclusively in economic rather than social terms.[9]

Athough Howard and Crompton make the point that public-service agencies must also apply social criteria to their program efforts, the reality is that when financial and marketing factors become preeminent, social considerations tend to become less important. The implication of the marketing model as a leisure-service orientation is that it tends to make an agency acutely aware of the fiscal potential of all programs and leadership efforts, and to subject possible plans for building new facilities or creating new services to the criterion of self-sufficiency—i.e., "Will it pay its own way?"

Although public departments have chiefly been identified with this approach, it has also influenced armed forces recreation, many voluntary agencies, and those therapeutic recreation service programs that have moved into reliance on third-party payments or outside reimbursement for patient or client services.

The rationale for adopting the marketing model of recreation service is presented convincingly by Bullaro:

> . . . successful leisure service managers must accept the fact that they have a business, and they must practice sound business strategies, however unglamorous they might be. Marketing techniques such as forecasting, pricing, advertising, selling, and distribution, are vital strategies if leisure service organizations intend to match their services with client needs and their cash flow with their expenses.
>
> Many successful leisure executives consider marketing their top priority. The leisure service organization that has a sound marketing program is equipped for survival.[10]

Human-Service Recreation Model

Sharply opposed to the marketing model, this orientation sees recreation and leisure as vital social concerns that play an important role in meeting human needs and contributing to community health and welfare. Stemming from the human potential movement of the 1960s, recreation came to be seen as a potentially powerful force in the enrichment of people's lives and as a way of addressing critical social problems.

Many of the programs and services described throughout this text that are designed to meet the needs of youth, the aging, or the handicapped, represent the human-service recreation model in action. Beyond providing services, however, this orientation suggests a total community role for recreation professionals which sees them as assuming leadership in identifying and meeting social needs of all sorts.

To illustrate this orientation, Niepoth cites a position statement developed by participants in a California and Southwest recreation and park conference:

> The economic, political, social and aesthetic conditions inherent in today's environment create a population replete with alienation, emotional deprivation, unemployment, poverty, crime and disintegrated sense of community. Citizens in urban communities are becoming increasingly mobile, involved in changing family relationships and life-styles, experiencing new or altered patterns of housing, work and leisure . . . in changing value systems.
>
> The recreation and park movement is not immune to the forces of social change which has altered the consciousness of women, minority groups, the poor, the elderly, the handicapped and the young. The use of leisure time has important implications for human development, community integration, mental health, conservation of resources and the quality of human existence. However, it is necessary to move beyond recreation activities, buildings, and parks, and accept the consequences of what we do in terms of making people stronger and improving the quality of community life. Our traditional role of taking care of the parks and offering a program of recreation activities is no longer effective in society's changing social environment.[11]

Obviously, the extent to which a recreation and park department accepts this view of the world and description of its responsibilities will have a major impact on its priorities and leadership roles and functions.

Whether or not it is committed to one of these philosophical approaches, each different type of leisure-service agency is likely to have a somewhat different kind of emphasis and set of program priorities. Public recreation and park departments, for example, tend to have diversified programs serving all age groups with popular, inexpensive activities, and are also most likely to operate extensive outdoor recreation and park facilities.

Typically, many voluntary, nonprofit youth-serving organizations provide a broad range of organized sports, social, and creative activities for children and youth.

Numerous private-membership associations serve the special interests of adults in areas such as sports, boating, hunting and fishing, social programs, the arts, and other leisure pursuits.

Commercial recreation provides an immense range of opportunities related to tourism, travel, and hospitality, instruction in special skills, entertainment, health and fitness activities, social pastimes, and similar activities.

Therapeutic recreation agencies are obviously primarily concerned with providing leisure services for special populations, and with using recreation as a form of treatment or rehabilitative modality.

Employee recreation associations meet the specialized needs of their members, as do armed forces and college or university recreation organizations. The final result is a vast, interrelated network of leisure programs and services that meet the varied recreational interests of all segments of the population.

Their success in doing so is obviously based on a number of factors, including their physical facilities and resources and other elements related to budgetary support. But probably the most critical element contributing to the effectiveness of recreation programs of all types is leadership. Leadership constitutes the human element that plans, organizes, and directs leisure-service programs on varied levels of participation. It provides the stimulus, encouragement, and guidance that are indispensable in recreation programming.

LEADERSHIP: THE FOCUS OF THIS TEXT

In moving to a direct consideration of leadership, the focus of this text, we will begin by examining its meaning. Exactly what *is* leadership, and why is it a key element in leisure-service programming?

Within the recreation field, the word "leader" usually describes the individual who works directly with participants in an organizing or instructional role, in carrying on program activities. The term "leader" is frequently used to describe an entry-level position, although in many large municipal recreation and park departments, individuals may remain at a leadership level throughout their entire professional careers.

In contrast, the term "leadership" applies to the combination of personal qualities and professional skills that an individual must possess in order to function effectively in interpersonal group situations. In recreation settings, employees on various levels of responsibility—including superintendents, commissioners, division heads, or other managerial personnel—all need to be able to apply leadership in working with varied groups. Indeed, the concept of leadership is found throughout the spectrum of human enterprises and institutions; generals and noncommissioned officers, presidents and mayors, business executives and assembly-line foremen and women are all expected to display personal leadership qualities and skills.

Beyond this, leadership may be thought of as a process, in which one or more individuals give a group direction and enable its members to function effectively together. Within the leisure service field, leadership can be seen at its most basic level, with a group leader conducting activities by teaching skills, organizing programs, or supervising recreation activities.

In analyzing and describing leadership, this text covers five key topical areas:

1. *Concepts of Recreation Leadership.* First, it examines leadership with emphasis on its contribution to successful program development in recreation, park, and leisure-service agencies. As part of this, it presents a number of key principles that underlie effective leadership in varied types of recreational settings.

2. *Group Dynamics and Leadership Functions.* Next, varied theories of leadership and group dynamics are presented, along with guidelines designed to help the leader learn to work effectively with groups of participants, co-workers, or community representatives. Specific functions of leadership are described, with assignments that contribute to the development of hands-on and problem-solving leadership skills.

3. *Program Activities.* Several major types of useful program activities are presented, to assist in developing direct leadership skills through class teaching or program-planning assignments. In each case, examples of useful activities are provided, along with suggestions for effective presentation in different settings or program formats.

4. *Settings for Leadership.* Throughout the text, recreation, parks, and leisure services are presented to the reader as a diverse and socially purposeful field of career opportunity. As part of this, the text provides a comprehensive overview of the major types of agencies offering recreation programs in the United States and Canada today.

5. *Philosophical Orientations for Recreational Leadership.* Finally, the book seeks to help the reader understand several basic orientations in organized recreation service today. Through these, the concept of recreation as a significant field of community service is documented, and the important role of leadership as part of the continuum of career development in leisure service is defined.

Throughout the book, the changing shape of modern society is depicted—together with those rapidly shifting social and demographic trends that influence the delivery of recreational programs today. New challenges, values, and opportunities for leisure-service professionals are presented, and emphasis is given to innovative programming and group leadership approaches.

The field of recreation leadership offers a challenging opportunity for rewarding career development for young people throughout our society. Their success, however, will depend heavily on their understanding of people and their leisure needs and interests, as well as their competence in developing and implementing programs to meet these needs and interests. Underlying such understanding and competence are a number of basic concepts of recreation leadership, which are presented in the chapters that follow.

NOTES

[1]Martin H. Neumeyer and Esther S. Neumeyer, *Leisure and Recreation* (New York: Ronald, 1961), p. 114.

[2]David E. Gray and Seymour Greben, "Future Perspectives," *Parks and Recreation* (July 1974): 49.

[3]"$262 Billion for Your Leisure Spending," *U.S. News and World Report* (26 July 1982): 47.

[4]Howard P. James, Chief Executive of Sheraton Corp., in "The Industry and the Economy," Advertising Supplement, *Time* (7 May 1984): n.p.

[5]A number of other important psychological benefits of recreation are identified by Seppo E. Iso-Ahola and Ellen Weissinger in "Leisure and Well-Being: Is There a Connection?" *Parks and Recreation* (June 1984): 40-44.

[6]York Onnen, cited in Kathleen Myler, "Exercise and Firm Up a Sagging Bottom Line," *Chicago Tribune* (17 October 1983): 3-1.

[7]"Crashing on Cocaine," *Time* (11 April 1983): 23.

[8]For a fuller discussion of the social values of recreation, see Richard Kraus, *Recreation and Leisure in Modern Society* (Glenview, Ill.: Scott, Foresman, 1984), Chapter 15.

[9]Dennis R. Howard and John R. Crompton, *Financing, Managing and Marketing Recreation and Park Resources* (Dubuque: William C. Brown, 1980), p. 1.

[10]John J. Bullaro, "The Business of Survival: Developing a Marketing Strategy," *Journal of Physical Education, Recreation and Dance* (April 1982): 64.

[11]"Human Services Statements," from *Leisure Lines: A Monthly Action Report of California Park and Recreation Society,* cited in E. William Niepoth, *Leisure Leadership* (Englewood Cliffs, N.J.: Prentice-Hall, 1983), p. 17.

QUESTIONS

1. What important social factors have helped recreation become a significant aspect of modern life? Illustrate with examples in your own community.
2. The text suggests several key purposes or values of recreation. Select a specific leisure-service organization and show which of these values it seeks to achieve, and how.
3. Which of the three models of leisure service ("quality-of-life," "marketing," and "human-service") do you feel is most desirable or justifiable in modern society? Why?

SUGGESTED READINGS

Reynold E. Carlson, Janet R. MacLean, Theodore R. Deppe, and James S. Peterson, *Recreation and Leisure: The Changing Scene* (Belmont, Calif.: Wadsworth, 1979).

Richard Kraus, *Recreation and Leisure in Modern Society* (Glenview, Ill.: Scott, Foresman, 1984).

H. Douglas Sessoms, *Leisure Services* (Englewood Cliffs, N.J.: Prentice-Hall, 1984).

_____

CHAPTER 2

Basic Concepts_____
of Recreation_____
Leadership_____

_____

_____

We now move to a more detailed analysis of recreation leadership, and to a number of concepts that are critical in the successful operation of leisure-service programs.

The term *leadership* is commonly used to describe the act of guiding or directing others in a mutual enterprise. For example, a typical dictionary definition suggests that a leader is "a person or thing that leads; directing, commanding, or guiding head, as of a group or activity."[1]

VARIED DEFINITIONS OF LEADERSHIP

Other definitions emphasize the relationship between leaders and group members. For example, Allport, a leading social psychologist, described leadership in the following words: "Leadership means direct, face-to-face contact between leader and followers; it is personal social control."[2]

Two authors in the field of social group work, Wilson and Ryland, wrote, "Leadership is a natural phenomenon in group life, a dynamic process which emerges in the interaction of individuals one with another."[3]

Davis suggested that leadership is the ability to persuade others to seek defined objectives enthusiastically. "It is the human factor which binds a group together and motivates it toward goals . . . the leader triggers the power of motivation in people and guides them toward goals."[4]

Tannenbaum and Massarik described leadership as "interpersonal influence, exercised in situations and directed, through the communication process, toward the attainment of a specified goal or goals."[5]

In terms of leadership within the field of recreation, Danford wrote, "Leadership is a process of stimulating and aiding groups to determine, or to accept, common goals, and to carry out effectively the measures leading to the attainment of these goals. . . . Leadership in recreation is concerned with all aspects of the situation which help to make it possible to achieve the objectives important to the department and to the group."[6]

Thus, we see leadership defined as a function, a relationship, a phenomenon in group life, an ability, a form of interpersonal influence, and finally as a process. While each of these views has merit, this chapter will focus on the three ways of understanding it that were identified in Chapter 1: (1) as a type of professional position or job level; (2) as a set of personal qualities and competencies that contribute to successful performance; and (3) as a process of working with others.

LEADERSHIP AS A POSITION OR JOB LEVEL

Since the beginning of the organized recreation movement, the term *Recreation Leader* has been widely used by many public and voluntary agencies to identify direct-service levels of professional responsibility. Usually, it is designated as one of several job levels that are found in personnel classification systems or textbooks on recreation and park management. For example, a common breakdown of such positions includes five titles:

1. *Executive:* top management level, often referred to as Superintendent, Commissioner, Director, or General Manager.
2. *Supervisor:* middle-management position, usually with responsibility for directing general or specialist program services within a large district or coordinating programs for a special population or form of activity.
3. *Facility Director:* similar to Supervisor, in that it involves management of a large recreation center, senior center, youth center, or specialized facility such as an aquatics or arts center.
4. *Leader:* the direct, face-to-face program leadership level, usually defined as general or specialist, in terms of program functions.
5. *Trainee:* often a part-time, seasonal, pre- or sub-professional position, this level may also be identified as Intern, Aide, or Assistant Leader.

Use of Title in Job Descriptions. Often in Civil Service codes or other personnel systems, the work of Recreation Leaders is described in such terms as:

Leadership Level: Leaders operate directly, in face-to-face relationships with groups of participants. Their primary responsibilities are: (a) to organize and direct a variety of programs; (b) to maintain inventories of supplies and equipment, and requisition new materials when necessary; (c) to carry out an effective program of local publicity and community relations; (d) to recruit and work with volunteers; (e) to be responsible for maintaining sound policies of safety, group control, and discipline among participants; (f) to keep records of attendance and special events, and to assist in the evaluation of department activities.

In some large recreation and park systems, leadership-level positions may be classified on several grades, such as *Leader I, II,* and *III;* or *Assistant Leader, Leader,* and *Senior Leader.* In others, the setting or area of program responsibility involved may be in the job title, such as *Playground Leader, Youth Leader,* or *Sports Leader.*

Other Titles.   Frequently, other titles may be used instead of leader, particularly in nonpublic or specialized types of agencies. Examples might be: *Recreation* or *Activity Therapist; Sports, Music,* or *Dance Specialist;* or even titles like *Ski Instructor, Fitness Director,* or *Activities Coordinator.* While such titles imply that the individual plays a coordinating or supervising role, the fact is that many leaders have such functions, as well as direct group leadership responsibilities.

SHIFT IN LEADERSHIP PRACTICES

Particularly in public agencies, the specific functions of recreation leaders have changed in many communities. For example, fewer individuals are being hired today as full-time, year-round leaders in playgrounds or community centers.

Instead, much of the actual program leadership is being done by part-time, seasonal, or volunteer workers. Increasingly, leadership-level personnel are likely to be attached to other types of special facilities, or are being assigned the role of helping others in the process of organizing or carrying out recreation programs.

Often, the function may best be described as *coordinating,* in the sense that the agency professional makes facilities available, schedules their use, acts as a consultant to community groups, and promotes cooperative relationships among groups. It is illustrated by a new title that has come to be assigned to many group leaders in French-speaking Canada and a number of European countries. The word is *animateur,* essentially meaning an individual who motivates and assists others in developing their own programs.

As part of this trend, leaders may find themselves carrying out a number of important functions related to the enrichment of community leisure services, such as advocacy efforts for disabled populations. Often, they play the role of planners, researchers, or evaluators, in terms of determining community needs. They may be resource persons, may train recreation paraprofessionals or volunteers, or may serve on planning teams with those representing other disciplines or social services.

Other Specialized Functions

More and more, those responsible for carrying on program activities in different types of agencies have become highly specialized in their responsibilities and skills. Often a high level of technical expertise may be required. In campus recreation as an example, a student union program specialist may be responsible for organizing mass concerts and social events, or for coordinating wilderness programs. In corporate/employee recreation programs, the task may be to develop fitness activities, stress management workshops, or similar functions.

In therapeutic recreation, there is increasing emphasis on assigning individuals to working with special populations and expecting them to have a specialized knowledge of disability, treatment approaches, assessment techniques, activity analysis and modification, and other functions which differ sharply from the traditional view of the recreation leader as a games or sports director. Similarly, leaders in a senior center may be responsible for planning and carrying out programs that relate to the varied needs of aging persons—including health, nutritional, legal, housing, family counseling, and similar concerns.

Summing up, the view of recreation leadership as a professional role or job title is entirely valid. However, today it encompasses many more variations and functions than in the past. Nonetheless, there are a number of generic skills and understandings that apply to recreation leadership in all kinds of settings. And, even for the individual who does not himself or herself directly work with groups, it is essential to be familiar with the principles and skills of leadership, in order to be able to supervise others effectively.

QUALITIES AND COMPETENCIES UNDERLYING SUCCESSFUL LEADERSHIP

A second way of understanding leadership is to see it not as a position title or set of assigned responsibilities, but rather as a set of personal qualities and abilities essential to working effectively with others in a stimulating or directing capacity.

In the field of recreation and parks, there has been widespread acceptance of the view that successful group leadership is heavily dependent on an individual's possessing certain personal traits that command the respect and cooperation of others.

Both the professional literature and leadership manuals published by many public or voluntary leisure-service organizations often identify the qualities which they believe to be essential to high-level performance. For example, Carlson, MacLean, Deppe, and Peterson cite as important leadership qualities knowledge of self and others, of the organization and its purposes, and the ability to plan and organize, encourage initiative, work democratically with others, make decisions, and communicate effectively.[7]

Other authorities describe the following qualities or personal traits as particularly relevant to recreation leadership:

1. A basic conviction that all human beings have worth and dignity, and that leisure can be a critical factor in helping to improve the quality of life for people of all ages and backgrounds.
2. The ability to be both visionary and pragmatic; having high ideals and yet at the same time being realistic and practical in facing present problems.
3. The willingness to trust others and encourage them to be fully productive; delegating responsibility and power and acting as an enabler.
4. A high level of personal motivation, including the ability to demonstrate initiative and confidence, to be a self-starter, and stay with a task.

Linked to this, the ability to learn and grow from defeats and mistakes, rather than be discouraged by them, and to make difficult decisions and stand by them.

5. A sound understanding of human nature, based in part on a formal knowledge of psychology, but also on an intuitive awareness of the feelings of people and how they typically behave and respond in life situations.

6. Linked to the preceding quality, other personal traits such as warmth, patience, empathy for the needs and feelings of others, and a sense of humor.

7. Other important traits, such as intelligence, flexibility, sound judgment, a strong sense of personal responsibility, and high moral standards in different areas of human relationships.

While many of these qualities would obviously be desirable in numerous other fields of endeavor, it is believed that they are particularly appropriate for those who work in the recreation field. Such elements as patience, flexibility, a sense of humor, and a high degree of personal motivation are especially important, along with a strong component of enthusiasm and the ability to relate to others in a cooperative way.

It should be stressed that different kinds of group situations may call for different qualities on the part of program leaders. Therefore the same set of personal qualities may not be as effective in all settings, a point discussed more fully in Chapter 3.

Values and Attitudes.   Several of the values just cited refer to the values and attitudes held by the leader. It is particularly important that recreation leaders have positive and constructive leisure values, and that they regard their work as having serious impact on the lives of those they serve. If they believe that what they are doing is trivial, or that their leadership role has no real meaning or value, then they are in the wrong field.

At the same time, it is necessary to recognize that the issue of values is a complex one. In any given recreation situation, different groups or individuals may have widely contrasting beliefs or sets of purposes—which may sometimes be at odds with each other. To illustrate, in a group program in a voluntary agency such as a Boys or Girls Club, each *individual* is likely to have a personal set of values and expectations, which may not be in harmony with those of other group members, or the *group as a whole*.

Certainly, the *overall agency* will have a set of standards or expectations, which it seeks to promote through group sponsorship. At the same time the *individual group leader* will have his or her own point of view and personal values system.

On a broader scale, the *parents* of group members and the *surrounding neighborhood* or *community* will also have values that they may seek to promote or impose on the group. The *recreation profession* itself certainly presents certain views of leadership goals through its literature and through meetings of professional societies. Finally, each *nation* has important cultural customs, beliefs, and values— although these may vary greatly by region, socioeconomic class, religious groupings, or other factors.

The point then is that there is likely to be great diversity in values and expectations surrounding any form of organized recreation participation. At the same time, the role of the leader is often central in determining how decisions are to be made, or in reconciling possible conflict situations.

Throughout the leadership process, it is essential that leaders be aware of their own values, and that they seek constantly not to impose these on others, but to promote a serious concern about the outcomes of recreational experience and on the nature of the group experience for all participants.

LEADERSHIP PROCESS

The third way of looking at leadership to be dealt with in this text involves understanding it as a process. Leadership is obviously something that happens as an interpersonal experience shared by those who are in charge of groups and those who participate in group activities. It is also a phenomenon that occurs among co-workers, where one individual assumes a role of leadership as they carry out assigned tasks.

Although it would be convenient to present a model of the leadership process within a particular agency or program setting, it is not possible to do so in a precise, orderly way. Leadership simply does not fall into a convenient, orderly time frame or sequence.

Instead, leaders carry out a variety of functions related to planning and directing activities, recruiting or attracting participants, working with community groups, or promoting, scheduling, organizing, and evaluating programs. It is often possible to describe such tasks in very specific steps which must be carried out in a regular, uniform way. Several sets of guidelines for leadership functions of this type are presented in Chapter 5, and other guidelines for directing specific recreational activities may be found in the chapters that follow.

Interpersonal Leadership Behaviors.   Many leadership functions involve interpersonal behaviors in which the leader works with group members to encourage and improve the quality of their participation, or to help the group itself make intelligent decisions or carry on program activities successfully. Such behaviors may involve communicating with others on various levels, praising or criticizing individuals where such actions may be called for, and inspiring or motivating group members. They may also involve clarifying department policies, issuing warnings about inappropriate behavior or imposing disciplinary measures, making referrals of participants or clients to other agencies, and similar tasks.

In carrying out such actions, leadership styles vary greatly. Some leaders may tend to be extremely dynamic, forceful, and outgoing, while others may be much quieter and nondirective in their approach.

Some types of organizations—such as armed forces or employee recreation departments or programs—are likely to place a high premium on leadership that is extremely well-organized, efficient, and productive. On the other hand, some agencies in the social-service field may encourage leadership that is more deeply concerned with the group process and individual growth, and in which the emphasis is on the dynamics of behavior and growth, rather than on statistics of attendance or revenue derived from programs.

Research in Leadership Styles.   As Chapter 3 will show, there has been considerable research on group leadership styles in recent years. While there is no single, universally-accepted model of effective leadership, there appears to be agreement that those individuals who are concerned with human relations and who are open and trusting with others, delegate responsibilities, and share decision-making powers, are generally more effective than authoritarian leaders who are task-oriented and who hold the reins of control tightly.

Beyond this general principle, effective leadership behavior appears to be very much a matter of commitment and enthusiasm, of thorough preparation, and of having a clearly understood set of objectives that help to guide one's action. These elements are dramatically illustrated in the following passage, which describes an actual group situation showing both effective and ineffective leadership behaviors.

Effective and Ineffective Leadership: A Case Analysis

The following excerpts are taken from a paper written by a graduate student in community recreation service at Teachers College, Columbia.[8] Her report is presented almost in its entirety; a few minor sections have been deleted:

> One of my daughters, during her eighth and ninth years, belonged to two different Brownie troops in two different locales. Her membership in one was very salutary, but her membership in the other was unrewarding. The most important element, in my judgment, was the difference in leadership.
>
> The first Brownie troop was led by two women who really believed that the girls could and would have a meaningful experience, not only as Brownies, or as potential Girl Scouts, but as citizens. They both acquainted themselves with the philosophy behind Scouting and felt the girls would grow as people if they themselves shared this ideology.
>
> They believed in the positive value of a group recreative experience which embodied immediate goals for the group as well as a far-reaching ideology. Both women had attended indoctrination sessions at the regional Scout office and both were familiar with the history of the movement. Although neither woman had had much previous experience leading a group of children, each liked children and wanted the experience to be successful. They met frequently to outline their program and to determine in which areas one might assume dominance, and in which areas they could be equally responsible. Before the children themselves were informed that a Brownie Troop was going to be formed, they informally sounded out all the mothers of all the girls in the grade and explained why they felt a troop was appropriate and how they felt the girls could benefit.
>
> After the meeting place and the time of meeting were established, they sent an attractive notice to the three classes involved, and invited the girls who might be interested to attend a meeting, at which the purpose of the formation of the troop and a

description of what the girls could expect if they became members was outlined. Although the facilities—the kindergarten school room—were not the best, they were centrally located for all the children. The schoolyard was used by many other children, but one of the mothers offered the use of her backyard for games and parties. Many of the other mothers offered either facilities or services, because the leaders had established excellent public relations.

The author goes on to comment that she felt that these two adult leaders possessed strong leadership qualities. They related well to each other and to the children, and were aware of the children's interests, desires, and needs. They were interested in developing the children's social and creative potential. They met together each week, two or three days before the troop assembled, to discuss the programs that had been held, to review the responses of children to earlier experiences, and to plan new activities. They had a flair, she felt, for making the Scout rituals dramatic and exciting, rather than silly or humdrum. They exercised democratic leadership by letting the children take over as many responsibilities as they could handle, and they made sure that each child had an equal opportunity to participate. They set the tone for the behavior of the group by their friendliness and interest.

They were both fair and firm. Although the group had some very lively youngsters, there were no disciplinary problems and the leaders were successful at enticing the more reticent girls to participate without coercing or embarrassing them in any way. They functioned as enablers, providing assistance to the group when the children asked for it. They understood the kinds of judgments and decisions which were appropriate for children of that age to make; they understood also which administrative duties were too difficult for the children to handle. As much as was possible, the children conducted the troop with stimulation and guidance from the adults.

So successful was the experience that the author comments, "Although we moved away from the area eight years ago (prior to the writing of this paper), my daughter still corresponds with her friends from this troop, although she retains no contact with our immediate neighbor's children. She still refers to this experience as the happiest group experience she has ever had." The author then continues:

> After we moved away from the area, my daughter wanted to join a new troop. The community into which we had moved had a fine Scout House with more than adequate indoor and outdoor facilities. None of the children she knew were Brownies, and when I called the Girl Scout Council, I was told that there was difficulty in starting a troop because there was no leadership available. I did not want to be a leader in my daughter's troop, and I managed to get two women to agree to lead the troop with a promise that I would assist them with the program.
>
> I was rather uneasy from the start, but I hoped that they would enjoy the experience once the troop was formed. They did not devote much energy to public relations or laying the groundwork before the troop met. I perhaps was not forceful enough in offering my services, since I did not know them very well and was not called upon for advice. My daughter managed to spread some of her enthusiasm around, and a group of girls did meet at the Scout House to form a troop. I do not believe these women had the inherent qualities of leadership or a real interest in leading young girls. They did little if any planning ahead for the meetings, and had constant disciplinary problems. They shouted to get order and frequently contradicted each other. I attended the

investiture, and felt that the spirit of the ritual had been lost completely; nor had the girls been imbued with any of the ideology of the Girl Scout movement.

When the leaders complained that they were glorified baby sitters and that these children "don't need this experience," they reflected their inability to relate to the principles behind Scouting and to the children involved. It was especially sad to me because I had pressured these women to become leaders and to assume roles for which they were unprepared as well as uninterested. As I look back, I feel that I also did the children a disservice, and they would have been better off if no troop had been formed. After several months, the troop disbanded. My daughter never again wanted to join the Girl Scouts. I think these women failed because they lacked the necessary personality traits for leadership. They did not understand how to inculcate group morale, how to achieve cohesiveness within the group, or democratic participation in a group activity. They failed also to establish any rapport with the parents of the children, and did not develop any kind of a meaningful program which would enhance the children's recreative experiences. Children are not easily fooled, and they responded to their leaders' lack of interest and inability to develop the social and creative potentialities the children possessed. The women never seemed to me to be aware of what was happening, nor to care very much. They said that the children's behavior confirmed their original opinion that there was no need for a troop and felt justified when the troop disbanded in chaos.

What conclusions may be reached from this case analysis?

First, that there are such things as leadership traits, but second, and more important, that these must be buttressed by thorough planning, conviction that what one is doing is important, and by a well thought out philosophy. The first two leaders were not successful solely because of intuitive skills, but because they believed in the goals of Scouting and in the potential of the children who came to them. They had a coherent set of objectives in mind, they enjoyed their task, and they worked hard at it.

These are the ingredients of success in recreation leadership.

GUIDELINES FOR GROUP LEADERSHIP IN RECREATION

This chapter has examined the nature of leadership in recreation service, both as a designated professional role, and as a process of group development and program management. It has emphasized the importance of leadership qualities, the possession of significant leisure values, and leadership behaviors and styles suited to the needs of groups in varied settings. Summing up, the following guidelines for effective group leadership may be presented:

1. *Concern with People.* Leaders should be chiefly concerned with people, rather than activities. Their primary focus should be on what happens to participants, rather than the successful accomplishment of program objectives stated in terms of attendance, activities carried out, or similar accomplishments.
2. *Possess Human Values.* Leaders should have a coherent set of human values, which regard participants as individuals with dignity and worth,

who need understanding, support, and encouragement. The recreational group experience offers an opportunity to make these values meaningful in practice, and to help shape the attitudes of group members constructively.

3. *Alert to Group Processes.* Leaders must be alert to group organization and group processes. They should be ready to provide assistance when it is needed, or to withdraw when group members are able to provide the needed leadership themselves. This principle of alternative assistance and withdrawal—skillfully applied—helps leaders become *enablers,* rather than *directors,* of groups.

4. *Aware of Individual Needs.* Recognizing that each person is an individual, with his or her own interests, values, needs, drives, and typical ways of behaving in group situations, leaders must be prepared to deal with a wide range of behaviors. They should be able to recognize and understand the meaning of variant behavior, including hostility, withdrawal, and other forms of apparently antisocial responses, although they should not be expected to be expert psychologists.

5. *Start Where Participants Are.* Leaders must start wherever the individuals comprising the group are (in their attitudes, skills, and patterns of behavior) and gradually strive to help them move in positive directions, and to help build their awareness of why and how they are changing.

Within this total framework, it is helpful for leaders to establish sets of personal objectives, toward which they are constantly working. These might include the following: (a) helping group members discover new and rewarding interests, skills, and personal capacities, broadening their recreation horizons; (b) helping group members gain increased social sensitivity, acceptance of others, and ways of behaving effectively and constructively in interpersonal relationships; (c) helping group members become capable of planning and carrying out programs successfully, accepting responsibilities, sharing in decision-making, and assuming leadership roles themselves. Perhaps the best way of defining this overall purpose is to stress that effective recreation leadership is always a form of *goal-oriented behavior*. It is essential that leaders know why they are presenting programs, what the needs and interests of participants are, and what they are trying to accomplish. Indeed, the ability to define and achieve concrete objectives is a key aspect of successful leisure-service practice.

OTHER LEADERSHIP EMPHASES

Finally, the reader should be reminded that recreation leadership is not always a matter of working directly with groups of participants on an intensive, face-to-face basis.

In many job settings, the leader may be responsible for making arrangements for other sponsors to use the facilities of an agency, or for planning a program and then assigning part-time, seasonal, or volunteer leaders to take direct responsibility for it. In such cases, the role of the professional leader tends to be a managerial one, rather than a direct leadership involvement.

Similarly, in some settings, the leader may be in charge of a facility which is used by participants in self-directed activity, or may conduct tours or interpretive sessions in which there is relatively little direct interchange with or among the participants. In some cases, leaders may coordinate large-scale events or programs without a meaningful degree of contact or group process taking place.

In still other agencies, recreation workers may be responsible for organizing or providing other services that are not really of a recreational nature—such as counseling, advocacy, referral, or vocational assistance. They may coordinate day-care, transportation, or discount-purchase services, or other forms of personnel or health-related functions.

At the same time, the recreation professional-to-be should recognize that his or her *unique* responsibility happens to be the organization and implementation of recreation programs. It should be understood that meeting leisure needs and using creative recreation programming as a medium of personal and community enrichment *must* represent the keystone of any agency's operation. And, to be most effective, the leader must operate within a personal philosophy and set of values that will make recreation both fun and a vital human experience.

To support and enrich a number of the concepts presented in this chapter, Chapter 3 examines the broad field of group dynamics, and presents additional analyses of leadership and leadership styles, based on past and present research findings.

NOTES

[1]*Webster's New International Dictionary* (Springfield, Mass.: G. C. Merriam, 1945), p. 1405.

[2]Gordon Allport, quoted in Ralph M. Stogdill, *Handbook of Leadership: A Survey of Theory and Research* (New York: Free Press, 1974), p. 9.

[3]Gertrude Wilson and Gladys Ryland, *Social Group Work Practice* (Boston: Houghton Mifflin, 1949), p. vii.

[4]K. Davis, quoted in Stogdill, *Handbook of Leadership,* p. 13.

[5]Robert Tannenbaum and Fred Massarik, "Leadership: A Frame of Reference," *Management Science* (October 1957): 3.

[6]Howard Danford, *Creative Leadership in Recreation* (Boston: Allyn and Bacon, 1964), p. 80.

[7]Reynold E. Carlson, Janet R. MacLean, Theodore R. Deppe, and James A. Peterson, *Recreation and Leisure: The Changing Scene* (Belmont, Calif.: Wadsworth, 1979), pp. 303–4.

[8]Hope Cramer, unpublished course paper, Teachers College, Columbia Univ., 1964; used by permission.

STUDENT PROJECTS

1. Select a leader you have known in a recreational agency, and analyze that leader in terms of the qualities described in this chapter. What were his or her most important strengths and weaknesses?

2. Visit a community leisure-service agency, and do a study of its leadership personnel, with respect to job title, qualifications, functions, and leadership styles.
3. Select a particular recreation group or program activity sponsored by a community organization. Identify its goals and values, and determine whether these are the same for the participants, leaders, and heads of the agency.

SUGGESTED READINGS

Edith L. Ball and Robert E. Cipriano, *Leisure Services Preparation* (Englewood Cliffs, N.J.: Prentice-Hall, 1978), Modules 7, 9.

Christopher R. Edginton and Charles A. Griffith, *The Recreation and Leisure Service Delivery System* (Philadelphia: Saunders College, 1983), Chapters 3, 6.

Richard Kraus, Gay Carpenter, and Barbara Bates, *Recreation Leadership and Supervision* (Philadelphia: Saunders College, 1981), Chapters 2, 3.

E. William Niepoth, *Leisure Leadership* (Englewood Cliffs, N.J.: Prentice-Hall, 1984), Chapters 2, 5.

_____

CHAPTER 3

Group Dynamics_____
and Leadership_____
Approaches_____

_____

_____

Visualize, if you will, two sharply contrasting styles of group leadership. On the one hand, there is the typical stereotype of the "win-at-all-costs" football coach, who exhorts his team with fiery harangues and paces up and down the sidelines shrieking invectives. On the other hand, there is the laid-back, casual style of the New Games festival leader, easygoing, relaxed, and bubbling over with good humor and sociability.

Both leaders are involved in directing forms of play. Who is the more effective leader? Obviously, there is no easy answer, since their purposes and philosophies are so different, and the demands of their group situation vary so greatly.

In reality, leadership styles cannot be as easily or sharply categorized as they are in these two descriptions. Instead, they tend to fall along a continuum, with leaders often adapting their approach to the needs of the group and the challenges of a particular program.

RECREATION LEADERSHIP: A COMPLEX ENTERPRISE

The point is that recreation leadership is a complex enterprise, in which practitioners must function with other human beings in a variety of relationships and task situations. As earlier chapters have shown, leaders must work closely with groups at various levels of professional practice. On administrative levels, recreation and park superintendents, general managers, or other agency executives play varied roles with civic groups, advisory boards and commissions, and subordinate employees. On supervisory and direct-leadership levels, there are numerous examples of group planning, team projects, committee assignments, and a host of other situations in which recreation practitioners work with groups to satisfy their common needs or reach agreed-upon objectives.

Because leadership is such an important part of management, there may be a tendency to confuse the terms with each other. However, Gibson, Ivancevich, and Donnelly point out that leadership is a distinctly different concept from management:

> A manager in a formal organization is responsible and entrusted to perform such functions as planning, organizing, and controlling. However, leaders also exist in informal groups. Informal leaders are not always formal managers performing managerial functions which are required by the organization. Consequently, leaders are only in some instances actually managers.[1]

Whether in formal or informal roles, leisure-service practitioners are constantly involved with group management processes. It is therefore essential that they become highly knowledgeable about group dynamics—an area of theoretical research in the field of social psychology but also the source of much useful information in applied fields like business management or public administration.

MEANING OF GROUP DYNAMICS

Group dynamics is essentially concerned with exploring and achieving an understanding of the nature and role of group in modern life, and in various social institutions:

> It examines the way groups are formed, the status and interrelationship of members, how different types of group structures affect the attitudes and productivity of members, how groups influence larger social institutions and, finally, how different types of leadership approaches affect group processes. Such knowledge is directly useful to those working on any level of leadership, supervision or administration.[2]

Group dynamics seeks to understand the interaction of group members. How effectively do they get along with each other? Are some individuals accepted fully, while others are rejected? How are decisions made? How are problems solved? What techniques of communication are used? Does the group have a harmonious climate? Do people like and work well with each other, or is there a pattern of bickering and personal antagonism? Does work get accomplished and projects get carried out, or do people refuse to take assignments or live up to their responsibilities?

Reeves points out that, simply by being human beings, we are concerned with group dynamics in many areas of our everyday lives. By being more knowledgeable about the nature of group interaction and our own relationship with others, we can become happier and more effective individuals:

> In striving to be a more effective member of the groups to which we belong, our first objective is to increase our sensitivity to the impact of our own personality on others. . . . The person who has a clear understanding of what makes him tick can, if he wishes, adjust more positively and more quickly to changes in a group situation. . . . Self-knowledge is closely related to intellectual and emotional maturity. The

more a person studies group dynamics, the more easily he will increase his own self-knowledge. And this in turn will make quicker and easier the necessary decisions about groups in which he wants to seek or maintain membership.[3]

THE NATURE OF GROUPS

In all social relationships and particularly in human-service fields like recreation leadership, it is important to practice sensitive and constructive human relations, built upon a foundation of mutual respect and faith in the dignity and worth of human beings. Beyond this, in working with people, leaders must be intensely aware of the nature of groups and group processes. Such knowledge and interpersonal skills are vital; good will is not enough. Group leadership skills can be learned and improved. But first, the leader needs to be aware of the nature of groups.

Groups should be regarded as units of two or more people who have a meaningful relationship with each other, in terms of sharing common goals, purposes, or needs. To the extent that their contact is a close and enduring one, they are likely to have common values and attitudes; membership in the group will influence both the behavior of group members and the overall setting in which the group exists.

Sociologists tend to view groups primarily in terms of organizational characteristics. Here is a typical definition of the term "group" in the sociological literature:

> . . . an organized system of two or more individuals who are interrelated so that the system performs some function, has a standard set of role relationships among its members, and has a set of norms that regulate the function of the group and each of its members.[4]

Obviously, there are many groups to which most of us belong in our lives: families, groups of friends, neighborhood associations or clubs, church groups, employment-centered groups, political clubs, hobby groups or associations, as well as other broader involvements.

These may be classified in different ways. A common means of classification has been to assign them to "primary" or "secondary" categories, depending on the degree of intimacy and closeness of interdependence and interaction in the group.

Another type of analysis classifies groups as *formal* and *informal*. *Formal* groups are those that are clearly and officially structured, with defined purposes—such as a squad of soldiers in the armed forces, or a task group of employees assigned to carry out a particular function. *Informal* groups are those which form naturally, rather than by deliberate design or command, in order to satisfy common interests or needs, and which do not have as clearly defined a structure.

Groups in Recreation Settings

Many different types of groups may be found in recreation and park programs, including the following examples:

1. *Socially Oriented Groups of Participants.* These include groups in which the primary emphasis is on social involvement; typical examples would be social clubs for children and youth, membership groups in senior centers, couples clubs in churches, or singles clubs in community centers or residential facilities.
2. *Therapy Oriented Groups.* Here the emphasis is on therapy or facilitating personal growth within a treatment program; examples might include therapy groups in hospitals or mental health centers, aftercare centers or sheltered workshops, or leisure counseling groups attached to such programs.
3. *Volunteer or Advisory Groups.* In a community setting, these might include groups of volunteers working with regular programs or on special events; parents' committees, neighborhood councils, coaches' committees, or other advisory groups of nonprofessionals.
4. *Groups of Co-Workers.* In all groups in which leaders or supervisors must work with teams of co-workers, group dynamics are a key factor. Often staff development processes, including in-service education, problem-solving, or task forces designed to improve motivation or productivity, make use of group dynamics techniques.
5. *Groups Involving Administrative Interaction.* These include planning groups or boards in which department or agency executives or high-level managers work closely with other civic officials, officers or other departments or organizations, members of trustees groups or other advisory bodies, and the like.

In addition to these examples, some agencies may develop other types of programs which rely very heavily on the interaction of members in order to meet the special needs of participants. For example, O'Connor describes "leisure clinics," "stress workshops," "women's worry clinics," and other mental-health oriented programs sponsored by community agencies in Colorado.[5] Pape and Walsh describe similar examples of programs dealing with women's issues, health care, and family needs that have been co-sponsored by Illinois park districts and mental health agencies.[6] Many YWCAs in particular have sponsored similar programs within a group-discussion or workshop format. In all such settings, effective group dynamics contribute greatly to each program's success.

Characteristics of Groups

Obviously, people join groups for various reasons. In some cases, they have no choice and become affiliated with groups because of factors such as the decision of school administrators, military authorities, or employers. In other cases, people join groups to satisfy personal needs for security, self-esteem, social affiliation, or sharing of interests and hobbies.

Within groups, there are certain characteristics which affect the experiences and satisfaction of members, as well as the overall effectiveness of the group itself. For example, each group has a more or less visible *structure* of relationships, in which certain group members have a high level of prestige and status, while others are regarded as less important or influential.

Linked to the idea of positions is that of *roles*. Within both formal and informal group settings, members are typically expected to carry out certain functions, or assume given responsibilities. In some cases, individuals may have a distorted or incorrect view of their own roles, or there may be *role conflict* when group members disagree about the roles they should be playing.

Another important characteristic of groups involves *norms*, or standards of behavior and performance that are shared by group members. The *cohesiveness* of groups involves the degree of closeness and unity among group members, while group *morale* consists of the level of positive and optimistic feeling about the group. All of these factors tend to affect both the motivation and productivity of group members, and the overall successful functioning of the group itself.

Awareness of the group process is extremely important, not only to the success of the group, but also in the effect the group has upon its members. It is known that the way in which individuals learn, their speed and retention of learning, and effective problem-solving are definitely influenced by the nature of the group experience. The group strongly influences the individual's formation of attitudes, levels of aspiration, self-perception and social behavior. The group process may be extremely important in determining whether its members satisfy their needs for affiliation, approval by others, social acceptance, and affection, and in developing a sense of self-worth, or meeting other psychological or social needs.

THEORIES OF GROUP LEADERSHIP

What are the underlying components of effective group leadership, and how do individuals gain influence among group members? Throughout history, there have been numerous efforts to explain the phenomenon of leadership in human society. For a period of time, the emphasis was on identifying the qualities of leadership in national leaders such as great military figures. In more recent years, political scientists and social psychologists have been concerned with studying the nature of group leadership on more mundane levels of society, in business, social, and community life.

Trait Theory of Leadership

One of the first attempts to analyze the nature of leadership in human society resulted in the so-called "great man" theory of leadership. This view saw the leader as a person endowed with unique qualities that captured the imagination of the masses. One author suggested that leadership can never come from large groups of people. Instead, a few individuals in every society possess different degrees of intelligence, energy, and moral force, and in whatever direction the masses may be influenced, they are always led by the "superior few."

In time, this approach was modified to the view that leadership in any human activity was based on the possession of certain personal qualities that enabled one to be effective in commanding the respect and cooperation of others.

The "trait theory" of leadership was challenged by research that demonstrated that only a few of the most common traits commonly thought of as components of leadership were found widely in leaders in different settings. Such qualities as a relatively high level of education and social status, intelligence, ability to communicate, adaptability, aggressiveness or assertiveness, emotional balance, self-confidence, achievement drive, willingness to take responsibility, persistence, sound judgment, and sociability or interpersonal skills were reported as related to successful leadership in a considerable number of research studies.[7] However, it was not possible to say that a specific grouping of these traits was found in *all* successful leaders, in *all* situations.

Beyond this, the *degree* to which a particular trait may be important varies greatly from situation to situation. For example, while intelligence has been shown to be a valuable component of leadership in many research studies, *too much* intelligence may actually be a detriment in some settings. Leaders who are considerably more intelligent than the members of their groups may have difficulty in communicating with them or being accepted by them, whereas leaders who are closer to group members in this respect are likely to be more effective.

What *does* appear to be present in all leaders is a drive *toward* assuming leadership roles, with their concomitant responsibilities and rewards. Jennings has observed that "the individual's . . . behavior . . . appears as an expression of needs which are, so to speak, so central to his personality that he must strive to fulfill them whether or not the possibility of fulfilling them is at hand."[8]

As Chapter 2 points out, the trait theory has generally been accepted in the recreation and parks field, in the sense that certain personal qualities have been accepted as characteristic of successful leisure-service practitioners.

However, other theories of leadership, such as the situational theory, also have important implications for recreational leaders.

Situational Theory of Group Leadership

Research in varied group situations led some behavioral scientists to conclude that it was essential that the personal characteristics of leaders be directly relevant to the characteristics or priorities of the groups they serve. Stogdill summarized research in this field:

> The evidence suggests that leadership is a relation that exists between persons in a social situation, and that leaders who are leaders in one situation may not necessarily be leaders in other situations. . . . Leadership is not a matter of the mere possession of some combination of traits. It appears rather to be a working relationship among members of a group, in which the leader acquires status through active participation and demonstration of his capacity for carrying cooperative tasks through to completion.[9]

Obviously, different situations require different kinds of competence from leaders, either in technical knowledge or interpersonal skills or qualities. For example, one situation may require bravery, determination, or the knowledge of how to survive in a particular kind of terrain (a military unit stranded in a hostile mountainous region), while another may require skills of argument or negotiation (a labor union committee involved in a difficult collective bargaining procedure). While most leaders are characterized by a high degree of task orientation, motivation, drive, and persistence, probably these traits would be more valuable in political, military, or business life than in a group devoted to the promotion of ''transcendental meditation'' or the study of Zen Buddhism, where other personal traits may be valued.

In terms of recreation leadership, while the general qualities described in the review of the Trait Theory are widely useful, specific job situations may require other special leadership abilities. For example, in developing programs, the ability to be innovative and creative may be extremely important. In working with community groups or other professionals, a knowledge of community resources or related social services might be especially valuable. If a serious conflict situation arose, the leader with the ability to communicate effectively and verbalize shared concerns and needs might emerge in a position of authority.

Functional Theory of Leadership

It has been pointed out that leadership involves an entire group, and that any or all of the group's members may perform specific acts of leadership at different times. The concept that leadership is found in what individuals *do,* rather than in who they *are* as people or what they *know,* is called the Functional Theory of leadership. It holds that leadership is a widely shared function of the group, rather than the unique possession of one person.

Such functional roles may be specifically described in terms of tasks such as public relations, budget-making, the ability to design a playground, organize a basketball tournament, or deal effectively with community representatives. On the other hand—in a deeper sense—they are identified as skills which relate or contribute to the healthy functioning of the group. Such skills might include: (1) helping to define goals and objectives; (2) facilitating group decision-making and problem-solving; or (3) maintaining group cohesiveness and member satisfaction.

Ideally, all members of a task-oriented group would be able to contribute in a meaningful way to one or another of these processes, and thus would assume, at least intermittently, leadership functions and identity in the eyes of the other group members.

Contingency Theory of Leadership

Other social psychologists have concluded that different styles of leadership are called for, depending on the interaction of such variables as: (a) the makeup of the group, and its values or felt needs regarding leadership styles or methods; (b) the actual demands of the situation, what the leader must accomplish and bring to the task; and (c) the qualities and capabilities, and personal needs or wishes of the leader.

Fiedler developed a complex analysis of leadership in different group situations, in which such variables as the leader's *position power* (meaning his or her degree of authority and ability to reward or punish group members), the *task structure* (the clarity of the group's goals and assignments) and *personal relationships* between the leader and group members all were studied intensively. His so-called Contingency Theory of Leadership concluded that the socially distant, or *work-oriented* leader tended to be more effective either in very simple work situations in which the goals were well understood and the solutions relatively easy, or in very difficult or demanding group assignments. On the other hand, the *interaction-oriented* leader tended to be more effective in situations imposing moderately difficult demands upon the group.[10]

Fiedler also comments that leadership is a very complicated issue that people have been working on ever since the time of Plato. He writes:

> In any leadership relationship, what we are concerned with is how much control and influence the leader has in a group or an organization. Some people do well with control and others don't. . . . It is a relationship between a person and other individuals. General George Patton was a very effective combat tank commander, but I doubt he'd be good as a chairman of the PTA.[11]

Attribution Theory and Path-Goal Model

There have been numerous other recent theories of leadership, including *attribution theory,* and the *path-goal* model of leadership effectiveness.

Attribution theory represents an approach under which leaders seek to analyze and understand rationally the behavior of their followers or subordinates—in other words, seeking "informational cues that explain why something is happening." For example, Kelley suggests that the primary attributional task of the leader is to analyze the causes of follower or subordinate behavior into three source dimensions: *person, entity,* or *context*.

> That is, for any given behavior, such as poor quality of productive output, the leader's job is to determine if the poor quality was caused by the person (e.g., inadequate ability), the task (entity), or some unique set of circumstances surrounding the event (context).[12]

By analyzing the leader's perception of such factors, it is possible to understand his or her behavior and to modify it in more positive directions.

The *path-goal* model of leadership attempts to predict leaders' effectiveness in different situations, based on their impact on followers' motivation, ability to perform, and satisfaction. This approach is called "path-goal" because it focuses on how leaders influence their followers' perceptions of work goals, personal development goals, and paths to goal achievement. It is particularly concerned with the leader's strategic use of rewards and other means of giving directions for goal accomplishment, and helping followers develop realistic expectations leading to satisfaction.[13]

Composite Approach to Understanding Recreation Leadership

Reviewing these various approaches, it is apparent that no single theory or model provides a complete explanation or guideline for developing effective recreation leadership.

Obviously, the trait theory is applicable, in that successful professionals in this field are believed to have certain important qualities which contribute to effective functioning in recreation leadership roles. In particular, it is important to have needed technical knowledge and skills, a sound philosophy of recreation, and the ability to communicate well, make effective judgments and decisions, organize efficiently, and command respect as a leader and spokesperson for the group.

Beyond this, it is obvious that different professional assignments or job situations may call for different leadership styles. In some cases, the *work-oriented* leader is likely to be more successful, and in others, the *interaction-oriented* leader.

Certain recurrent functions in groups may be carried on by different members of the group. Thus, leadership may be regarded as a shared process and, at times, will be in the hands of other individuals than the formal or appointed group leader. Finally, leaders should be aware of the findings of research regarding ways of motivating subordinates and followers, resolving conflict situations effectively, and developing a high level of satisfaction stemming from goal attainment on various levels.

SOURCES OF LEADERSHIP STATUS

In actual practice, it is important to recognize that leaders may gain power or authority in a number of different ways. In some cases, they are formally appointed to positions of authority, or hold job titles which confirm their leadership roles. In other cases, they may not be formally identified or acknowledged as leaders, but may function in this capacity. Sources of leadership status include the following:

1. *Elected Leaders*. In membership organizations, special-interest groups, or in political or governmental life, it is customary for leaders to be selected by choice of the majority through formal voting procedures. This process may also apply to committees, clubs, or other smaller group settings.

2. *Appointed Leaders*. In many governmental or business organizations, it is customary for high-level administrators to appoint individuals to leadership roles as heads of divisions, committees, district programs, or other operational units, usually based on their past performance.

3. *Career-Ladder Leaders*. Particularly in government or other large bureaucratic structures, many individuals achieve leadership posts by gradually climbing the "career ladder." They gain advancement by taking examinations, meeting Civil Service requirements, applying for promotions or transfer, or simply through seniority on the job.

4. *Inherited Leaders*. In contrast to leaders who "earn their spurs"

through past performance, some leaders "inherit" their posts either through family affiliation (most obviously when the post is passed from parent to child, as in the case of monarchies), or in political life, when a wife, brother, or close associate of a leading figure assumes the mantle of leadership when that person becomes ill, dies, or otherwise terminates office.

5. *Emergent Leaders.* This describes the type of leader who gains status within a group because, over a period of time or in a critical situation, he or she demonstrates the qualities necessary to help the group achieve its goals. Often, emergent leaders assume high-status positions without formal recognition, although they may also be elected by group members.

Types of Leader Influence

Leaders may derive their influence or power from several kinds of different sources. Some individuals have *legitimate power,* in the sense that they are formally elected or appointed to leadership posts which give them authority over the group and its actions. Other leaders have what is called *referent power,* because they exemplify the ideals and values of group members, who accept them as role models and respect their authority.

Still other leaders are influential because of their *expertise,* which group members respect, or because they are able to *reward* others financially, or with other types of positive reinforcement. Finally, some leaders are influential because they are able to exert *coercion,* or other forms of negative reinforcement or punishment on group members.

Recreation leaders play important roles, in terms of helping groups of participants or co-workers function to their maximum potential. In so doing, they seek to promote positive group and staff relationships, and to mobilize the efforts of group members toward the achievement of organizational goals. Sessoms and Stevenson discuss a number of key roles and functions of leaders, including the following:

1. To develop a *sense of "we-ness,"* so that group members are able to pull together and work toward common goals.
2. To develop a positive *hedonic* tone, or pleasant group climate, which in turn enhances the group's productivity.
3. To help group members identify their *goals* and *objectives.* While these might appear to be self-evident, often they are not, and the leader must help group members select appropriate goals, in keeping with their overall purposes and agency philosophy, along with their capability.
4. To help the group *organize for goal achievement.* This function involves establishing priorities, responsibilities, and necessary group structures.
5. To initiate *action* that will lead to achieving the group's goals.[14]

Linked to these functions are others which involve helping the group develop and implement an overall *philosophy,* and establishing a pattern of effective *communi-*

cation. In recreation-related settings, these tasks may differ somewhat according to whether the group situation is work-oriented or program-oriented.

Work-Oriented Groups

These are groups of recreation leaders, specialists, supervisors, volunteers, or other individuals who are concerned with carrying out professional responsibilities. Frequently, such co-workers must share the process of formulating plans, making decisions, and solving problems, and reviewing possible recommendations or courses of action. At such times, the leader is instrumental in helping group members initiate and carry out a course of action while maintaining a high level of cohesion and group satisfaction.

Program-Oriented Groups

Leaders who are responsible for working with groups of recreational participants where the activity itself is of major importance may feel that understanding group dynamics is not particularly critical in their work. Instead, they may feel that the chief task is to teach skills, or to supervise participation, in such areas as games or craft activities, sports, dance, or music. However, they should recognize that even in such assignments, there are often problems involving interpersonal relationships, scheduling, special events, programs, or exhibitions, irregular attendance, and poor morale. Thus even in an activity-centered group, group dynamics represent an important concern.

In both work-oriented and program-oriented groups, leaders may need to assume a variety of different roles, including the following:

Policy-maker: helping the group make decisions about relating to goals, membership, meeting time and place, dues, and similar matters.

Planner: helping the group develop specific plans for activities, programs, trips, special events, and other projects.

Organizer: helping the group evolve ways of structuring themselves, of making concrete plans for action.

Resource Person: acting as a source of information, knowledge, skills, and contacts.

Referee: helping the group resolve conflicts and disagreements.

Disciplinarian: in a constructive sense, helping the group members develop rules and other forms of control and impose them of their own volition; exerting controls directly when necessary.

Group Symbol: acting as a model, one who group members admire and respect, and whose values and behavior they emulate.

In addition to these functions, the leader may seek to help the group affirm its identity, by capitalizing on techniques that build a sense of belonging. Studies have shown that slogans and songs, uniforms or T-shirts, customs and traditions, and similar devices help strengthen group members' feelings of loyalty and commitment, as well as sense that the group's well-being is their concern, and that it serves to meet their needs.

EFFECTIVE GROUP LEADERSHIP STYLES

How does one assess the overall quality of leadership behavior? What leadership styles are most effective? We tend to speak of the "democratic" group leader, as if this were the only desirable approach. What *is* democratic leadership, and *is* it the most effective and appropriate style for group leaders in recreation settings?

Research in Leadership Approaches

During the 1930s and 1940s, an extensive series of research studies in group leadership methods were carried out by Lewin, Lippitt, and White, among others.[15] These studies identified three major orientations, or leadership approaches: the *autocratic*, or highly authoritarian; the *laissez faire,* or permissive; and the *democratic* approach, in which the leader offers support, advice, technical assistance, and similar forms of help, but strives also to have group members take over the functions of decision making, planning, and other group tasks.

Briefly summarized, these studies found that while autocratically-led groups tended to be productive, they also resulted in group members' becoming highly dependent on the direction of the leader. When he absented himself, the group was unable to function effectively or to meet emergencies well. In the permissively-directed groups, there tended to be poor activity output, as well as uncertainty, confusion, and frustration. In general, the democratically-led groups were most successful, both in task accomplishment and in the morale and cohesion of group members.

A number of other research studies in the 1950s and 1960s showed how leadership techniques could be used to modify the nature of group relationships, and to manipulate the attitudes and behavior of group members. These studies emphasized the *power* of group leadership as well as the ease through which both negative or hostile values and more constructive and desirable intergroup relationships could be developed.

Exploration of Other Leadership Styles

Over the last two decades, research into leadership methods resulted in new ways of identifying alternative group approaches. Instead of the three basic styles (autocratic, permissive, democratic), numerous unique styles were described in different business or government agency settings, often using popular or "catchy" terminology. For example, some of the different types of business managers today are said to include:

1. *The Craftsman:* This is the type of individual who is production-oriented, concerned with quality, and interested in building a sound record.
2. *The Jungle Fighter:* This type of individual is interested in gaining power. Life and work are viewed as a jungle. Others are viewed as accomplices or enemies.
3. *The Company Man (or Woman):* This individual is interested in cooperation, commitment, and security.
4. *Gamesman (or Woman):* This new type of leader thrives on challenge, competitive activity, and new and fresh approaches. The main goal of this type of person is to be a winner. This person is interested in developing the tactics and strategies needed to be a winner.[16]

Gradually, however, most analyses of leadership styles began to resolve themselves around two basic orientations: *task-oriented* and *person-oriented.*

Task-Oriented Leadership: Task-oriented leaders are primarily concerned with the work to be done. They get their chief satisfaction from successful work accomplishment; they tend to be autocratic, restrictive, distant, directive, and structured in their approach. In general, they subscribe to what McGregor has called Theory X—the traditional view of employees or workers as individuals who will "goof off" if not carefully supervised, and who require carefully structured work assignments, clearly stated task expectations, and a clear-cut system of punishments and rewards in order to guarantee effective performance. In some texts, the task-oriented leadership approach is referred to as the productivity-oriented approach.

Person-Oriented Leadership: This approach describes leaders who enjoy group interaction and emphasize interpersonal relationships more than they do task-accomplishment. Basically, such leaders believe strongly in open communication, employee participation in goal setting and group decision making, and mutual trust rather than more coercive ways of enforcing productivity. They subscribe to McGregor's Theory Y, which holds that workers will be far more productive under a trusting, participative, job-enrichment system of management, than under the traditional autocratic, highly structured system. This approach is sometimes referred to as the "relationship-oriented" or "interaction-oriented" approach.[17] A more complete discussion of McGregor's theories is found in Chapter 13.

While the latter approach sounds far more appealing, does it actually work more effectively in all leader-group situations? Belasco suggests that the evidence is mixed. Considerable research in industrial plants, military research laboratories, schools, and various government agencies has led to the following conclusions:

1. Supervisors of high productivity departments had employee-oriented, supportive leadership styles, emphasizing member participation and satisfaction.
2. Supervisors who practiced employee-oriented leadership had lower turnover, more cooperation, and higher employee satisfaction.[18]

However, he also found that not all high-producing industrial or military units were characterized by employee-centered leadership, nor did all person-oriented supervisors have high-producing units. Other factors apparently affected this relationship. A series of midwestern studies concluded:

1. Supervisors who plan and schedule the work of subordinates in a directive way were rated very highly by their superiors and generally had high productivity and low cost and scrap rates. They also had higher grievance and employee turnover rates.
2. Supervisors who emphasized employee consideration had low grievance and employee turnover rates, but low productivity rates as well.
3. There was substantial unexplained variation between group performance and leadership styles. That is, many initiating-structure leaders had low performance groups, and many employee-consideration leaders had high performance groups.[19]

In general, the prevailing trend in personnel management theory today is to favor the person-oriented approach. However, many managers and supervisors who actually work in business, government, or the military appear reluctant to abandon the more traditional values expressed in McGregor's Theory X, and appear to adhere to the task-oriented approach. Research seems to confirm that successful leadership depends very heavily on the special circumstances involved:

> Task-motivated leaders tend to be very pleasant and very considerate when everything is under control. They tend to get uptight and more punitive and controlling when the situation is less under their control.
>
> Relationship-motivated people tend to be a little more businesslike when everything is under control and more concerned with personal relationships when things are a little less controlled and more touchy.[20]

In general, the style that works best depends on the power of the leader's position, the difficulty of the task, and the attitudes and relationships of the leader's subordinates.

TRENDS IN GROUP-MANAGEMENT APPROACHES

The strongest thrust in the area of groups dynamics today, in such fields as business, government, or social service, is in the direction of participative management. This approach suggests that leaders—on whatever level—should seek to establish an atmosphere of trust and free communication, and that they should involve co-workers, subordinate employees, or program participants in a genuinely-shared process of group planning and cooperative action.

Participative Management Emphasis

This approach has generally become known as the "participative management" style of leadership, and has strongly influenced current business and government management methods. As an example, Schmitt identified a continuum of leadership behavior with respect to the decision-making process; it extends from *Autocratic Leadership* at one end of the continuum, to *Participative Leadership* at the other, in seven distinct stages (see Table 3–1).[21]

TABLE 3–1 Managerial Decision-Making

Autocratic Leadership Approach				Participative Leadership Approach	
Use of authority by the manager				Area of freedom for employees	
Manager makes decision and announces it	Manager "sells" decisions	Manager presents tentative decision, subject to change	Manager presents problem, gets suggestions, makes decision	Manager defines limits, asks group to make decision	Manager permits employees to function within limits of agency policy

Adapted from *Supervisory Behavior in Decision-Making*, (Robert Tannenbaum and Warren H. Schmitt: "How to Choose a Leadership Pattern." *Harvard Business Review*, March–April, 1958): 96.

It generally reflects the view that people *want* to make a significant contribution in the work environment, and that work can be creative and interesting. It is the responsibility of management to release their energies through trust and encouragement, and by giving them meaningful assignments, rather than through a "carrot-and-stick" approach to motivating by punishments and rewards, or through a rigid system of authoritarian supervision.

When individuals have been accustomed to other leadership styles in work-related situations, it may not be easy for them to adapt positively to such approaches. Often, at the outset, people may abuse trust, and may take advantage of a superior's flexibility or openness to loaf on the job and fail to produce. Through the group process, it is essential to develop a mutually supportive climate in which group values emerge that all workers or participants can support, and that help to build their own level of motivation.

By sharing in decision-making and problem-solving, and by having a real voice in planning programs and determining the nature of their own work assignments, the assumption is that leaders and participants alike will take greater pride and satisfaction in the group effort, will support its decisions, and will be more fully productive.

This growing emphasis is illustrated by a number of key trends identified in John Naisbitt's popular book, *Megatrends*.[22] On a governmental level, Naisbitt points out that we are steadily moving away from a "top-down" approach to authority and decision-making, in which the centralized or higher levels of authority have traditionally been the source of much power, to a decentralized or lower level of authority, which he describes as a "bottom-up" philosophy.

Naisbitt also points out that networking, the process in which different organizations and individuals join together in cooperative projects, is becoming increasingly popular in many areas of public service. Hudson sums up the linkage of the two elements:

"Participatory democracy" is a concept that is intertwined with both decentralization and networking. The guiding principle of participatory democracy is that people must be part of the process of arriving at decisions that affect their lives. . . . As Naisbitt states, "People must feel that they have 'ownership' in a decision if they are to support it with any enthusiasm."[23]

Several aspects of this approach to recreation and leisure-service management and group leadership include: (1) cooperative goal structuring; (2) the role of delegation in problem-solving; (3) the consensus approach to decision-making and group problem-solving; and (4) the influence of attitudes in the management process. Each of these reflects an important aspect of current group dynamics thinking that is useful both in staff operations and in the leadership of recreation groups of various types.

Cooperative Goal Structuring. Shared goal-setting has great potential for creating a climate in which both individual and organizational goals can be realized—as compared with situations in which group members compete to have their goals accepted by others, or simply forge ahead individualistically, without accepting common aims. Since many functions of leisure-service agencies can best be carried out through cooperative action, it makes sense to use this approach even in the initial phases of planning and goal development. Little writes:

> The leisure-service manager serves an important role in articulating congruency between organizational and employee goals. To structure goals cooperatively, managers should present a task or problem to everyone in the organization who affects or is affected by it, establish group ownership of the task, design nonthreatening ways to exchange information and ideas, develop problem-solving groups based on individual strengths, and reinforce successful completion of each step through feedback.[24]

When all members of a work team or recreation program group have shared in establishing their group's goals, they are much more likely to support them than if they were "handed down" by higher levels of authority.

Delegation of Authority. This term refers to the assignment of a specific task or area of responsibility to subordinate employees or group members. In delegating authority, the manager or group leader is expressing his or her confidence in those who have been given the added responsibility. Logically, this approach fits well with the idea of cooperative goal structuring. Once all members of a team have shared the problem-solving or priority-setting process, they should also play significant roles in implementing the group decisions that have been made. However, Bannon points out that, although delegation sounds simple, it is difficult for many managers to put it into action:

> They may believe they have delegated tasks through fancy organizational charts and detailed job descriptions, yet they still maintain restrictive control over the organization's daily activities. Even those managers who sincerely want to delegate a burdensome workload among competent and promising staff members are easily confounded by what sounds so easy at first. Organizational theorists admit that few managers are able to put delegation of authority into practice.[25]

There are a number of reasons why this is the case. Managers may be reluctant to delegate authority because they do not have confidence in their employees or because they are unwilling to take the "risk" that this may involve. They may fail to understand the advantages of successful delegation, or may have a desire for nothing "short of perfection." On the other hand, they may fear to delegate because they are unwilling to give up the reins of power, or because they may fear that employees will "outshine" them by doing the tasks too well.

Similarly, employees or recreation group members may not welcome additional responsibilities, and may indeed resist the entire idea of participative management. Many leaders have experienced the situation where only a few members of a social club or program committee are *willing* to take responsibility and do the work necessary to carry on special events or other activities.

This suggests that the process of delegating authority must be carefully initiated, with subordinate employees or group members encouraged to assume new leadership roles, and given assistance that will make it possible for them to achieve success. Rewards and "stroking" in the form of praise and recognition are essential elements, in reinforcing this process.

Consensus Approach to Decision-Making.

A related principle of effective group management holds that decision-making should be a shared process, in which all concerned individuals play a meaningful role, and in which every effort is made to arrive at decisions acceptable to all.

This approach has received fresh emphasis in recent years by those who have studied Japanese approaches to business management. Yoshioka, Nilson, and Edginton point out that decision-making in the Western world is often made by higher-level executives on an individual basis, and passed down the chain of command. They point out:

> By contrast, Japanese managers use consensus as a method of decision-making, involving appropriate parties within the organization. This strategy produces a commitment to an organization's actions. . . . Employee motivation and self-worth are increased significantly because each individual knows his views have been reviewed. The resulting job satisfaction increases productivity.[26]

A key element in the Japanese approach to improving worker productivity is the "quality circle." A quality circle usually consists of between two and ten employees who meet voluntarily one hour a week to identify, interpret, and solve work problems, and to improve the quality of each worker's contribution. Quality circle discussions seek to build more humanistic and meaningful work environments, and to solve problems that individual employees may have within the organization.

Other important elements in the Japanese approach to participative management include: (a) a free flow of information from frontline employees to top management to facilitate better and quicker decision-making processes; (b) employee rotation among departments, resulting in better cooperation within the overall organization; (c) commitment to common goals and a sense of two-way loyalty between workers and management, with a strong sense of job security; and (d) emphasis on collective values within the organization, rather than individuality and self-sufficiency.

A particularly important aspect of the participative management approach involves problem-solving. Group-centered problem-solving techniques may include values-clarification or sensitivity training exercises, which help individuals work together openly and cooperatively. Role-playing, such as sociodrama or psychodrama, is often helpful in exploring issues and creating better understanding of different viewpoints held in the group. Brainstorming is also valuable as a means of developing a large number of creative solutions or ideas that might not surface through ordinary group processes.

Probably the most widely used problem-solving technique is group discussion. Groups are usually able to generate more ideas than single individuals can, and the combined judgement of the group is usually sounder than the views of individual members. It is also assumed that when all group members have had a real opportunity to express their views and be part of the process, they will accept and support the decision that is made.

As the group engages in a problem-solving discussion, different members should assist in playing such important roles as initiating discussion, regulating it, bringing information or opinion to the group, encouraging others to take part, harmonizing or compromising different points of view, and ultimately helping move the group toward decision or action.

The leader's role is to help group members define the problem they face, keep the discussion focused on the central issues rather than extraneous ones, clarify contributions where necessary, and maintain an atmosphere where cooperation and maximum group productivity can be achieved.

One of the key elements in cooperative group efforts of this kind is the effort to arrive at a "win-win" solution, rather than a "win-lose" solution, in which one individual or faction overcomes others, or a "lose-lose" outcome, where nobody gets what they want. Group problem-solving processes are discussed more fully in Chapter 12 with a discussion of such techniques as brainstorming and role-playing.

Importance of Attitudes. A final critical element in the participative management approach has to do with the overall attitudinal set of the manager or leader. Studies have shown, for example, that the most effective managers are those who genuinely trust and like their subordinates, are positive about their organization's goals and programs, and are willing to share responsibility and delegate authority.

To illustrate, a recent study of over 1000 executives of major American corporations found that these individuals possessed certain common traits and attitudes. They were able to learn from failures and on-the-job difficulties and to redirect negative energy into positive, constructive performance. Successful managers, the study revealed, tend to think positively, be perceptive about their subordinates' needs and motivations, strive for meaningful communication with them, and be persuasive in dealing with their co-workers and raising their performance expectations.[27]

Similarly, recreation program leaders must have positive, upbeat attitudes, if they are to be effective. The case study of Girl Scout leaders presented in Chapter 2 reveals how the two women who were convinced that the work they were doing was important, and who committed themselves fully to the task, were successful—while other leaders who lacked these attributes failed.

The implications are clear. Recreation leaders at every level must be aware of the human relationships within their agencies and co-workers, and must strive to enhance positive group dynamics with them and with the participants they serve. Effective performance is a product of such attitudes and leadership approaches, and of sound knowledge of the competencies that underly day-by-day program leadership in varied agency settings.

REASSURANCE FOR THE READER

In concluding this chapter, the reader deserves a word of reassurance. First, it is recognized that much of the material presented in it has been drawn from the literature in the social and behavioral sciences, and may appear to be somewhat dry and technical.

However, it is important for recreation leaders to understand the concepts that have been summarized, and to apply them whenever possible in their own work. Beyond this, the reader should recognize that one's ability to work effectively with others in group situations may stem very heavily from one's own personality traits and common sense, as well as from group leadership skills that are developed through experience.

Often, people who have almost no theoretical background in the scientific understanding of group dynamics are *extremely* successful in working with others, because of the warmth of their own personalities, their enthusiasm, and their good judgment.

Finally, it should be stressed that skills related to group process are only *part* of the leader's essential repertoire of competencies. Beyond these, recreation leaders must have specific abilities related to teaching or directing various types of program activities, as well as other skills involved in managing recreation areas or carrying out other important functions.

Before examining these specific methods of activity leadership, however, this text will provide an overview of the different types of agencies in which recreation leaders are employed. Following this, the functions and roles of leaders will be presented, with examples drawn from each of the different kinds of organizations.

NOTES

[1]James L. Gibson, John M. Ivancevich, and James H. Donnelly, Jr., *Organization: Behavior, Structure, Processes* (Plano, Tex.: Business Publications, Inc., 1982), p. 230.

[2]Richard Kraus, Barbara Bates, and Gaylene Carpenter, *Recreation Leadership and Supervision* (Philadelphia: Saunders College Publishing, 1981), p. 65.

[3]Elton T. Reeves, cited in Kraus, pp. 65–66.

[4]Kraus, p. 180.

[5]Constance O'Connor, "Self-Awareness Programs: A New Frontier in Recreation," *Parks and Recreation* (October 1979): 43–45.

[6]Carolyn Pape and Joseph A. Walsh, "Prevention in the Park: Recreation and Mental Health," *Parks and Recreation* (October 1979): 40–41.

[7]Ralph M. Stogdill, *Handbook of Leadership: A Survey of Theory and Research* (New York: Free Press, 1974), p. 30.

[8]Stogdill, p. 64.

[9]Stogdill, pp. 64–65.

[10]See Marvin E. Shaw, *Group Dynamics: The Psychology of Small Group Behavior* (New York: McGraw-Hill, 1971), pp. 275–78.

[11]Gibson et al., p. 255.

[12]Gibson et al., p. 246.

[13]Gibson et al., pp. 268–70.

[14]H. Douglas Sessoms and Jack L. Stevenson, *Leadership and Group Dynamics in Recreation Services* (Boston: Allyn and Bacon, 1981), pp. 6–7.

[15]See Ralph K. White and Ronald Lippitt, *Autocracy and Democracy* (New York: Harper Bros., 1960).

[16]See Michael Maccoby, *The Gamesman* (New York: Simon and Schuster, 1976).

[17]E. William Niepoth, *Leisure Leadership* (Englewood Cliffs, N.J.: Prentice-Hall, 1983), pp. 140–44.

[18]James A. Belasco, David R. Hampton, and Karl F. Price, *Management Today* (New York: Wiley, 1975), pp. 86–87.

[19]Belasco et al., pp. 86–87.

[20]Sessoms and Stevenson, p. 43.

[21]See Robert Tannenbaum and Warren H. Schmitt, "How to Choose a Leadership Pattern," *Harvard Business Review* (March–April 1958): 96.

[22]John Naisbitt, *Megatrends: Ten New Directions Transforming Our Lives* (New York: Warner, 1982).

[23]Naisbitt, pp. 221–22.

[24]Sandra L. Little, "Cooperative Goal Structuring," *Journal of Physical Education, Recreation and Dance* (April 1982): 43.

[25]Joseph J. Bannon, *Problem-Solving in Recreation and Parks* (Englewood Cliffs, N.J.: Prentice-Hall, 1981), p. 10; see also "Reduce Stress and Increase Effectiveness Through Time Management," *Parks and Recreation* (November 1982): 40–41.

[26]Carlton F. Yoshioka, Ralph A. Nilson, Christopher R. Edginton, "What Park and Leisure Services Can Learn from Japanese Managers," *Journal of Physical Education, Recreation and Dance* (April 1982): 61.

[27]Allan Cox, *Cox Report on the American Corporation* (New York: Delacorte, 1983).

QUESTIONS

1. Why is an understanding of group dynamics extremely important for recreation leaders? Illustrate your reply with examples of different program situations in which leaders work directly with groups.
2. Of the various theories of leadership presented in this chapter, which do you feel are most applicable to recreation situations? Why?
3. Under what circumstances do you feel that "relationship-oriented" leaders are likely to be most effective? "Task-oriented" leaders? What are the arguments supporting participative management or shared decision-making as effective group approaches?

STUDENT PROJECT

As a class exercise, divide into small groups, and demonstrate how a meeting might be conducted using autocratic, democratic, or laissez-faire leadership techniques. What are the reactions of the group members and spectators to each of these approaches?

SUGGESTED READINGS

Christopher R. Edginton and Charles A. Griffith. *The Recreation and Leisure Service Delivery System* (Philadelphia: W. B. Saunders, 1983), Chapters 4, 10.

Richard Kraus, Gay Carpenter, and Barbara Bates, *Recreation Leadership and Supervision* (Philadelphia: W. B. Saunders, 1981), Chapter 4.

E. William Niepoth, *Leisure Leadership* (Englewood Cliffs, N.J.: Prentice-Hall, 1984), Chapter 6.

H. Douglas Sessoms and Jack L. Stevenson, *Leadership and Group Dynamics in Recreation Services* (Boston: Allyn and Bacon, 1981), Chapters 1, 2, 3, 5.

Settings for_____
Leadership:_____
An Eight-by-Eight_____
Model_____

We now move into an analysis of the eight major types of agencies that comprise the present-day leisure-service system. These include the following categories: (1) public, or governmental; (2) voluntary, nonprofit; (3) private membership; (4) commercial; (5) armed forces; (6) college or university-sponsored; (7) corporate/employee; and (8) therapeutic.

This chapter will first define these categories and provide appropriate illustrations or examples, and will then analyze each in turn, based on eight elements or characteristics. The elements are: (1) nature of sponsorship or administrative control; (2) sources of funding; (3) philosophy and organizational goals; (4) typical structure, related to lines of authority and functions; (5) populations served; (6) staffing patterns; (7) facilities and physical settings used for programming; and (8) major program elements and formats.

Essentially, the analysis provides an eight-by-eight model (see Table 4–1), with 64 cells showing how each of the different types of agencies may be described, based on each of the elements or characteristics. Since the information is too detailed to be presented in a single diagram, it takes the following format. First, each of the eight categories of organizations is briefly defined. Then, one by one, they are analyzed with respect to the eight elements, with emphasis on their special implications for program leadership.

DEFINITION AND EXAMPLES OF THE EIGHT CATEGORIES

1. Public, Governmental. This category includes all publicly sponsored leisure-service agencies which are officially a part of government on several levels: federal, state or provincial, or local. As an example, in the United States, on the

TABLE 4–1 Model of Agency Types and Characteristics

Types of Agencies	Characteristics of Agencies							
	Sponsorship or Administrative Control	Sources of Funding	Philosophy and Organizational Goals	Typical Organizational Structure	Populations Served	Staffing Patterns	Facilities and Physical Settings	Major Program Elements
Public, Governmental		*taxes fund raising*				*Forestry Trail hiking naturalist*	*Informational day acara to reve l*	
Voluntary, Nonprofit		*gifts United way*						
Private Membership								
Commercial								
Armed Forces								
College or University-Sponsored								
Corporate/Employee								
Therapeutic								

federal and state levels, there are hundreds of recreation and park departments, bureaus, or other governmental agencies concerned with open space, natural resource management, the promotion of recreation as an economic function or the provision of services for special populations.

On the local level, public recreation agencies include municipal (city, town, village) recreation and park departments, as well as programs sponsored by county governments or special park and/or recreation and park districts. In this chapter and throughout the text, primary emphasis is given to examining the functions of local recreation and park agencies, since this is the level most directly concerned with meeting leisure needs and interests as a primary form of governmental responsibility.

2. Voluntary, Nonprofit. Voluntary, nonprofit agencies represent organizations which serve the public with a wide range of programs and services intended to achieve desirable social outcomes. While they may charge for membership or participation in programs, they are not profit-making. Often referred to as youth-serving, character-building, or social-service organizations, they typically provide a variety of programs intended to meet needs related to education, health, welfare, vocational adjustment, social adjustment, and constructive use of leisure.

There are hundreds of examples of voluntary, nonprofit agencies in modern society, such as the Boy or Girl Scouts; the YMCA, YWCA, or YM-YWHA; the Police Athletic League or 4-H Clubs; or organizations designed to meet the needs of the handicapped, special-interest organizations, or programs designed to serve the economically disadvantaged or promote environmental or religious values.

3. Private Membership. These are organizations which are somewhat narrower in their scope than the first two described, both in terms of those who participate and the kinds of recreational programs they provide. Customarily, they include organizations with clearly defined memberships; and do not provide programming for the public at large. Their memberships may or may not be restrictive in nature; country clubs, golf clubs, tennis clubs, or hunting and fishing clubs may have exclusive admission policies requiring careful review and screening by a membership committee, or may be relatively easy to join.

Other examples of private membership organizations may include fraternal or service clubs, or recreation programs linked to one's residence (as in condominium developments with recreational facilities).

4. Commercial. This category of leisure-service agency includes any type of business or company that provides recreational programs, services, products, or equipment to the public at large, on a for-profit basis. It includes companies in the field of travel and tourism, commercial entertainment or sports, health and fitness centers, private instruction in recreational activities, or the manufacture of leisure-related supplies.

Examples include theme parks, resorts, private camps, dance studios, bowling alleys, racquetball centers or health spas, playground equipment manufacturers, or video game arcades.

5. Armed Forces.   While armed forces recreation programs are actually sponsored and largely financed by the federal governments in the United States and Canada, they represent such a uniquely different, large-scale category of service that they are presented here as a separate type of sponsor. Examples incude administrative units responsible for meeting morale, welfare, and recreation needs of servicemen and women in all branches of the armed forces.

6. College or University-Sponsored.   Often referred to as "campus recreation," this category of sponsorship includes recreation-related programs provided or assisted by colleges or universities designed to meet the leisure needs of students, faculty members, or sometimes others living in the adjacent community.

Specific examples of such programs include intramural sports associations, sports clubs, social programs, cultural arts series, outing associations, or other recreational activities which are carried on under the direct sponsorship or supervision of the college or university administration.

7. Corporate/Employee Programs.   These are recreation programs designed to serve the employees of a given company. Originally titled "industrial recreation," today they are often referred to as "employee recreation and services," or as "corporate" programs. These newer titles are combined in this text, in the term "corporate/employee" programs. The organizations involved may be extremely diverse, including manufacturing concerns; insurance companies, banks, or high-tech enterprises; government agencies; airlines companies; drug manufacturers; or numerous other types of businesses.

8. Therapeutic Recreation Service.   These are recreation programs serving individuals who are disabled in some form (emotional, mental, physical, or social) with specially designed leisure-related activities. They may be clearly intended as a form of therapy or leisure education, or may simply provide modified forms of recreation for special populations.

Operating both in institutional and community settings, they include recreation programs in nursing homes, psychiatric hospitals, or physical rehabilitation centers, as examples. Other illustrations include programs sponsored in the community by wheelchair sports associations, Special Olympics, or similar groups.

Following this initial explanation of the eight categories of recreation sponsors, we now move into a more detailed analysis, based on the eight characteristics shown in Table 4–1 (p. 54).

PUBLIC, GOVERNMENTAL AGENCIES

1. Sponsorship or Administrative Control.   Local public agencies, the form of government sponsor stressed in this chapter, are operated as branches of government which have been established primarily to carry out recreation and park functions. In some cases, other government units may also have leisure-service responsibilities as a secondary function. Their authority and responsibilities are usually defined in the legislation that authorized them initially, or in municipal charters, educational codes, or other legal documents.

Beyond this, specific operational responsibilities and policies have often been built up over a period of time through later ordinances, changes in the municipal code, or internal policy decisions or statements. Typically, a municipal, county, or park district program will be administered by a director, superintendent, or general manager who has been appointed by a mayor, county executive, township board, city manager, or other governing authority.

In many municipalities, counties, or special districts, there will be an elected or appointed board or commission to which the agency's director is responsible, which approves budget plans, personnel decisions, and policies.

2. Sources of Funding. For several decades, public recreation and park agencies were commonly referred to as "tax-supported" governmental bodies, with the assumption that their primary source of income would be general tax funds allocated to their support, with possibly 5 or 10 percent of their operational budget derived from fees and charges.

Today, it is probably safe to say that general tax funds are still the primary means of support for most public local agencies, but that a much higher percentage of the annual budget is derived from registration, admissions, rental or use fees, and charges. Other means of support include: (1) bond issues, which are usually applied to capital expenditures; (2) concession and leasing arrangements which provide the department with a share of profits from the operation of their facilities by private businesses; (3) grants from federal or state funding sources or foundations; (4) gifts and other forms of funding assistance or cosponsorship arrangements with local business or industry; or (5) other fund-raising events, drives, or special arrangements with groups of volunteer citizens.

3. Philosophy and Organizational Goals. In general, the philosophy of local, municipal recreation and park agencies has been drawn chiefly from the "quality-of-life" and "human services" approaches. It was widely accepted that recreation and park facilities and programs contributed to health, physical fitness, and varied aspects of community life. Often the point was stressed that recreation helped to prevent or reduce juvenile delinquency, to build positive forms of leisure participation, and to contribute to cooperation and understanding among different community groups.

Such beliefs stress the values and purposes of recreation as a form of community service, and are often expressed as external goals—outcomes that recreation may achieve *for* the community. Internal goals—outcomes that recreation and park agencies seek to achieve for *themselves*—usually encompass achieving a strong measure of community support and understanding, or having adequate budgetary support and a viable political constituency.

4. Organizational Structure. While there are many different types of local public organizations in the leisure-service field, the most common type today is the combined recreation and park agency. Usually, this is a separate department or administrative unit within the overall governmental structure, under the direction of an appointed department head, with the title of commissioner, superintendent, general manager, or director.

In a large public agency, there will typically be a number of separate service divisions: for administration; facilities planning, construction and maintenance; and program. Under program, there may be several service units for major areas of program activity, as well as geographical subdivisions for different sections of the community. In smaller departments, this structure is likely to be simplified, with an administrative director and several assistants, each one in charge of a major management or program function.

5. Populations Served.

Public, tax-supported recreation and park departments normally have a stated responsibility for serving all segments of the community, including those of all ages, socioeconomic backgrounds, races, religions, life-styles, and leisure interests. In reality, they cannot possibly meet all such needs, and therefore tend to restrict themselves heavily to serving the younger and more active age groups in the population, with a heavy emphasis on sports, games, aquatics, and outdoor recreation activities. In addition, special programs are often developed for adults and elderly residents, or the physically or mentally handicapped.

6. Staffing Patterns.

Based on the structural patterns of recreation and park departments on the local community level, most programs are conducted by generalist or specialist leaders. In the past they tended to be assigned heavily to playgrounds and community centers; today, a growing proportion of full-time, year-round personnel are assigned to special facilities to carry out supervisory functions.

In addition, many public agencies employ a substantial number of part-time personnel to teach special classes, or seasonal employees to augment regular staff during the summer months. Public departments usually have the highest percentage of professionally educated staff members who are affiliated with the organized recreation movement, with the possible exception of therapeutic recreation employees, who also have a high level of professional identification.

7. Facilities and Physical Settings for Programs.

As the term "recreation and park" implies, most public local agencies involve the related functions of planning and carrying out recreation programs, and operating park systems. Together, these functions involve the acquisition, design, construction, and maintenance of an extremely broad range of indoor, outdoor, and other specialized facilities.

These include such elements as playgrounds, parks, community centers, senior or youth centers, swimming pools, sports fields, tennis courts, golf courses, marinas, beachfronts, nature centers, sportsmen's centers, skating rinks, stadiums, arts centers, auditoriums, and numerous other types of facilities large and small. In addition, many public recreation and park departments use school facilities extensively for indoor sports and instructional programs, and in some cases operate programs in housing projects or other community facilities. Some departments even rent or own campsites at a considerable distance from their community's borders.

8. Major Program Elements and Formats.   As later chapters will show, the major areas of programming in local recreation and park departments include sports and games; outdoor recreation activities; swimming and other forms of aquatic recreation; arts and crafts; music, drama, and dance; social recreation; special events and other human-service functions. These in turn are scheduled in appropriate formats and at suitable times for different age groups or special populations, and geographically distributed so all areas of the community have adequate access to the chief program activities, and other specialized programs are available in more centralized locations.

VOLUNTARY, NONPROFIT AGENCIES

1. Sponsorship or Administrative Control.   These consist essentially of two types: (1) those organizations that constitute a large-scale national or regional federation, with local districts or units; and (2) independent agencies that have their own trustees, boards, or other policy-making supervisory councils. Most such organizations are incorporated, and thus must meet the legal requirements of the state in which they are situated.

In terms of formal policies, agencies that are part of larger federations may have considerable autonomy (with the national body suggesting goals, personnel, or program policies), or may be required to follow very precise policies in these areas. Often, a number of such agencies within a region or large metropolitan area (such as a large metropolitan YWCA council) will have its budget allocation, staffing decisions, and program policies subject to review/approval by a central board in the area. Completely independent organizations, in contrast, are able to make their own decisions, subject to approval by their boards.

2. Sources of Funding.   Such organizations tend to rely on several sources of revenue. Membership organizations like the YMCA, YWCA, or YM–YWHA usually have fees for annual memberships for individuals or families, plus other charges for enrollment in classes, use of facilities, or attendance at events. Youth-serving organizations in particular may operate their own national or local fund-raising drives, or may receive a portion of money raised by Community Chest, United Way, Red Feather, or similar campaigns.

In some cases, they may conduct certain programs on contract with governmental agencies, which provide revenue for them. Organizations like the Boys Clubs or Police Athletic League frequently have boards or advisory committees composed largely of successful professional or business executives, who assist strongly in fund-raising efforts.

3. Philosophy and Organizational Goals.   Relatively few voluntary agencies tend to think of themselves as primarily recreational; instead, they are regarded as youth-serving or character-building organizations. Their goals may vary; often they are linked to broad religious and spiritual values and outcomes, when they are connected to specific denominations or religious groups. Others may have sharply defined purposes, such as reducing juvenile delinquency and crime, helping girls and young women become better able to function effectively and independently in society, or assisting in education, counseling, or similar areas of social adjustment and community living.

Within this context, recreation is often viewed as a "threshold" activity that is useful in attracting new participants. In addition, recreation and leisure may be perceived as important aspects of community life, and the sponsoring agency may regard its purpose as helping members use their leisure constructively and creatively, in developing richer and more positive life-styles.

Often such organizations have as goals helping their members learn to function effectively in a democratic society, creating positive attitudes and relationships with those of different racial or ethnic backgrounds, or even promoting world peace and international fellowship through intercultural experiences and travel exchanges. Here, too, recreation may play an important role in promoting such values and outcomes.

4. Organizational Structure.   These organizations vary greatly in terms of their make-up and complexity of organization. On the one hand, agencies which operate within a single major facility, such as a YMCA or YWCA building, a Boys' or Girls' club, or a Police Athletic League center, tend to have a centralized bureaucratic structure, with direct lines of authority to the executive director of the organization, and other individuals heading up service or program units. Organizations like the Boy or Girl Scouts, in contrast, usually have a limited number of professional staff members who work in a coordinating and enabling role with regional or district boards or councils composed primarily of volunteers, who plan and direct local programs.

The national organization usually dictates the goals and levels of membership and program activities in broad outline. More sharply defined programs and projects are developed on the regional or district level, while individual units, such as troops or clubs, plan and carry out their own programs subject to the general approval of the district professionals.

5. Populations Served.   Like public agencies, these tend to focus more heavily on younger age brackets, although organizations, particularly special-interest groups, also serve adults and senior citizens.

A substantial number of voluntary organizations have religious affiliations, and serve only members of their own denomination. Others are geared specially to meeting the needs of the socially or economically deprived. Still others are designed to attract and involve only those with a particular leisure interest, such as camping, the arts, or a given area of sports programming. Thus, while the nonprofit field is broad in its overall scope, individual agencies are relatively selective in the audience they serve.

6. Staffing Patterns.   Most nonprofit community organizations have administrative personnel and program specialists in key service areas. In addition, they often rely heavily on part-time leaders in areas of special competence, and, to a much greater degree than public agencies, on volunteers. Many youth-serving organizations, such as the Boy and Girl Scouts, depend almost totally on volunteers for direct group leadership. While most voluntary agencies require professional employees to have college degrees, they tend not to give strong preference to recreation as an area of special training. Instead, they often hire personnel with education, physical education, psychology, sociology, or social work backgrounds.

7. Facilities and Physical Settings for Programs. Many voluntary agencies, such as YMCAs, YWCAs, YM-YMHAs, Boys Clubs, Girls Clubs, Salvation Army units, Police Athletic Leagues, and similar groups, own their own large facilities—usually in the form of a community center type building. Usually, they do not own or operate outdoor facilities, but rely on those owned by public authorities, with the exception of many Y's or youth clubs that own their own campgrounds. Customarily, Boy and Girl Scout groups do not own their own buildings, but instead meet in schools, churches or synagogues, or even private homes.

8. Major Program Elements and Formats. Because they serve a more specialized type of population, the programs of voluntary agencies are often less diverse than those of public departments. In addition, the youth-serving goals or other social-service functions of nonprofit organizations means that they are likely to emphasize certain types of programs designed to achieve designated outcomes.

For example, an organization like the Police Athletic League will sponsor sports, games, hobby, and club activities that attract young people, but will also promote contests, campaigns, special events and counseling programs or other functions to help build good citizenship and law-abiding values.

PRIVATE MEMBERSHIP ORGANIZATIONS

1. Sponsorship or Administrative Control. These are generally constituted in either of two ways: (1) an organization that has been established by a group of private citizens who maintain control over it through an elected group of officers and various committees; or (2) an organization that is commercially owned, with the format of a private-membership body.

An example of the first would be a country club owned and operated cooperatively by its membership. An example of the second would be a recreation facility and program designed to serve residents in a retirement community owned by a corporation and operated for profit. As a "mix" between these two types, a commercially owned private membership group might involve the membership in establishing policies and carrying out various administrative functions.

2. Sources of Funding. Organizations of this type are generally self-sufficient, depending on their own internal fund-raising efforts to support annual budgets. Typically, private clubs have substantial annual dues, plus other revenues from restaurants, bar income, and similar sources. Since they normally seek to serve only their own members, they do not meet public needs and do not usually conduct fund-raising drives or seek outside fiscal support. The exception would be those fraternal orders or service organizations whose members provide programs for special populations, and who raise money for this purpose.

3. Philosophy and Organizational Goals.

Private membership organizations tend to be primarily concerned with meeting the personal needs of their members, rather than with broader or more abstract social values. Thus, their goals are likely to be to provide social opportunities for members with others who are like themselves; often, clubs of various types represent a degree of exclusiveness and social snobbery. They are intended to provide recreational activities like yachting, fishing, tennis, golf, bridge, or similar pastimes in an attractive and uncrowded environment, with other compatible participants or families.

Again, an exception to this approach may be found in those fraternal or service groups that seek to assist special populations or promote community welfare in specific areas of social concern. Obviously, their philosophy and goals are very much like those of voluntary agencies in this respect.

4. Organizational Structure.

These are usually organized on a very simple plan, with in some cases the membership forming management committees responsible for budget and fiscal control, building operations, membership and program planning, and with a professional manager and staff responsible for carrying out each of these functions. In other cases, when the membership organization is privately owned, as in the case of a retirement community or vacation community operated by a real estate corporation, they simply hire professional staff members in various specialties, with company officers carrying out management functions, as in any business.

5. Populations Served.

These are often relatively exclusive in nature; they tend to serve middle- and upper-class families with fairly sharply defined social and recreational interests. Quite homogeneous in nature, they are therefore able to focus on specific areas of activity and to provide these in depth.

6. Staffing Patterns.

Country clubs, golf clubs, tennis clubs, yacht clubs, and similar organizations tend to employ individuals primarily on the basis of their managerial ability and experience or technical skills, rather than their college background or professional affiliations. In other words, the manager of such an organization must have strong business skills, just as a ski instructor or golf pro must have special skills in his or her area of expertise. In general, such organizations have relatively few job openings for professionally trained recreation personnel.

7. Facilities and Physical Settings for Programs.

Customarily, private membership organizations own and operate their own extensive facilities, usually at a level of attractiveness and comfort that few public or voluntary agencies can meet. In addition to golf courses, tennis courts, swimming pools, or other areas for sports activity, they sometimes operate restaurants, bars, ballrooms, and similar facilities both for their own members and to rent privately for added income, with the option of catering weddings, parties, and similar events.

8. Major Program Elements and Formats. As indicated earlier, these organizations usually have very limited programs, in terms of the range of activities, although they often present them on an impressive level of expertise and with highly skilled leadership.

COMMERCIAL AGENCIES

1. Sponsorship or Administrative Control. Like any form of business, a commercial recreation enterprise is typically managed as a corporation, either publicly or privately owned. Usually, it would be under the administrative control of a chief officer or board of directors, who in turn assign administrative and supervisory powers down the chain of command, to individuals on successive layers of authority.

2. Sources of Funding. Obviously, commercial businesses in the leisure-service field gain their revenues from fees, charges, and sales. A large successful ski-center enterprise, for example, might have not only the ski complex itself, with several slopes at different levels of difficulty, lifts, and other necessary facilities, but would probably also operate one or more lodges, and might possibly have a complex of privately owned condominium units. It would probably also house restaurants, bars, or cocktail lounges, discos, shops, and other facilities. At the ski area, income would be derived from lift tickets, equipment rental, classes, and similar services.

3. Philosophy and Organizational Goals. Recreation businesses normally have a very simple and direct philosophy and set of goals, which is to provide a needed product or service to the public and to earn a profit while doing it. However, this does not mean that they are oblivious to other goals and values. Many commercial recreation sponsors are highly responsible and serve to provide significant forms of leisure service. For example, private camps for children and youth often offer outstanding programs of outdoor recreation, education, and overall character development. Similarly, many health and fitness centers provide sound guidance and excellent facilities for physical development, often linked to nutritional and related areas of counseling. Many resorts and tourist attractions provide wholesome family activities and entertainment that is unmatched within the spectrum of leisure activity.

In contrast, of course, commercial recreation sponsors who are vending "products" related to sex, gambling, or drugs exploit their market with little concern about values or human outcomes.

4. Organizational Structure. As in the case of private membership bodies, recreation businesses are typically organized so that there is a vertical chain of command, under an executive director. Depending on the complexity of the operation, there is also likely to be a horizontal, or side-by-side separation of functions related to planning, marketing, fiscal control, product development, facilities management, and similar elements. Unlike public or voluntary agencies, program services tend not to be identified as a separate function; instead, the operation of facilities or product management is likely to be the focus of the entire organization.

5. Populations Served.   Like public agencies, commercial recreation organizations serve a broad range of population groups with diverse program attractions. However, since they must charge for their services, they do not usually attract the economically disadvantaged, the disabled, or the very young or old as targets for involvement.

6. Staffing Patterns.   Like private membership organizations, recreation businesses are concerned with the "bottom line"—that is, the ability of an employee to do the job effectively, rather than whether he or she has been professionally trained in recreation as such. However, a growing number are employing recreation-trained individuals as planners, supervisors, or in other staff roles. As more and more colleges and universities prepare specialists in commercial recreation, and assign students to field placements in commercial settings, this number will undoubtedly grow.

7. Facilities and Physical Settings for Programs.   Commercial recreation businesses operate many types of highly developed facilities. These include bowling alleys, ski complexes, aquatic complexes, hotels, resorts, health spas and racquetball centers, sports stadiums, dance studios, marinas, and, most often places where entertainment and sociability are offered, including night clubs, bars and taverns, movie houses, casinos, dinner theaters, and similar locations.

8. Major Program Elements and Formats.   Commercial recreation organizations literally offer every conceivable type of recreational pastime or service, including many (such as large-scale entertainment events or extensive travel-and-tourism opportunities) that public or voluntary agencies cannot provide. In addition, they represent the source of all forms of recreational equipment, clothing, or supplies that are used in outdoor recreation, sports, home electronic entertainment, and other areas of popular leisure activity. Without question, the sheer volume of profit-oriented recreation far outweighs the leisure programs provided by other types of sponsors, in terms of the amount of money spent and the variety of different activities enjoyed.

ARMED FORCES RECREATION PROGRAMS

1. Sponsorship or Administrative Control.   Recreation programs within the various branches of military service in the United States are part of a system officially designated as the Department of Defense (DOD) Morale, Welfare, and Recreation (MWR) Program. System-wide policies for each branch of the armed forces are developed by a centralized unit of that branch. For example, the Navy's program manager for policy and technical guidance is the Recreational Services Division of the Naval Military Personnel Command. Within general policies set forth in this way, the commanding officer of a particular base is responsible for conducting MWR programs which are actually planned and directed by both military and civilian personnel on the base.

In addition, specific aspects of programming may be promoted or coordinated on an interservice basis by such groups as the Interservice Sports Committee (ISC) of the Department of Defense ISC Secretariat, within the office of the Assistant Secretary of Defense for Public Affairs.

2. Sources of Funding.   Fiscal support of military recreation programs is provided by both *appropriated* (money allocated by Congress for general support of the armed forces) and *nonappropriated* funding. This includes money raised from liquor sales, post-exchange profits, vending machines, or fees for participation in programs. As shown earlier, the proportion of nonappropriated funding has risen steadily since the mid- and late-1970s, and many recreation programs in the armed forces are expected to be relatively self-supporting today.

3. Philosophy and Organizational Goals.   Historically and at the present time, the purpose of armed forces recreation has been to make a career in the military more attractive and to provide many of the benefits and opportunities that are normally available in civilian life.

Beyond this, armed forces recreation is viewed as an integral part of the entire morale and welfare program, and is intended to make an important contribution to the physical fitness and emotional well-being of participants. Competitive sports in particular are believed to build a feeling of esprit de corps and pride. In many isolated or dangerous settings, military recreation helps to prevent burnout and boredom; in high-tension situations, it serves to provide relaxation and release from stress. In today's armed forces, the goal of promoting family stability is especially high, since the conditions of military living often tend to make normal family life difficult, resulting in poor morale on the part of military personnel.

4. Organizational Structure.   There is a different organizational structure within each of the major military service branches. Normally, there is a strict chain of command under the authority of the commanding officer of each base, ship, or other service unit, with all civilian or military personnel subject to his or her authority. Military procedures and policies dictated by the Department of Defense govern the operation, with specific program goals and policies for Morale, Welfare, and Recreation that apply to all service units.

5. Populations Served.   By definition, military recreation is designed primarily to serve members of the armed forces and their dependents, as well as other base personnel. In some cases, they may also provide limited programming opportunities for community residents. Their participants therefore tend to be primarily younger adults and children, with some participation by middle-aged and older adults—all with a relatively similar life-style and set of values shaped by being part of or affiliated with the military.

6. Staffing Patterns.   Managerial and leadership personnel in military recreation fall into two categories: members of the uniformed forces, and civilian personnel. In the latter group, one segment consists of Civil Service employees who are paid by appropriated funds allocated by Congress. A second group involves civilian employees who are not Civil Service personnel, and who are paid by nonappropriated funds. Armed Forces recreation personnel are drawn from many disciplines, and include specialists in sports, music, crafts, library work, and a number of other areas of special expertise.

7. Facilities and Physical Settings for Programs.   These tend to include facilities for the most popular sports, hobbies, and social activities, including recreation centers and bars. In some cases, such as on isolated posts or smaller ships, they may be very limited, consisting of little more than a library, scheduled motion pictures, and equipment for a few games and fitness activities. On other, larger bases, they may be extremely varied and impressive.

8. Major Program Elements and Formats.   Programs in military settings usually give chief emphasis to sports and games, physical fitness, hobbies, social activities, and similar pastimes, including entertainment, such as films and shows. Many programs also include extensive activities in various crafts areas, as well as stress-management, day-care activities, assistance in trip planning, and a variety of other useful personal services.

COLLEGE OR UNIVERSITY-SPONSORED PROGRAMS

1. Sponsorship or Administrative Control.   Recreation programs on college and university campuses may be administered by a Dean of Student Life or Student Affairs, who is responsible for directing all student personnel services not of an academic nature. Often, they are split with respect to sponsorship and administrative control, with intramural sports, sports clubs, or fitness or outdoor recreation activities coming under the authority of a department or school of physical education and recreation, or division of athletics, while other leisure programs are directed by a campus office concerned generally with student-life programs.

In some institutions, a student-run recreation association may be given the responsibility for planning, coordinating, and managing all campus recreation and social activities, and of scheduling major facilities for such programs.

2. Sources of Funding.   Normally, the overall funds for supervising and staffing a campus recreation program and for providing and maintaining needed facilities would come directly from the college or university budget. In some cases, student activity fees are charged along with tuition, and may include free admission to sports events and other activity programs. Special trips, concerts, or other events or attractions might require additional fees to be paid by those taking part.

3. Philosophy and Organizational Goals.

Institutions of higher education that sponsor campus recreation programs do so for several reasons. Historically, many such programs were initiated as a means of social control, and to insure that students did not take part in off-campus leisure activities that might be dangerous, immoral, or destructive in other ways.

Today, campus recreation is generally viewed as an important part of the spectrum of student services, including housing, health care, personal counseling, and academic advisement. Recreation is recognized as being part of a full life, and integral to a rich educational experience; indeed, many cocurricular leisure programs are carried out in direct cooperation with academic departments and help to extend the experience of students in these subject fields. Other nonacademic experiences in areas involving student leadership, political activity, publications, or business management promote the overall development of students and often lead to career opportunities following graduation.

4. Organizational Structure.

As described under the heading of sponsorship and administrative control, these programs are usually under the administrative direction of a Dean of Students or Student Life, or of a Director of Campus Recreation or Intramural Sports. Customarily, there will be several professional staff members who work with students in organizing and carrying out programs. Often there is a loose structure for decision-making or overseeing programs. Although funds are often allocated through student government to subsidize various activities, frequently there are relatively few control and evaluation procedures, and students may have a considerable amount of freedom in planning and carrying out programs.

5. Populations Served.

As in the armed forces, campus recreation programs are designed to serve a somewhat limited audience: students, faculty, staff, and sometimes community residents. The emphasis, then, is primarily on involving a relatively young, well-educated population with broad cultural interests and a diversified life-style.

6. Staffing Patterns.

Staff members in campus recreation programs are drawn from many fields of study. Those who run intramural and sports clubs programs tend to have backgrounds in physical education or recreation. Others who work in cultural, social, or other program fields may have degrees in fields related to their program specialization. A sizable number of staff members in student life programs are likely to have backgrounds in guidance or counseling psychology, while the overall heads of services on administrative levels often are trained in student personnel administration, or in other academic fields, before moving into student-life roles.

A relatively small number of such individuals belong to the National Recreation and Park Association or the American Association for Recreation and Leisure. Instead, they often are affiliated with organizations like NIRSA (National Intramural and Recreational Sports Association), or other groups concerned with higher education or student union management.

7. Facilities and Physical Settings for Programs.   Campus recreation facilities usually include extensive provision for indoor and outdoor sports and aquatic programs, as well as lounges, theaters, auditoriums, and halls for social and aesthetic programming. Frequently, the same areas used for academic instruction are also used for cocurricular leisure programming. In general, leisure facilities may be found in student union buildings, gymnasium and outdoor athletic areas, dormitories, and academic buildings. In addition, many campus recreation programs involve adventure programs and trips to distant sites for skiing, scuba diving, and similar pastimes.

8. Major Program Elements and Formats.   These programs differ from those of other agencies in that they tend to reflect the young adult population of those attending colleges and universities, as well as the cultural and academic background of higher education institutions. Thus, in addition to sports and games and social activities, campus cocurricular programs are likely to include a wide range of experiences related to publications, political activity and current affairs, performances in the arts, outings, and environmental activities and similar events.

CORPORATE/EMPLOYEE RECREATION

1. Sponsorship or Administrative Control.   There are a number of different administrative patterns in company-sponsored recreation programs. These include: (1) the company taking total or almost total responsibility for providing facilities and staff to direct recreation programs, with employees providing direction through an advisory council; (2) the company providing a number of major facilities, one or two professional staff program directors, and some financial subsidy, but with an employee council or recreation committee taking major responsibility for planning and carrying out programs; (3) the company providing a number of facilities, but with employees responsible for running the program; and (4) the company playing no formal role, and employees organizing activities which normally are carried on away from the work site.

2. Sources of Funding.   As indicated in the section on sponsorship and administrative control, patterns vary greatly in employee recreation programs and services. The most common situation, however, would be one in which a company assigns the task of administering employee programs to an individual responsible for personnel activities. This individual's salary, along with facility maintenance and full or partial subsidy of different programs, are provided by the company.

In many companies, programs that are directly concerned with promoting health and fitness, reducing stress and burnout, or generally improving the effective functioning of employees, are fully paid for by management, while other activities of a social or clearly recreational nature must be paid for, at least in part, by participants.

Many companies use funds gathered from vending machines, cafeteria profits, or similar sources, to help subsidize employee recreation activities.

3. Philosophy and Organizational Goals.

The overall philosophy of many company executives who support and assist employee recreation programs is that it helps to make workers more fit and efficient, to reduce absenteeism and accidents, and to create a sense of camaraderie and loyalty to the company. Personnel on different levels come to know and respect each other, and work together in planning and carrying out programs.

The health of employees has become a particularly important concern, with many large concerns sponsoring cardiovascular fitness programs, along with stress management, weight reduction, smoking cessation, and similar activities. In some cases, employee recreation programs also extend to providing leisure activities for those living in the surrounding community or region; here, the goal is obviously one of providing a needed community service, and maintaining positive public relations.

4. Organizational Structure.

Customarily, such programs are under the administrative direction of a director of personnel benefits and services with, as indicated, one or more professional staff members responsible for planning and directing activities. The most recent trend in this field has been to have companies provide less financial support and direct assistance to recreation programs, and to expect employee committees, councils, or volunteer organizers to play a fuller role in program development.

5. Populations Served.

The population served is usually drawn from those employed by the company and their families. While they may therefore include a wide range of socioeconomic backgrounds and interests, with participants ranging from laborers or blue-collar workers to top executives or professionals, they all have the common characteristic of being involved in a similar work setting.

6. Staffing Patterns.

Relatively few individuals employed in this field have specialized backgrounds in recreation education. Instead, they are often drawn from the overall field of personnel management, or in some cases are employed in a company and become active as participants and volunteers in employee programs, before they are transferred to personnel responsibilities. Another key aspect of staffing in many corporate/employee programs is that often individuals supervise or direct recreation programs as only one of several areas of responsibility, including other personnel services and benefit programs.

7. Facilities and Physical Settings for Programs.

Relatively few companies have developed extensive recreation facilities, although a number have built gymnasiums with additional classrooms, lounges, and meeting rooms for varied programming. The largest single push today is in the direction of physical fitness facilities, with many companies providing weight-training and other exercise machines, indoor and outdoor tracks, rooms for aerobic dancing, pools, and racquetball courts. Others have developed country clubs with attached golf courses, or other special outdoor facilities for use by employees and their families. When employee recreation programs have extensive sports leagues and events, they usually make heavy use of publicly owned facilities to carry these on.

8. Major Program Elements and Formats. In the past, such programs tended to be extremely limited, with emphasis on a few team sports, such as softball or bowling, along with annual events such as a Christmas party or summertime picnic. Today, employee recreation activities are much broader, including extensive charter travel programs, hobby or personal-development classes, fitness activities, and numerous other special interest groups. As indicated earlier, physical fitness is a major concern in many such companies today, and recreation is often administratively linked to other employee services, including benefits and personal-needs programs.

THERAPEUTIC RECREATION SERVICE

1. Sponsorship or Administrative Control. Therapeutic recreation is unlike the other seven categories in that it does not represent a type of sponsorship. Instead, it involves recreation programs for special populations, which may then be sponsored or organized by any of the other types of agencies.

For example, a public recreation department or a voluntary youth-serving agency may sponsor special clubs for the mentally retarded or orthopedically handicapped. A commercially operated nursing home will normally provide activity programs for residents and may in fact be required to do so by law. A private membership organization like the Kiwanis may operate a summer camp for disabled children and youth, and the armed forces may provide recreation as a morale or treatment service in military hospitals.

Despite the fact that it is not in itself a distinct type of sponsorship or category of agency, therapeutic recreation is discussed separately in this chapter because it represents a major professional specialization and area of needed leisure service in the modern community.

2. Sources of Funding. Depending on the type of institution or sponsoring agency, fiscal support of therapeutic recreation service can vary greatly. When it is provided as part of a treatment center's normal care, it is usually included as part of the overall expense of the institution and paid for through patient/client charges, or moneys received from health insurance, Medicaid, or similar plans. Under the latter circumstances, recreation may be billed separately, as a reimbursable service (like occupational therapy or physical therapy) but this is not normally the case.

When recreation for the handicapped is provided by a municipal leisure-service department, it is typically paid for by tax funds, although special charges to participants may supplement this form of support. Other organizations, such as special summer camps for disabled children and youth, may rely heavily on grants from Community Chest campaigns, or special fund-raising drives. Often, they may sponsor large-scale tournaments, shows, bazaars, or lotteries, raffles, or Las Vegas nights (gambling events) to raise funds.

3. Philosophy and Organizational Goals.   Again, therapeutic recreation may have many different kinds of goals, depending on the population being served and the type of setting in which the program is being carried on. As a general philosophical statement, the overall purpose of recreation for individuals with a disability is to meet their need for satisfying and enriching leisure activity, and to help make their lives as full as possible.

Beyond this, recreation provided in a treatment setting may actually be designed as a form of therapy, intended to restore or extend physical abilities, improve social function, maintain or improve morale, or teach needed skills. Often, treatment programs are designed to help a disabled person learn to live independently in the community, and to use his or her leisure positively.

When recreation is provided for individuals who are not undergoing treatment, usually the rationale is exactly what it would be for nondisabled persons—except that it may be necessary to modify activities somewhat, to insure successful performance and satisfaction. Related to this, another important goal of community recreation for the disabled is to promote "mainstreaming" with nondisabled participants.

4. Organizational Structure.   The structure of therapeutic recreation agencies varies according to the setting and type of agency. In a large-scale, community-based operation like the San Francisco Recreation Center for the Handicapped, there will be a full administrative staff, operating with numerous advisory groups, and separate divisions and professional specialists dealing with different aspects of facility management, programming, transportation, and other support services.

In a smaller, institutional setting, there is likely to be a single level of direct service in the form of recreation specialists, activity therapists, or face-to-face leaders, working under a rehabilitation services coordinator, or treatment unit head.

5. Populations Served.   The single common denominator here is that the population served should have some significant mental, emotional, physical, or social disability which puts them at a disadvantage in terms of recreational involvement, or in which recreation may serve as a significant and important form of personal growth or treatment medium.

Beyond this, participants in therapeutic recreation programs vary greatly in the nature and degree of their disability. They may be hospitalized or institutionalized and be almost totally dependent on others, or they may live independently in the community or with their families. In terms of their recreational backgrounds and interests, these vary as widely as those of the nondisabled members of the community.

6. Staffing Patterns.   As indicated earlier, personnel in this field are employed in many settings, on different levels of responsibility. The most common role is that of therapeutic recreation specialist or activity leader or therapist. Increasingly, such individuals have been receiving college or university training in this specialization, and a growing number have applied for and received special credentialing through the professional registration program of the National Therapeutic Recreation Society, or similar state certification systems. In addition, community-based therapeutic recreation programs often rely heavily on volunteers; those in institutions much less so.

7. Facilities and Physical Settings for Programs.   These tend to be rather limited in many hospitals and treatment centers or nursing homes, often consisting of lounges or other rooms that are converted for social programs. However, some institutions—particularly special schools or youth homes—have gymnasiums, auditoriums, hobby and craft shops, and a good variety of outdoor fields for sports programming. Community-based therapeutic recreation programs often make use of facilities owned by public or voluntary agencies on a free or rental basis.

8. Major Program Elements and Formats.   Obviously, the activities provided for disabled individuals vary greatly, depending on their disability and their rehabilitative or other personal needs and interests. Often, arts and crafts, music, hobby skills, and social recreation are among the key activities. Adapted sports and aquatics are often popular, and with the mentally retarded or developmentally disabled, many basic leisure skills, such as bowling, skating, or swimming are used to teach basic motor skills.

With most populations, a key purpose of therapeutic recreation is to promote independent functioning and the ability to use community leisure resources confidently. In some treatment programs, activities of daily living (ADL) or trips and outings are stressed to achieve such goals. In others, recreation leaders may also conduct discussion groups and provide leisure counseling and other forms of assistance, such as referral and advocacy, to assist their patients or clients in meeting their social needs in the community setting.

SUMMING UP: IMPLICATIONS FOR LEADERSHIP

This chapter has provided a systematic analysis of eight of the major types of agencies in which recreation leaders are employed, based on eight key elements or characteristics of each type of leisure-service organization. One of these elements had to do with staffing patterns; beyond what has already been presented, a number of additional implications for recreation leadership may be identified.

Career Opportunities in Areas of Service

As indicated earlier, the public sector has traditionally been seen as the chief source of career opportunities in leisure-service—particularly in terms of available job opportunities for entry-level employment. Today, it must be recognized that, while a substantial number of individuals continue to be employed in local governmental recreation and park agencies, such programs are generally not expanding and there is a limited flow of new job openings in them because of tight budget limitations.

Voluntary agencies are similarly constrained in terms of the volume of new openings because of budgetary considerations. The greatest volume of new job opportunities that are generally available to recreation and park majors would appear to lie in the areas of commercial, private, and therapeutic recreation service. In addition, a growing number of recreation majors are finding employment in the areas of campus, armed forces, and corporate/employee recreation programs, although the strategies for obtaining positions in these fields are rather complex.

Professional Identification.   Leaders and supervisors in public recreation and park agencies generally identify with the recreation movement, and are members of its professional organizations. A growing number of such individuals have specialized college training in the field, and the trend toward more demanding certification or registration of personnel seems to be promoting such requirements.

Leaders and supervisors in voluntary agencies tend also to require college degrees for professional-level positions, although in many cases social group work, education, the social sciences, or other related fields are regarded as acceptable degree fields for professional preparation. In commercial and private agencies, there is generally less concern about the academic preparation of program personnel, with chief emphasis being given to their on-the-job competence and experience.

Therapeutic recreation service is giving increasingly stronger attention to employing professional staff members with specialized degrees in this field, while the other fields described tend to be more flexible, with a growing emphasis on training in business management practices.

Range of Opportunities and Job Mobility.   In contrasting different types of leisure-service agencies, it is worth considering the range of career opportunities they offer, as well as their degree of job mobility.

In smaller public agencies, with limited numbers of staff members, the most logical form of career advancement has usually involved moving to another, larger department at a higher level of job responsibility. In some larger departments, it has been possible for employees to move up a career ladder to executive-level positions, but, given the pyramidal nature of most large bureaucratic organizations (with many more jobs on the lower levels than at the top) usually such possibilities are limited. A fairly common practice, however, in many public agencies, has been for successful recreation and park managers to move to more general roles in county or municipal government. Typically, a successful recreation and park professional may become a county supervisor, city manager, or other executive working with a broader range of governmental responsibilities. Similarly, an effective nursing home activities director may well move into the broader area of health service administration.

In voluntary agencies, many of the larger national bodies maintain personnel services and newsletters which facilitate transfer and career advancement for their employees, who may move from one agency in an overall federation to another. Finally, in private and commercial organizations, the situation is similar to any form of personnel practice in business concerns, with considerable opportunity to move ahead within a given organization or to transfer to a better position in a different one—depending on one's ability and professional drive.

Lacking the job security, union support, or Civil Service procedures that often buttress public employment, or the personnel practices that provide uniformity or stability in voluntary agencies, those working in private and commercial fields tend to follow more entrepreneurial styles. With a higher level of risk in terms of job security, they also have a better potential for advancement to higher-paying jobs or even to begin their own businesses. A substantial number of public recreation and park employees who left their agencies following budget cuts in the late 1970s moved into leisure-contracting services, or other forms of personal enterprise in the recreation field, often with a high level of success. Many others have transferred laterally into other forms of recreation service—such as employee, armed forces, campus, or therapeutic recreation.

Appropriate Leadership Styles

In both public and voluntary recreation agencies today, effective job performance tends to place a high premium on the ability to work with people and with varied community groups, as well as a strong emphasis on achieving desirable social outcomes through leisure-service programming. In commercial and private organizations, a high level of competence in specific job skills is important, as well as the knack of "selling" the agency's programs and services, and satisfying customers, clients, or members.

Management skills, including particularly those connected to marketing and fiscal management, are becoming increasingly important in many types of recreation organizations. Particularly in armed forces and corporate/employee recreation programs, there tend to be clearly outlined policies and procedural guidelines, and a strong bureaucratic structure within which the recreation leader must operate. Following the chain of command, efficient organization and follow-through, and careful documentation of values and outcomes are essential in such programs. In addition, because of the increased expectation that recreation programs become as economically self-sufficient as possible, it is extremely useful for entry-level staff members to have well-developed business skills related to marketing, accounting, and similar functions.

In campus programs, leadership style must emphasize the enabling function, in which staff members strive to involve students as leaders, recruit volunteers, and build ties with other campus organizations and the overall academic life of the institution. In addition, since recreation specialists are closely integrated within the overall student personnel operation, it is important to understand the general goals of higher education, and to be familiar with the current thinking with respect to the psychosocial development and needs of college-age students, as well as specific aspects of counseling and guidance.

In therapeutic recreation, there is increased emphasis on goal-oriented programming, and on prescriptive treatment plans designed to meet important therapeutic goals. Patient or client assessment and techniques of evaluating activity outcomes are also critical. Therapeutic recreation specialists must be able to play a wide variety of professional roles, including those of counselor, educator, organizer, evaluator, advocate, and team member within the overall service network.

Summing up, college students who seek to prepare themselves for professional roles in such organizations would be wise to gain as much early experience as possible in the specific type of setting concerned—either through part-time or seasonal work, or by volunteering informally or as part of field work or internship courses. In addition, they should carefully examine the needs of the type of leisure-service agency they are interested in, and concentrate on building their own positive strengths and remedying possible deficiencies, as part of an intelligent career-development strategy.

STUDENT PROJECTS

1. Select one of the eight elements through which agencies are analyzed in this chapter, such as *Sources of Funding,* or *Philosophy and Organizational Goals.* Then identify at least three different recreation agencies in the community and compare them, based on this element.
2. As a team project, survey the various recreation sponsors in the community (if it is a large city or county, do this within a defined district). Show how different agencies provide varied types of activities, or meet the leisure needs of different population groups. Identify apparent overlapping programs among agencies, and gaps in service throughout the community.
3. As a follow-up to Project 2, examine the staffing patterns of a number of representative leisure-service agencies and determine the nature of their leadership practices, in terms of their emphasis on professionalism.

SUGGESTED READINGS

Reynold E. Carlson, Janet R. MacLean, Theodore R. Deppe, and James S. Peterson, *Recreation and Leisure: The Changing Scene* (Belmont, Calif.: Wadsworth, 1979).

H. Douglas Sessoms, *Leisure Services* (Englewood Cliffs, N.J.: Prentice-Hall, 1984).

Donald C. Weiskopf, *Recreation and Leisure: Improving the Quality of Life* (Boston: Allyn and Bacon, 1982).

CHAPTER 5

Roles and Functions of Recreation Leaders

Having examined the theoretical base of recreational leadership and the kinds of agency settings in which leaders are employed, we are now ready to look at their actual roles and functions.

This chapter presents an up-to-date picture of the day-by-day responsibilities of leisure-service personnel in a cross-section of public, voluntary, therapeutic, armed forces, and other types of agencies. In addition to describing the actual tasks, it presents guidelines for carrying them out effectively, as well as examples of general agency expectations of recreation personnel.

AN OVERVIEW OF ROLES AND FUNCTIONS

Obviously, leaders' responsibilities vary considerably from organization to organization. They are influenced by the size and complexity of the agency itself, its goals and range of program services, and the population being served.

Beyond this, a number of other factors affect the roles and functions of leaders. *Junior* leaders or other subprofessional employees are likely to have more direct, face-to-face group leadership responsibilities, while *senior* leaders or center directors are likely to have more managerial or supervisory responsibilities.

Some leaders are defined as *specialists* and focus on a given activity area or category of participants, while others are *generalists*. Some leaders work in a *single setting* year-round, such as a playground or community center, while others *rotate* from facility to facility and assignment to assignment. In some cases, leaders are responsible only for directing recreational activities, while in others they must also provide other services.

To clarify this picture, the following section outlines the responsibilities of recreation leaders under two major headings: (1) tasks related directly to program leadership; and (2) tasks of a general supervisory or managerial nature. Following that, a number of guidelines for carrying out specific leadership functions are presented, based on the operational manuals of a number of representative leisure-service agencies.

TASKS RELATED TO PROGRAM LEADERSHIP

Usually, this is regarded as the primary responsibility of recreation leaders. It is assumed that their chief function is to conduct sports and games; lead music, drama, or dance activities; teach outdoor recreation skills; or plan social programs or other special events.

The reality of course is that program leadership involves much more than simply leading activities. Instead, it includes the following important elements:

1. Program Planning and Implementation. This task involves the overall development of recreation programs from the initial planning stage to the final evaluation and report stage.

> **a.** *Program Planning and Design.* This involves assessing the needs and interests of participants, as well as the goals and resources of the agency, and developing a systematic plan for varied types of program activities. It includes making decisions as to the age levels or other characteristics of groups that are to be served, the format of program activities, and the schedule that is to be followed.
>
> **b.** *Organizing and Implementing.* Here the leader must promote and publicize the activity, determine the location and make sure that all needed equipment or supplies are available. If additional leadership is needed, such as volunteer coaches, officials, or others with special skills, it must be recruited or arranged for. Each of these tasks must be carried out before the program is set in motion.
>
> **c.** *Monitoring and Evaluating.* Once program activities have begun, they must be observed or monitored. If problems occur, steps should be taken to solve or remedy them. At the conclusion of programs, it is usually necessary to evaluate them, formally or informally, and to submit required reports.

2. Direct Activity Leadership. In addition to these program-related responsibilities, leaders typically have a number of functions related to conducting face-to-face program activities, such as:

> **a.** *Activity Leadership.* This task involves the actual leadership of program activities, including such functions as teaching basic skills, organizing and conducting group activities, supervising free-play activities, acting as an official or coach, or similar tasks.

b. *Group Leadership.* Here the leader acts as an advisor to groups, helping them plan and carry out activities, and maintaining a constructive and cooperative social climate. This may involve helping group members themselves assume fuller leadership responsibilities, resolving disagreements, solving problems, and similar tasks.

c. *Providing Individual Guidance.* In many recreation situations, the leader also strives to act as a counselor with individual members of the group, helping them by providing a positive role model, offering personal support and guidance when appropriate, and making it possible for them to gain satisfaction from the activity and the group experience.

d. *Safety-Related Functions.* An important part of direct activity leadership involves health and safety. Leaders are responsible for accident prevention, safety education, and emergency procedures, regular inspection of areas and facilities, and similar tasks. Maintaining appropriate controls over the behavior of participants and making sure that agency policies are followed in all risk-related areas or situations where guidelines have been established is essential.

3. Provision of Related Program Services.   Most activities provided by leisure-service agencies are clearly recognized as recreational. However, many such organizations are multiservice in nature, and frequently their supervisors or leaders may be expected to organize or direct activities that are *not* recreational. Particularly as the leisure-service field has diversified into new types of sponsorship or formats for service, such responsibilities have become increasingly common. Several examples follow:

a. *Programs for Elderly.* Golden Age Clubs or Senior Centers, which are often directed by recreation-trained individuals, are likely to have program components in the following areas: dental, medical or other health-related services; nutritional (hot lunch) programs; personal counseling, legal aid, voter registration or similar services; transportation, home-visiting, family-service, or social-service referral activities.

b. *Programs for Youth.* Activities for teenagers which are provided by public agencies or voluntary organizations like the Y's or Boys' or Girls' Clubs often include: educational counseling and tutorial programs; vocational guidance and in some cases work-study programs; drug and alcohol abuse groups; other forms of family or personal counseling; and, in some agencies, "roving" or "detached" leaders who work with unaffiliated or gang youth.

c. *Other Nonrecreation Functions.* In other types of settings, such as employee or armed forces recreation programs, such services may be provided as day-care programs for children of working parents; carpool or other forms of transportation assistance; discount purchase services or group-buying plans; stress counseling, drug or alcohol abuse, or weight-reduction programs; preretirement planning or other forms of personal counseling or workshops.

In some cases, such services must be provided by specially skilled or qualified personnel, rather than by recreation leaders. An obvious example would involve dental or medical services. In such situations, it is customary to make use of part-time specialists who may be brought into an agency to provide the needed expertise, or to jointly sponsor programs or services with other agencies able to provide qualified personnel in the needed program areas.

4. Supervision of Special Facilities.   Most of the preceding functions deal with the leadership or supervision of activities or programs, including group management tasks. Many leadership-level personnel, however, may be assigned to supervising facilities with a minimum of actual program leadership responsibilities. Examples include:

   a. *Outdoor Recreation Sites.* Such facilities or areas as tennis courts, golf courses, sports fields, picnic grounds, nature preserves, or other outdoor recreation sites may require supervision that carries out the following functions: (1) checking use permits or assigning individuals or teams to areas for organized play; (2) overseeing the maintenance of areas and facilities; (3) registering and assigning individuals or groups to picnic sites, camp sites, or other locations; and (4) supervising participants to insure that agency policies or rules are being followed.

   b. *Special Activity Facilities.* These may include facilities such as nature centers or environmental education sites; historical museums; performing arts centers with outdoor music, dance, or theater performances; marinas or boating facilities; riding stables and trails; sportsmen's centers, with riflery, archery, fishing/bait-casting facilities, and similar areas.

   In some cases, agency staff members may be assigned to instructional or interpretive functions in such locations. However, often their role is simply one of overseeing the area or facility, making arrangements with participating groups, employing specialist instructors, supervising admissions and maintenance procedures, and similar tasks. In a broad sense, these are program-related functions. However, they are quite different from the traditional concept of the recreational leader's role as being solely concerned with the direct leadership of program activities and groups in familiar activities like sports and games, arts and crafts, storytelling, trips and outings, or special events.

TASKS OF A GENERAL SUPERVISORY NATURE

In addition to such program-related responsibilities, many leaders may be called upon to carry out other functions within their agencies, of a general supervisory nature.

   Although these might be regarded as appropriate responsibilities for managerial personnel, the reality is that often employees who hold the title of Leader—or who are on comparable job levels—are expected to carry them out. They must therefore be included within the total context of leadership roles and functions.

To a great degree, the nature of the agency will determine whether or not leaders are assigned such tasks. For example, community relations might be an extremely important responsibility for employees of a public recreation and park department, but not for recreation staff members on a geographically isolated military base. Similarly, staff members in a nonprofit voluntary agency may be heavily concerned with recruiting and supervising volunteers, while employees of a commercial leisure-service business might make no use of volunteers at all.

Recognizing these differences, the following represent supervisory functions that leaders in leisure-service organizations may be called upon to assume.

1. Policy-Making and Planning Functions.   In many organizations, policy-making is done at a fairly high level of administrative responsibility, and may need to be approved by boards, commissioners, or trustees, if it deals with critical or politically sensitive issues. However, in other leisure-service agencies, policies may involve sharing the views of staff members on all levels—particularly if there is acceptance of the ''participative management'' approach to planning and problem-solving.

In such situations, leaders may serve on study groups or committees to develop plans or program objectives. It is essential that leaders take advantage of such opportunities to make positive and constructive contributions to agency planning. Grass-roots leaders often have the most accurate picture of what is actually happening in the field, and can provide information and opinions that are extremely valuable in this process.

2. Budget Development and Fiscal Process.   Although leaders are not usually involved in high-level budget negotiations, they are often asked to contribute to the analysis of agency priorities and programs that provide the basis for budget requests.

Beyond this, leaders may become involved in fund-raising in a number of ways: (1) through charging and collecting fees for registration or other program involvements; (2) through carrying out varied fund-raising projects, such as raffles, bake sales, or similar events; (3) by working with parents' groups or neighborhood councils that may contribute funds to support programs and purchase equipment; or (4) through concessions at major facilities, cooperation with business or other community organizations that cosponsor or assist programs financially, and in similar ways.

Beyond this, leaders are generally involved in the fiscal process when they carry out inventories and requisition supplies and equipment, or when they transmit funds, make reports, do cost-benefit analysis, or perform other functions that involve the collection, use, or transfer of funds.

3. Personnel Functions.   Leaders in many cases must oversee or direct subordinate employees, including seasonal, part-time or ''session'' workers, assistant leaders or aides, or volunteers.

Often, leaders may be expected to recruit or enlist such assistants, subject to administrative approval or clearance within the department. Full-time professional leaders often must help orient, train, assign, and supervise other personnel, to ensure that they are making a useful contribution to the program. In addition to helping part-time, seasonal, or volunteer workers improve their leadership skills, the leader must also seek to build their understanding of the values and goals of the agency.

4. Public Relations.   Public relations are often thought of in a limited way as consisting primarily of publicity—letting the public know about the programs offered in one's center or other facility. The techniques for doing this are obvious. They include the use of fliers and handbills, posters in stores and schools, announce-ments made in churches or synagogues, public-service messages over the radio or on television, and schedules or special-interest features in local newspapers.

In a broader sense, public relations consists of more than a one-way dissemi-nation of information from the recreation department to the public at large. Instead, it should be a two-way process of sharing information and ideas, of getting inputs from the public in terms of planning recreation programs and events, and of building a fuller and more positive image of the agency. The purpose of public relations is not only to encourage participation in recreation programs, but to help build more varied interest and support, and to make sure that the program genuinely meets the needs of commu-nity groups.

5. Community Relations.   Closely linked to public relations as a leader-ship responsibility is community relations. This involves a full range of cooperative activities between the recreation staff and varied community groups. Ideally, it includes the use of neighborhood advisory committees or councils, parents or busi-nessmen's groups, and cosponsored programs with voluntary organizations, local sports leagues, and other special-interest groups. The principle of networking is particularly essential today because of the limited financial resources of many agen-cies. By pooling their resources, coordinating their services, and planning jointly to meet community needs, recreation leaders are able to maximize their efforts and results.

To give a comprehensive picture of the overall functions of recreation leaders, this chapter will now present a more detailed analysis of the following three elements: (1) specific tasks and responsibilities of leaders in several types of leisure-service settings; (2) guidelines indicating exactly how such responsibilities are to be carried out; and (3) general agency statements describing their expectations of leadership personnel, in terms of job performance and other aspects of personal behavior.

SPECIFIC TASKS AND RESPONSIBILITIES OF LEADERS

Among the most familiar settings for recreation leadership are neighborhood playgrounds and recreation centers. To illustrate the traditional functions of leaders in such settings, the following list of job functions has been compiled from a number of different recreation and park department manuals.

Job Functions of Playground/Recreation Center Leaders

The most important and widely accepted responsibilities of leaders in such settings have been identified as the following:

1. *Plan, Organize, and Conduct Programs.* The leader is responsible, under the general direction of his or her district supervisor or department head, for planning, organizing, and carrying out a full range of attractive and enjoyable activities designed to achieve the key goals of the sponsoring agency, and to promote both the learning of useful leisure skills and the development of the constructive social values of sportsmanship and good citizenship.

2. *Lead and Direct Activities.* In addition to his or her overall program responsibilities, the leader is normally expected to teach, lead, direct, coach, or officiate in a variety of program activity areas, including arts and crafts, storytelling, dance, drama, sports, trips, and nature activities.

3. *Guide and Direct Participants.* The leader must work with individuals or groups of participants to promote positive and socially constructive forms of behavior. This includes guiding them in cooperative group relationships, effective group planning and decision-making, and respect for public property and community social values.

4. *Maintain Control and Discipline.* The leader must obviously maintain order and discipline on the playground or in the center, preventing vandalism, fighting, or other antisocial behavior. In addition, he or she is usually expected to enforce departmental regulations devoted to smoking, gambling, drinking, the use of undesirable language, or other prohibited acts, and to apply disciplinary measures when required.

5. *Provide a Desirable Model.* Leaders are expected to provide desirable adult models for children and youth in their own behavior and personal habits, and to represent the department positively in all contacts with the public or other municipal employees. This involves strict adherence to departmental regulations and seizing every opportunity to present a favorable image of the department and recreation itself as an important form of community service.

6. *Accident Prevention and First Aid.* An essential leadership function is to maintain an effective safety and accident prevention program. This includes vigilant attention to all possible safety hazards, such as defective equipment, and immediate follow-up on having them repaired, as well as constant teaching and enforcement of desirable safety attitudes and practices in *all* areas of playground or center activity.

7. *Facilities, Equipment, and Supplies.* As indicated, the leader is responsible for regular inspection and supervision of facilities, and for reporting problems of cleanliness or maintenance, as well as safety hazards. He or she is also responsible for maintaining an up-to-date

inventory of equipment and supplies, for supervising their use, and for requisitioning new materials when necessary. In some departments, leaders also are in charge of scheduling recreation facilities (such as ball fields) for use by other community groups.

8. *Supervise Volunteers.* An important function of recreation leaders or center directors is to recruit or enlist volunteers from the community, to train and assign them, and generally to supervise them in program service. When volunteers are intelligently selected, guided, and rewarded—with recognition and appreciation—they make a significant contribution to many recreation programs.

9. *Public and Community Relations.* Recreation leaders are normally expected to publicize their programs thoroughly, through announcements, fliers, bulletin boards, releases to newspapers and TV stations, and similar methods. In addition, they must maintain cordial and cooperative relationships with neighborhood residents, business people, and community organizations, in order to better meet neighborhood recreation needs and to be able to call upon community resources for various forms of help. In larger departments, such efforts are often coordinated through a central office of public and community relations.

10. *Reports, Forms, and Evaluations.* The recreation leader is required to keep accurate records of general playground or center attendance, as well as participation in special events or trips. Reports must also be made out and submitted for other administrative reasons, such as accidents or other special incidents, collection of fees, or disciplinary infractions. The leader is expected to fill out and submit such reports accurately and promptly, according to departmental guidelines, and to carry out program evaluations as required.

11. *Adhere to Department Regulations.* All recreation and park departments have a code of personnel practices and regulations. Some of these simply describe departmental procedures in areas such as pay, leave or vacation, probation and promotion, and retirement and other "fringe" benefits. Othes are in the form of regulations governing leaders' responsibilities and behavior in a variety of areas. Leaders must be thoroughly familiar with such procedures and regulations, and must adhere to them carefully.

12. *Overall Departmental Role.* Finally, playground or center leaders and directors are expected to play a significant role in the department as a whole. This may involve accepting alternative assignments, serving on special committees or task forces, assisting other individuals as requested, making suggestions to improve programs or joining in problem-solving groups, representing the department in community meetings, and generally maintaining favorable relationships with other employees. Leaders are also expected to take part in in-service training programs sponsored by their departments.

LEADERSHIP FUNCTIONS IN OTHER SETTINGS

In contrast to the assigned responsibilities of playground or recreation center leaders, personnel working in other types of settings may have specialized job functions related to the mission of their program. For example, the San Francisco Recreation Center for the Handicapped has outlined the following set of general responsibilities for leadership personnel.

San Francisco Recreation Center for the Handicapped

Job description: Recreation leader

Under close supervision the recreation leader is responsible for the promotion, organization, and personal leadership of a variety of recreation activities either indoors or outdoors of the Recreation Center for severely handicapped children and adults. The leader conducts activities with assigned groups, and may supervise the work of nonprofessional personnel. The leader's work is subject to review and direction by the Recreation Supervisor.

General responsibilities:

1. Organizes, promotes, leads, teaches, and conducts diversified recreation activities such as arts and crafts, low organized games, team games and sports, modern, social, creative, round, folk, and square dancing, drama, social recreation, study clubs, nature activities, camping, community singing, informal music activities, and journalism.
2. Consults with individuals and groups to determine their recreational interests, needs, and desires.
3. Leads a well-rounded program of diversified and adaptive activities suited to the needs and interests of handicapped persons attending the Center.
4. Assists in organizing, promoting, and directing tournaments, shows, socials, play productions, dances, exhibits, festivals, and special events.
5. Cooperates and assists in the conduct of community-wide events.
6. Maintains assigned functional areas of the center such as the game room or crafts room, library, and social hall.
7. Assists in recruiting, training, and supervising seasonal and part-time paid and volunteer recreation leaders.
8. Works with community groups in organizing and planning recreational activities for participants of the Center.
9. Ensures that safety precautions are observed in all activities and gives first aid. Also must know emergency procedures for special individuals, fire and doctor contact.
10. Reports to Recreation Supervisor orally or in writing on activities, groups or individuals, plans, and problems; recommends action, and carries out policies in dealing with the group.

11. Requisitions, issues, receives, and oversees the use of equipment and materials; cares for and maintains equipment, and recommends the acquisition or disposal of equipment and materials for the recreation center program.
12. Assists in the preparation of manuals, programs, announcements, bulletins, and related materials needed in the program.
13. Substitutes as needed for the immediate supervisor and acts in his or her absence.
14. Assists handicapped participants in feeding, in bathroom needs, lifting, and so forth.
    a. Must be familiar with and interested in each participant of his or her program, his or her recreational needs and growth.
    b. Responsible for supervision of volunteers in the program, to assure that volunteers will be treated with the respect they deserve and placed as their potential indicates.
    c. Assumes a general responsibility for the appearance of the Recreation Center building and all its facilities, and also proper cleanup and closing procedures.
    d. Is cooperative with all staff and volunteers and conforms to the professional code of ethics of our Recreation Association.[1]

This listing of job responsibilities illustrates many of the typical functions of therapeutic recreation specialists working in community-based settings. In treatment centers, there tends to be a heavier emphasis on functions that contribute to a systematic and scientifically based approach to treatment. Leaders are expected to assess patient or client needs, develop goals and objectives and individual treatment plans, and work closely with team members representing other medical or rehabilitative disciplines. They are expected to analyze and modify activities to meet patient/client needs, to develop "curriculum" formats, and to evaluate and document program outcomes.

It should be stressed that therapeutic recreation specialists are not solely concerned with providing leisure programs. Instead, they may also serve as counselors, community educators, advocates, or in similar roles, and often must function as full-fledged members of interdisciplinary treatment teams or other work groups.

Job Descriptions in Voluntary Agencies

Many nonprofit community organizations have detailed classification systems of employees in various categories. Such positions in the Young Men's Christian Association are usually classified under such titles as *General Director, Youth Director, Physical Education Director, Membership Director,* or *Business Director.* Within this framework, each position has a set of assigned functions. Those of the YMCA *Youth Director* are as follows:

Responsibilities of YMCA youth director

1. Assists boys and girls through organized groups and informal education to develop attitudes and social habits consistent with Christian principles.
2. Integrates programs and activities with efforts of parents, school, church, and community leaders.
3. Guides the Youth Program Committee of the Board of Directors in formulating policies for youth programs.
4. Identifies youth needs and organizes group programs to meet these.
5. Enlists, trains, and supervises volunteer group leaders.
6. Interprets YMCA to youth members, parents, and public.
7. Manages business aspects of youth department.
8. Is generally responsible for day camp and sometimes for resident camp program direction.
9. Maintains adequate records and makes reports.[2]

Functions in Military Recreation

Within each branch of the armed forces, the functions of recreation employees are defined in a number of different program areas, and on different levels of responsibility.

In the Air Force, for example, there is an extensive program of sports activities, including the following elements: (a) *instruction* in basic sports skills; (b) a *"self-directed"* program of informal participation, with little supervision or direction; (c) an *intramural* program of competition among personnel on a given base; (d) an *extramural* program involving competition with representatives of other Air Force bases or community sports programs; (e) a *varsity* program involving higher-level competition, which may extend to national or even international play; and (f) a program for *women* in the Air Force.

The individual serving as *Sports Director* must perform varied functions. Working with a Sports Council that consists of the squadron sports directors, members of base standing committees, team managers, and others, the Director must develop policies and supervise the entire program. With respect to the *intramural* element in the program, for example, this includes the following responsibilities:

U.S. Air Force: Responsibilities of intramural sports director

1. Plan, direct, and supervise the general conduct of all intramural activities.
2. Assist group and squadron sports directors and team managers in an advisory capacity.
3. Develop intramural policies in collaboration with the base sports director, the sports council, the sports staff, and the participants.
4. Systematically publicize and promote the program.

5. Draw up schedules, organize leagues, meets, and tournaments, and plan special events.
6. Select, train, assign, and supervise intramural officials.
7. Interpret the intramural program to base personnel.
8. Provide for the safety and well-being of all participants.
9. Evaluate the program.
10. Compile and publish game results and individual and team records.
11. Develop and publish rules relating to program administration.
12. Develop and supply to squadron sports directors and organization managers the necessary forms for reporting game results, signing out equipment, reserving practice areas, making a protest, and so forth.
13. Control equipment furnished for contests.
14. Prepare budget estimates.[3]

Functions in Commercial Recreation

The job responsibilities of program personnel in commercial recreation vary greatly, since there are so many different types of organizations and services offered to the public. In general, they are concerned with creating, marketing, and managing a product or service that will be attractive to the public at large, and that can be delivered in the most efficient and economical way possible, in order to maximize profits. They may center about the performance of a single specialized task within a large, complex organization, such as a theme park, or may involve a variety of business, technical, and person-related skills.

For example, in a research study of the types of competence needed by ski center personnel, a Michigan State University team found that the fifteen most frequently performed functions involved the following:

1. Personnel management
2. Labor cost control
3. General administration and management techniques
4. Utilize basic meteorology (Snow farming techniques)
5. Control ticket sales (Winter revenue producing facilities)
6. Identify snow types (Snow farming procedures)
7. Determine amounts and types of equipment needed (Short ski, cross-country, etc.; Winter revenue producing facilities)
8. Institute inventory control system (Sports equipment maintenance)
9. Develop ski packages (Winter revenue producing facilities)
10. Personal selling
11. Marketing
12. Set up security and rental retrieval procedures (Winter revenue producing facilities)
13. Set up, operate, or integrate ski rentals and repairs (Winter revenue producing facilities)

14. Apply safety regulations and understand liability (Lift operations)
15. Business office operations[4]

Obviously, many of these skills are of a highly technical and specialized nature. At the same time, in order for ski managers or assistants to be effective, they must be able to understand the motivations, interests, and needs of potential visitors to the area, and should be able to relate to other leisure-service organizations, in order to develop courses and clinics, promotional packages, joint programs, and other marketing efforts.

GUIDELINES FOR CARRYING OUT JOB RESPONSIBILITIES

In addition to such formal statements of the functions of recreation leadership personnel, many agencies also have developed manuals or training programs which indicate *how* the work is to be done. In some cases, the exact procedures which must be followed are indicated. In others, instructions are of a more general nature, in the form of suggestions or recommended courses of action.

For example, leadership manuals for those working in playgrounds or recreation centers typically include concise guidelines covering the following areas: (1) responsibility of leaders for prompt and regular attendance and for giving a "full day's work"; (2) leaders becoming familiar with all relevant personnel and community offices; (3) illness or emergency notification procedures; (4) safety inspection of facilities; (5) getting to know participants; (6) responsibility for carrying out planned programs; (7) responsibility for serving all potential participants; (8) enforcing regulations for appropriate behavior by participants, and maintaining a safe and orderly environment for play; (9) arrangements for developing cooperative programs with other groups or organizations; (10) publicizing playground or center activities; (11) assigning volunteer leadership tasks to program participants, where feasible; (12) being alert to the needs of possible "problem" participants; (13) promoting desirable citizenship values and social behavior; (14) keeping accurate daily and weekly records of attendance; (15) filing special forms or reports involving accidents or personal injury; (16) maintaining positive, professional relationships with other staff members, and with the public; and (17) involving participants and representatives of the community in program planning.

Obviously, this listing is only a summary of the kinds of suggestions that might be made to leaders for effective program management in a center or neighborhood playground. More detailed instructions are often listed in departmental leadership manuals in such areas as accident prevention and first aid, publicity and community relations, and maintenance of control and discipline.

As an illustration, many leisure-service organizations have detailed procedural manuals covering the operation of swimming pools or beach swimming areas, where failure to provide thorough professional lifeguard supervision might result in a tragic accident or a costly lawsuit.

The following set of rules for lifeguards, taken from the Aquatic Program

Manual of the St. Louis, Missouri, Department of Parks, Recreation, and Forestry, is typical:

Rules for lifeguards

While on duty, a Guard should:

a. Report, ready for duty, at least 15 minutes before assigned shift, and be in proper position when his or her shift starts.

b. Be professional, alert, courteous, and always tactful.

c. Maintain an erect and alert position while on the stand so he or she can observe signals from the other guards and note anything unusual in the water area he or she is guarding.

d. Refrain from unnecessary talk or visiting with the public. If talk is necessary, do so while keeping assigned area under observation.

e. Make requests and issue orders in a courteous and determined manner. If orders are not executed in full and at once, report the incident to the Senior Guard on duty.

f. On stand duty, take the proper position in the seat. On walking patrol, concentrate primarily on the water area.

g. Always have a whistle and wear an approved type of identification.

h. Keep swimmers and bathers from congregating on walk area in the immediate vicinity of the guard stands.

i. Refer detailed inquiries to the Pool Manager or Aquatic Program Supervisor.

j. Pool Manager or assistant will be responsible for clearing all swimmers out of water during an electrical storm.

k. Not only guard the lives of the patrons, but also maintain discipline among the more active ones so as to ensure the comfort and pleasure of others. Do not tolerate any rowdyism.

l. Promptly enforce all facility rules.

m. Keep the facility fit for inspection at all times; keep all litter picked up and keep all lifeguard, life-saving, and first aid equipment in readiness.

n. At the time each shift ends, make a survey of the bottom of pool and then the entire locker room. Make sure everyone is out of the building.

o. Know your specific duties in the event of a major emergency.

p. Check to make certain all doors and gates to facility are locked when a life guard is not on duty.[5]

Such detailed statements of required leadership procedures tend to be found in functional areas where there might be a risk to health and safety or where it is particularly important that careful controls be maintained.

For example, the Eighth United States Army Recreation Services Operation in Korea (EUSA RSOK) has an extensive Youth Activities (YA) program designed to serve the dependents of armed forces personnel. As part of the sports program, when youth sports teams travel to compete against other teams, the following guidelines must be rigidly observed:

Rules for overnight trips and out-of-country travel (EUSA RSOK)

1. Coaches/chaperones will establish a curfew that must be observed by all participants.
2. An adult/youth ratio of at least 1:10 must be maintained at all times. Participants are restricted to on-post activities except that off-post activities may be permitted if specifically approved by the coach/chaperones.
3. Coaches/chaperones must be billeted in the same facilities with team members.
4. Coaches/chaperones will determine the appropriate action to deal with minor disciplinary problems (e.g., benching, non-suiting, restrictions, etc.).
5. In case of major disciplinary problems (e.g., theft, fighting, vandalism, disruptive conduct) coaches/chaperones may take any or all of the following actions:
   a. Recommend that the participant not be eligible for any YA participation or achievement awards for that sport or activity.
   b. Recommend that the participant not be allowed to participate in any future overnight trips sponsored by the YA program.
   c. Recommend to the Area Commander that the participant be referred to the Youth Conduct Review Board for possible sanctions as prescribed in paragraph 8 UNC/USFK/EA Reg 600-52, "Dependent Misconduct" dated 15 May 1978.
   d. In the case of out-of-country trips, arrange for immediate return of participant to Korea via MAC Aircraft or via commercial airline at the expense of the parents/guardians, with their consent.
6. The size of groups traveling out-of-country for competition is limited to not more than 50 youths plus coaches and chaperones for each trip.
7. The duration of out-of-country trips is limited to scheduled days of competition plus travel days.[6]

Similarly, voluntary agencies serving children and youth normally establish detailed and precise procedural manuals in areas related to health and safety. The Girl Scouts of the United States of America, for example, publish an extensive manual on health and safety practices, which all leadership personnel must observe. This manual includes rules with respect to meeting places and other program sites, transportation practices, emergency procedures and first aid, camping standards, and activity "checkpoints" governing the leadership of various program activities with a risk potential.

Leadership Guidelines in Therapeutic Recreation

Many therapeutic recreation leadership manuals contain detailed procedural guidelines governing all aspects of the activity program. For example, the Children's Seashore House, a treatment center for physically disabled children and youth in Atlantic City, New Jersey, has developed instruments and procedures for carrying out assessments of patients, including the use of referral forms, social-behavior and group-interaction rating scales, leisure interest inventory forms and diagnostic batteries, as well as guidelines for writing assessments and progress notes. Beyond this, the Children's Seashore House has a formal procedure for developing therapeutic recreation plans for patients, including guidelines for writing objectives. Leaders are instructed to follow medically-approved procedures in working with children with different types of illnesses or disabilities, or for handling emergencies that may occur during the course of programming.

To illustrate, guidelines for involving children with *Spina Bifida* (a form of physical disability primarily of the lower extremities, with the potential for injury because of decreased sensation and neuromuscular impairment), include the following elements:

Examples of guidelines in the therapeutic recreation plan

A. *In-House Activities*—require special precautions due to decreased sensation.

B. *Cooking*—avoid transferring hot liquids across child's lap. Child should be positioned with legs under food preparation table. Instruct child on how to pass sharp kitchen utensils.

C. *Sports and Games*—child should wear braces for floor or mat activities to prevent fractures. When out of braces, child's legs should be positioned directly in front of child when child is sitting on the floor. Provide close supervision; protect child's legs from other children.

D. *Ocean Activities*—one-to-one supervision required when child is sitting in water waist high. Watch wave action to insure child is not knocked over. *Do not turn your back to this child;* child could float away.

E. *Pool Activities*—one-to-one supervision required to prevent other swimmers from dunking this child. (Remember, if this child is dunked he cannot push off the bottom of the pool to get air.)[7]

In addition to these required procedures for involvement in activity, the Treatment Plan includes specific descriptions of the child's need or problem, as well as the purpose or expected outcome of the recreational experience.

Hiking unit for mentally retarded

As a second example of leadership guidelines in the field of therapeutic recreation, Joswiak has developed extensive recreation therapy program descriptions for use at the Patton Developmental Center in California. In a description of a *Hiking Unit* for use with mentally retarded clients at the Developmental Center, he outlines appropriate Entrance Criteria, Exit Criteria, and Objectives for the program. Examples of objectives include:

To walk on uneven terrain characterized by numerous rocks, branches, etc. Criteria: The client will walk on the described terrain in a manner characterized by:

a. Feet shoulder-width apart (if deemed appropriate for the terrain).

b. Hands and arms maintained at the side of the body in a relaxed position.

c. Maintaining balance without swaying, bending or rocking.
d. No inappropriate tension visible in the body (no overflow).
e. Looking at the ground periodically when appropriate.
f. A rate of speed generally considered to be average.
g. Smoothly integrating the above components.
h. Assistance may be given. Recreation Therapist may hold hand(s) of the client.

To demonstrate the ability to utilize hiking-related skills. Criteria: The client will:

a. Put on a day pack appropriately.
b. Take off a day pack appropriately.
c. Fill a canteen with water from a stream.
d. Unzip a day pack.
e. Zip a day pack.
f. Take a canteen out of the day pack.

In teaching clients these hiking and hiking-related skills, Joswiak suggests that leaders use the following techniques:

a. Physical manipulation and prompts, e.g., grasping the client's legs to help him pick up his/her feet, holding onto one or more hands to help provide balance.
b. Verbal directions and prompts, e.g., "bend your knees."
c. Modeling the correct behavior, e.g., "make your feet wide like me."
d. Co-active movements, e.g., "let's both walk picking our feet up."
e. Guided discovery, e.g., "what is the right way to put on your pack?"
f. The client will be given one-to-one attention for a minimum of _____ minutes per session.
g. Appropriate behavior or approximation will be reinforced with _____.[8]

Numerous other therapeutic recreation agencies develop similar leadership guidelines to assist their program specialists in working effectively with different populations. Other examples of effective leadership approaches in such fields as corporate/employee, private membership, and campus recreation programs are found in later chapters of this text.

Overall Department/Agency Expectations of Leaders

Apart from developing guidelines which show exactly how programs are to be carried out, or services provided, many leisure-service agencies have prepared statements outlining in general terms the kinds of performance they expect from their leadership personnel.

Typically, they expect leaders to demonstrate a degree of personal commitment and dedication, and a human relations approach which will enhance their effectiveness in working with participants and the general public. For example, the Los Angeles, California, Department of Recreation and Parks publishes an extensive *Recreation Branch Manual* which outlines in full detail the attributes of successful leadership. It includes the following passages as part of a comprehensive description of the recreation leader's responsibility, under the heading of *Job Conduct*.

Work Performance Standards

Each employee must fully understand that public service is the primary goal. Every public contact should be used to perform a public service and create good will for the City.

Recreation Branch employees are expected to meet reasonable standards of professional and personal behavior. . . . The changing needs of the community, along with special demands of permit groups, make it doubly important for an employee to be able to work under pressure (and) to adapt to new conditions and work hours not normally scheduled.

During the normal working day, attention to duty is important and a definite obligation of the employee. During working hours, do not visit unnecessarily with other employees. Do not conduct personal business, write personal communications, study on Department time, or engage in activities in conflict with the best interests of the City.

Success in recreation requires the ability to plan, work and get along well with people . . . employees (must) reflect consideration for others regardless of position. . . . Employees should develop a team spirit, involve others in planning, implementing, and evaluating programs while at the same time developing a unity of purpose.

Recreation requires unfailing patience, consideration, and courtesy at all times. The manner in which the service is rendered is as important as the service itself.

The person who is outstanding in any group is the one who is enthusiastic about his job, profession, or the activities he directs. Without enthusiasm, employees cannot be inspired to best efforts.

Statements, records, and reports must be accurate. For example, games and activities should be conducted according to accepted standards and rules. . . . Recreation employees should live up to the tradition that City service is businesslike, exact, and economical.

Recreation personnel are entrusted with the care of thousands of dollars worth of equipment and properties. They deal with people who expect honest and fair treatment and who expect promises to be fulfilled. Also, they handle records, valuables, reports, and receipts. . . . Employees who are entrusted with such responsibilities must be honest and not deviate from absolute integrity in these and other respects.[9]

The Los Angeles Recreation Branch also urges its employees to continue to add to their formal knowledge and skills through a continuous program of education and self-development in appropriate college curricula, and by taking part in department training meetings, by maintaining a professional library, and by joining and being active in both community organizations and professional recreation associations. All these are essential both to personal growth and to professional advancement.

Prescribed Employee Behavior or Appearance

In some cases, leisure-service agencies may be very specific in prescribing approved forms of behavior, or ways of meeting the public, for their employees. This is particularly true in commercial recreation, which tends constantly to be aware of the need to maintain an attractive, appealing image, and to be perceived by the public in a favorable light. In such settings, leaders may often be called upon to play a marketing or "selling" role while on the job.

For example, in health spas and fitness centers, dance studios, or similar commercial recreation settings where patrons typically sign up for periods of active membership, or extended courses, professional staff members are normally expected to play the role of salesperson, and to "sign up" patrons either for first memberships, or for renewals. In such situations, the basic criterion for judging a leader is not so much his or her competence in instructing an activity or providing other services, as it is the individual's sales record and ability to sign up customers.

Designing the Leader's Image.   In some commercial recreation settings, such as major theme parks like Walt Disney World, the very appearance and make-up of staff members may be determined by management—not only for performers in various shows, but for all employees who meet the public in any capacity. The official staff handbook, *Walt Disney World and You,* makes this clear in an introductory section that explains:

> Walt Disney World is a giant outdoor show played on more than 27,000 acres of resort-hotels, campgrounds, golf courses, and of course, the Magic Kingdom Theme Park. Your stage is more than twice the size of the island of Manhattan.
> You've been cast to perform a specific role at Walt Disney World. When you "play a part," you have to "look the part," whether you are on stage, presenting the show . . . or back stage, preparing the show. You may even wear a costume, specifically designed . . . by the best designers . . . to fit the role you'll be playing.[10]

All staff members are responsible for wearing assigned costumes, for maintaining hair with specific guidelines as to length, coloring, accessories, cosmetics, length of fingernails, make-up, jewelry, and other details of personal appearance. Similarly, prescribed ways of meeting and dealing with the public are clearly outlined and presented to new employees in staff training sessions.

In contrast, leaders at Club Med resorts must fit an entirely different kind of image—appropriate for guests of this worldwide organization with over 90 "villages" that uses the devil's pitchfork as its corporate logo. Club Med advertises itself as "the antidote for civilization," and caters successfully to a sophisticated, adult singles market that is drawn to its mix of active water and land sports, entertainment, informality, and enthusiastic social participation in exotic seaside environments. Nudel writes that Club Med's leadership staff is not composed of recreational professionals or physical fitness buffs, although they usually have sports or other useful performing skills.

> Rather, they're healthy, toothy, enthusiastic people, ranging from early 20s to their 40s, whose very demeanor encourages participation.
>
> Club Med changes its resort staff every six months. It is the lure of travel rather than high salary scales that entice personnel to join the Club Med organization and induce them to stay.
>
> While expertise in a sport or recreation is vital, it appears almost secondary. Club Med is more concerned about the interaction of individuals and the psychological tools that can be subtly used, to bring out the child in everyone.[11]

Within this program, leaders are not expected to fit the carefully conforming model imposed by organizations such as Disney World. Instead, they are encouraged to be themselves, to mingle freely with guests, and to enjoy themselves fully—to create and sustain an atmosphere that will make the entire experience pleasurable for all.

Other types of recreation sponsors, such as corporate/employee or armed forces recreation, generally impose an image which is harmonious with the general tone of the organization itself. In such settings, recreation personnel normally must fit into the appropriate mold, in terms of appearance, leadership style, and program values.

CREATIVITY: THE ESSENCE OF LEADERSHIP

A final essential aspect of leadership that must be stressed here has to do with the leader's taking the initiative to suggest or develop new creative approaches to agency programming. It is one thing for the leader to observe rules and "go by the book" in following required departmental procedures and guidelines. It is something else to participate actively in the overall operation of the department, to present new and exciting ideas, and to inspire participants and other staff members with one's enthusiasm.

The five chapters that follow are devoted to a presentation of useful recreation activities that are found in many leisure-service programs today. They offer a cross-section of games, sports, arts and crafts, music, drama, dance, and other pastimes. They may be used to practice leadership skills as part of course assignments or projects, or simply to enrich the leadership capability of the reader. Obviously, they do not represent a truly comprehensive collection of activities. However, they provide *enough* to give a reasonable picture of each type of program activity, as well as the leadership methods most commonly used to carry it on.

In reading these chapters, students should be aware that recreation and leisure are constantly changing phenomena. While some program activities and events will probably remain popular for many years to come, others rise and fall rapidly in popularity. New program services and agency functions are constantly evolving. As part of this picture, an important function of recreation leaders is to contribute creatively to dynamic and constructive change.

NOTES

[1]*Staff Manual*, Recreation Center for the Handicapped, San Francisco, California, n.d.

[2]Personnel Policies Manual of National YMCA, summarized in Richard Kraus, Barbara Bates, and Gaylene Carpenter, *Recreation Leadership and Supervision* (Philadelphia: Saunders College Publishing, 1981), pp. 42–43.

[3]*Air Force Sports Program Manual* (Washington, D.C.: Air Force Publication No. 215–2, Oct. 1966).

[4]*Job Specifications and Skills Necessary for Ski Area Managers* (East Lansing, Mich.: Research Report 408, Recreation and Tourism, Michigan State Univ., October 1980).

[5]*Aquatic Program Manual*, Department of Parks, Recreation, and Forestry, St. Louis, Missouri, n.d.

[6]*Youth Activities*, EUSA RSOK (Korea: Department of the Army, Recreation Services Manual, August 1982), p. 20.

[7]Karen Fernsten, ed., *Clinical Manual* (Atlantic City, N.J.: Children's Seashore House, July 1984): p. 374.

[8]Kenneth F. Joswiak and Karen Shartle, *Treatment and Therapy Modalities: Recreation Therapy* (Patton Developmental Center, 1978).

[9]*Recreation Branch Manual* (Los Angeles, Calif.: Dept. of Recreation and Parks, 1974).

[10]For fuller description, see Kraus et al., *Recreation Leadership and Supervision*, pp. 285–86.

[11]Martha Nudel, "Club Med: At the Forefront of the Singles Tourism Market," *Parks and Recreation* (November 1982): 32.

STUDENT PROJECTS

1. As a team project, identify direct-service program leaders in several types of leisure-service agencies. Using a diary approach or an intensive interview technique, determine the exact tasks they carry out over a typical two-week period and the amounts of time devoted to each type of task. Have them rate the importance of each type of task in rank order, and determine whether the two elements (time spent on each task, and its degree of importance) tend to agree or disagree.

2. As a follow-up to Project 1, determine which tasks are generic and are found in all types of agencies, and which are unique to certain agencies and not found in others. Determine the implications of these findings to professional preparation in recreation service.

3. Select one major area of responsibility, such as public relations or the recruitment and supervision of volunteers, and develop a set of guidelines or a manual showing how this overall function should be carried out in a given setting. Base it both on field observation and the literature.

SUGGESTED READINGS——————————————————————

Edith L. Ball and Robert E. Cipriano, *Leisure Services Preparation* (Englewood Cliffs, N.J.: Prentice-Hall, 1978).

Christopher R. Edginton and Charles A. Griffith, *The Recreation and Leisure Service Delivery System* (Philadelphia: Saunders College, 1983), Chapters 3, 6, 8, 9.

Richard Kraus, Gay Carpenter, and Barbara Bates, *Recreation Leadership and Supervision* (Philadelphia: Saunders College, 1981), Chapters 5, 6, 7, 8, 9.

PART 2

Activities
for Recreation
Leaders

Program activities vary widely. Here, several handicapped participants take part in a paddle-rafting trip in Portland, Oregon, sponsored by S.O.A.R. (Shared Outdoor Adventure Recreation). Reading, Pennsylvania, children enjoy arts and crafts, and adult women participate in a corporate/employee fitness program in Glenview, Illinois. Vigorous sports are keynoted in the Hershey National Track and Field Youth Program, and a Reading summer recreation session. Employees and their families take part in a clowning workshop sponsored by the Honeywell Corporation's recreation program.

CHAPTER 6 _____

Sports, _____
Active Games, and _____
Fitness Activities _____

_____

_____

In examining the major types of recreational activities that leaders are responsible for conducting in organized leisure-service programs, it is obvious that the most popular and widely found type of activity involves sports and games.

In 1984, *U.S. News & World Report* provided statistics of involvement by Americans in varied forms of active recreation (see Table 6–1). Of the top twelve pastimes, several were sports and active games. While the leading team sports, such as baseball, basketball, or football, are not on this list, they also represent a major form of leisure involvement for younger males in our society and a tremendously popular form of spectator interest for all age groups. Increasingly, sports like soccer, volleyball, and racquetball are gaining greater success, and more and more girls and young women are participating in a wide range of athletic events.

TABLE 6–1 Participation in Selected Forms of Active Recreation[1]

Activities	Number of Participants (in Millions)
Swimming	102.3
Bicycling	72.3
Fishing	63.7
Camping	61.6
Boating	42.0
Bowling	40.3
Body building (with equipment)	34.9
Jogging	34.3
Roller skating	30.2
Softball	28.0
Tennis	25.5

Reported in *U.S. News & World Report*, August 1984, based on A. C. Nielsen Company data.

The sponsors of sports programs include public recreation and park departments; schools and colleges; Y's and other voluntary organizations, such as the Police Athletic League, Boys and Girls Clubs, and Catholic Youth Organization; corporate/employee recreation associations; and numerous special interest organizations.

In addition to individual and team sports, active games form a major part of the daily programs of many public, voluntary, camping, and other recreation agencies. Finally, fitness activities have become increasingly widespread, and clearly represent an important aspect of leisure participation today.

Far from being a trivial aspect of modern culture, sports apparently represent something very basic and important in our lives. It is essential that recreation professionals recognize this, and that they make every effort to understand and satisfy the psychological, physical, and social motivations for participating in sports and games.

MOTIVATIONS FOR SPORTS PARTICIPATION

Given the great diversity of different types of sports, games, and outdoor pursuits which fit under this heading, it is difficult to identify any single set of personal goals or values that would apply to all forms of participation. However, certainly the following values would apply very widely.

Psychological Aspects.   Sports provide an opportunity to "let off steam," and to express aggression or hostility either directly or vicariously, as spectators. It has been argued that in past centuries, people had to overcome natural obstacles and dangers found in their primitive environments; today, we have created sports and games which represent mock struggles with artificial dangers.

Whether or not one fully accepts this view, there is no doubt that sports, particularly those which are highly combative or physically dangerous, such as football, boxing, bobsledding, or parachute jumping, offer modern men and women a challenge they cannot find elsewhere in their lives.

Beyond the element of physical risk and daring, the urge to compete with others or with oneself, to overcome odds and obstacles and to reach new levels of personal accomplishment, is a powerful motivation behind participation in sports.

Social Aspects.   Sports also offer the chance to be a member of a team—a closely-knit human group—with all the reassurance and warmth that may imply. This factor is particularly important today. Many social commentators have described a growth of *alienation,* a lack of belonging and commitment, on the part of young people today.

Sports, while obviously not the total answer to the problem, do provide a direct and forceful kind of identification and human contact that is the very opposite of alienation. A team under pressure is a very tightly knit group. And even in a nonteam sport, with a player competing against a single opponent, there is contact. The athlete identifies closely with his or her rival; they are sharing the same impulses, pressures, and emotions. In other sports or active games which do not stress competition as heavily, the social rewards may be based on a sense of fellowship and companionship, and on sharing experiences with others.

Physical Aspects.   The recent explosion of interest in physical fitness as part of a total "wellness" approach was discussed at an earlier point in this text. While many individuals are willing to undergo rigorous conditioning programs—particularly when they are in training for sports competition—the majority of youth and adults in our society prefer to combine their fitness efforts with more enjoyable recreational pursuits.

As a result, many public, voluntary, educational, commercial, and corporate/ employee physical fitness programs have been established. These tend to stress not only weight-training or the use of exercise machines, but activities like jogging, running, swimming, aerobic dancing, and racquet sports—all of which have strong recreational components and may be carried on in group or club settings.

Serving Varied Populations Through Sport and Physical Activity

In the past, although lip-service might have been given to the goal of involving different groups through sports and active games, the reality was that the bulk of sports programming was for boys and young men. Today, there is much greater diversity in organized recreational participation in sports and active games. There are many outstanding examples of sports leagues for middle-aged or senior participants, and of fitness programs serving such groups with vigorous and sustained activity that helps keep them young!

Today, programs for girls and women are being given increased emphasis in both recreational and interscholastic and intercollegiate athletic competition. In the early 1970s, Gilbert and Williamson wrote:

> There may be worse forms of prejudice in the United States today, but there is no sharper example of discrimination than that which operates against girls and women in competitive sports. No matter what her age, education, race, or talent, the female's right to play is severely restricted. The funds, facilities, coaching, and rewards allotted women are grossly inferior those allotted men.[2]

More and more public recreation and park departments are today making an effort to equal the scope and variety of programs already being sponsored for boys and men, in offering new sports opportunities for girls and women. In so doing, many are taking a lead from schools and colleges that have initiated corecreational classes and clubs in a wide variety of sports and outdoor recreation interests. Some colleges today sponsor clubs and intramural competition with mixed teams of men and women in sports like flag football, volleyball, softball, fencing, and various aquatic activities.

In particular, there is greatly increased sports programming for the mentally or physically disabled. Through Special Olympics, wheelchair sports programs, and numerous similar efforts, great numbers of disabled persons young and old are today being involved in sports and active games—including the visually disabled, those with spinal cord injuries, and other groups that would never have had an opportunity to play in the past.

SPORTS AS A MAJOR COMPONENT OF COMMUNITY RECREATION PROGRAMS

Sports have the following special values for public recreation and park departments: (a) they represent a most effective public relations medium and a means of easily reaching and serving large numbers of people; (b) they are a useful means of providing spectator events for adults; (c) they meet varying needs of people of different ages; (d) they serve to motivate physical fitness, develop sportsmanship and character, and release tension; (e) they create interest in the entire recreation program; and (f) they are valuable because they afford an opportunity for general participation and mass enjoyment rather than intensive competition and the development of champions.

In addition, sports have traditionally been an important part of public recreation programs because they can be offered on various levels of skill, ranging from the complete beginner to the advanced competitor. While some sports activities may require close supervision or instruction, many of them almost run themselves once leagues, teams, and schedules have been established. It is possible, therefore, to serve comparatively large groups of people with a minimum of professional leadership, in contrast to certain other recreational activities.

Functions of Public Recreation and Park Departments

In addition to building sports facilities of all types, both for its own programs and for other community groups and organizations, the public recreation and park department should perform the following functions in programming sports:

1. Survey and analyze total community needs, interests, and capabilities, in order to develop a comprehensive and diversified offering of sports activities.
2. Provide direct participant services, including the following:
   a. offer instruction on a variety of levels, from beginning skills to advanced or high-level performance;
   b. schedule opportunities for free play, or casual participation, on playgrounds or play fields, or in after-school centers, in those sports which can be carried on with a minimum of supervision or leadership;
   c. organize, or assist other groups in carrying on programs of league competition or scheduled play throughout the sports season.
3. Stimulate community-wide interest and participation in sports in general or in specific activities by sponsoring clinics, workshops, demonstrations, or other special events—including tournaments and competition.

4. Train and develop leadership in the form of leaders and coaches, both within professional staff and the community at large, including many parents or other adults who may serve as volunteer leaders or officials.

5. Assist in coordinating the total community sports program, so that overlap is avoided, and major events or similar activities are not scheduled against each other; to provide facilities for other community agencies, such as churches, "Y's," and industrial leagues, and assist them with problems of leagues and public relations.

Each of the other types of leisure-service agencies described in this text contributes to recreational sports and fitness programming—usually by serving a particular population with instruction or competitive leagues. Campus recreation programs and corporate/employee agencies, for example, typically sponsor a wide range of sports activities.

Obviously, it is not possible for this book to present instructional or coaching methods in a wide range of recreational sports. However, to provide a picture of useful activities and leadership approaches in this area, it does present a sampling of active games and modified sports activities, guidelines for coaching and conducting tournaments, and examples of fitness programming and special services for disabled populations.

Lead-Up Games

One useful category of recreational activities consists of lead-up games. These are active group contests which are highly athletic in nature, and which help to equip young boys and girls with the skills needed to take part in popular team sports. They are especially important for youngsters who have not yet acquired the coordination or physical ability needed to engage in more complex or demanding activities.

By developing specific techniques related to ball handling, throwing, catching, kicking, or other skills, youngsters are given confidence. In addition, they learn to work as part of a team, to cooperate with their fellow players, and to understand the concepts and rules of different sports. Several examples of such lead-up games follow; suggestions for leading games effectively are provided in Chapter 10 (*see* page 197).

Punch-A-Cat
Baseball Lead-Up Game

May be played by six to ten participants. There is only one base and home plate. One player is at bat; the others are in the field (Figure 6–1). The player at bat bounces a rubber or tennis ball once, and then punches it toward the field. The object is for him to run to first base and back before the ball can be fielded and returned to the base before him, making him "out." A fly ball caught is also an "out." A player scores one point each time he runs to the base and back to home plate safely. He remains at bat until he is put out. Then he goes to the outfield, and all the other players move up one position. All take a turn at bat.

Flies Up
Baseball Lead-Up Game

May be played by six to ten participants. One player is at bat; the others are in the field. There is no base running. The player at bat

FIGURE 6-1

tosses up a softball or baseball, and then hits it to the field. If a fielder catches it on the fly, he becomes the new batter. If he catches a grounder, the batter must place the bat flat on the ground, and the fielder "bowls" the ball toward the bat (Figure 6–2). If he succeeds in hitting it (the ball usually bounces up into the air), the batter must catch the ball before it touches the ground again in order to remain at the plate. If he cannot, the fielder goes up to bat. If the "bowled" ball does not hit the bat, the batter remains at the plate. No score is kept.

Guard Basketball
Basketball Lead-Up Game

Six to ten players on a team. One team stands behind an outer circle (with one teammate in the center). The other team stands on the inner circle, evenly spaced (Figure 6–3). Using a basketball or rubber playground ball, players on the team outside the larger circle must pass the ball to their teammate in the center, while players on the inner circle try to prevent the pass from being completed. The "guarding" team may hit or kick the ball away, but may not catch it. Each time the ball

is caught by the center player, it is passed out to the outer circle without interference, and the play is resumed. Each time a pass is completed to the center player, one point is scored for his team. After about five minutes of play, the teams reverse positions. The team with the highest total at the end wins. Emphasizes skills of passing, catching, and guarding.

Twenty-One
Basketball Lead-Up Game

Four to six players line up at the free-throw line, facing the basket. The purpose of the game is to score exactly twenty-one points, by making basketball shots as follows. Each player is given three successive shots at the basket. The first shot is from the free-throw line, and is worth five points if made. The next two shots are made from wherever the ball is recovered. The second basket is worth three points if made, and the third basket is worth one. When the first player has taken his three shots, each of the other players has his or her turn. The game continues until one player gets exactly 21 points. If a player makes more than 21 points, his score goes back to zero, and he must begin the game all over again.

FIGURE 6–2

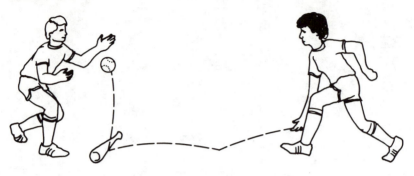

FIGURE 6–3

FIGURE 6–4

Square Soccer
Soccer Lead-Up Game

Eight to twelve players on a team, standing along two adjacent sides of a square, and with two players behind a center dividing line (Figure 6–4). Using a soccer ball or rubber playground ball, the two active players try to kick the ball below shoulder height through the opposing team. Defending players may use any part of the body to block the ball, but may not catch it with their hands. The ball stays in play until it goes through a team and over the boundary line. One point is scored when this happens. After each score, the two active players on each side change places with others on their team, and the team that was scored against is given the ball to begin play. *Only* the active players may score.

Other Modified Sports

Games of the type just described are extremely useful for playground or indoor gymnasium situations, because they may be played by large numbers of children without a high degree of skill. For youth in general, and also for adults who are past the age of highly vigorous play, the recreation leader may wish to modify certain major sports. The point of the modification may be to permit larger numbers to enjoy the game, to make it safer, or to encourage less skilled players to take part. A good example of this would be "Flag Football"—a modification of the game in which players do not tackle and block each other, but in which most of the other elements of football have been retained. Here are other examples of modified sports:

Slow-pitch Softball

This game differs from regular softball in the following ways:

1. The ball is sixteen inches in circumference, compared to twelve inches for the regulation softball. Gloves are therefore not needed. The ball is easier to hit and catch and does not travel as far or as fast as the regulation ball.
2. The ball, when pitched, must describe an arc (reaching a point above the batter's head) before it reaches the plate. This slows it up, makes it easier to hit, and prevents speedy pitchers from dominating the play. There is more action for both hitters and fielders.
3. An additional player, a "short centerfielder," is added to the team, giving more players a chance to join in.

This version of softball has become a popular recreational sport in the Midwest in recent years, with many older players (including some teams with no one under the age of 60) taking part. Recently it has spread to the West Coast and has caught on there. Other variations of the game (some make use of a fourteen-inch ball, and are called "Mush Ball") have become popular elsewhere in the country.

Indoor Hockey

This game was carried on originally in the recreation department of Battle Creek, Michigan, and has since spread to a number of other communities. It represented an attempt to develop a variation of hockey that could be played in any community, without a rink, that would be fast and strenuous but safe, that would give smaller and younger children a chance to play, and that would use simple and inexpensive equipment. The game is played with lightweight plastic or wooden sticks and pucks that may be purchased commercially or manufactured in a woodworking shop. It has simple rules, and may be learned in fifteen minutes or less. It may be played on any smooth surface, including a gymnasium floor, and is useful for children in the middle elementary grades and older, including both boys and girls—and in many cases, disabled youngsters as well.

Four Square

This game is a variation of handball. The essential differences are that it is played on a flat hard surface without a vertical back wall, and that it uses a volleyball. The game is played on four adjacent squares, each ten feet square (Figure 6–5). The ball is served with an underhand scooping motion by the first player into any square or box not his own. It must be received on one bounce and directed to any other square. A player commits a foul (and receives a penalty point) when he does one of the following: (a) fails to direct the ball into another square; (b) hits the ball downward (known as "spiking"); (c) volleys (ball must bounce in his square before being played); (d) plays the ball on more than one bounce; (e) hits the ball so it touches a line; (f) hits it into the same square twice in a row; or (g) holds or catches the ball. As the game is played, a player stays in the same square, but the serve rotates from player to player. Each time a player commits a foul, a point is scored against him. The player with the least number of points after a set time is the winner.

Still other forms of such sports have been developed, which make them easier games to play, for younger children or those lacking developed motor skills. Volleyball may be played, for example, with the ball being hit after a bounce, or with

FIGURE 6–5

modification of the playing lines, to make the game simpler. Softball may be played with batters using a batting tee, until players are able to hit a pitched ball confidently. Numerous other examples of modified sports may be found.

Active Playground Games

In addition to the lead-up games and modified sports just described, there are many active playground games which are useful in working with younger children in a wide variety of recreation or physical education settings. These include tag games, relays and races, and dodge ball activities. A sampling of some of the most useful playground games follows.

Tag Games

Tag games include many different kinds of competition, but all with one common element: trying to tag another player or players.

Exchange Tag
8–30 players

Children squat or stand in a large circle, except for one child chosen to be "It" who stands in the center. The leader calls out the names of any two players (if they do not all know one another's names, she may give them numbers, and then call out two numbers). These two try to exchange places in the circle before "It" can tag one of them. If a runner is tagged, she becomes "It," and the old 'It' takes her place in the circle. If no player is tagged, the leader calls out two new names or numbers.

Howdy, Neighbors
12–40 players

Players take partners and stand in couples around the circle. One couple goes around the outside, slaps the joined hands of any couple, and then these two couples race around the outside in opposite directions to get back to the empty place. When they meet on the opposite side of the circle, they must stop, bow, and say "Howdy, Neighbors!" before continuing.

Cat and Rat
12–40 players

Children stand in a circle about two feet apart, facing the center. One player becomes the *Cat* and another the *Rat*. They stand on opposite sides of the circle. At a signal, the *Cat* chases the *Rat*. The *Rat* may run between any of the openings between the players in the circle, but they must then immediately join hands, closing the hole. The *Rat* is permitted to run through the closed openings, but the *Cat* may not. The object of the game is for the *Rat* to close up all the gaps before the *Cat* can tag her.

Bronco Tag
12–30 players

Children scatter in groups of two. One child becomes the front end, or "head" of the *Bronco,* and the other, with her hands clasped around her partner's waist from behind, is the "tail." In addition, one child becomes a *Chaser* and another a *Runner.* At a signal, the *Chaser* pursues the *Runner.* To avoid getting caught, the *Runner* tries to put her arms around the "tail" of any *Bronco.* If she does this, she becomes the new "tail," and the child who had been the "head" of that Bronco now becomes the *Runner* and must try to escape. If the *Runner* is caught before she can

become part of a *Bronco,* she reverses roles with the *Chaser,* and pursues her. As the *Runner* approaches them, *Broncos* may try to dodge about and avoid her, but may not use hands or arms to push her away.

Steal the Bacon
8–20 players

Players are divided into two equal teams with each team standing on a line facing the other, and about twenty feet between the lines. Players on each line are numbered consecutively (1, 2, 3, 4), with the numbering beginning at opposite ends of the lines. A large handkerchief, beanbag, or other object is placed in the center between the lines. This is the "bacon." The leader calls out a number and the two players with that number run forward. The object is to steal the "bacon" and get back to the player's place in line without being tagged. Players may simply run up, grab the bacon, and run back, or may circle about much more cautiously before stealing it. If a player steals it successfully, her team gets one point. If she is tagged, the other team gets one point. If players take too long to make a move, the leader may warn them and count to five as a time limit for them to make a move. She makes sure to call all the numbers, although not in order. The first team to win a set number of points, such as fifteen, is the winner.

Relay Games

This category includes both active relays and party games which are more humorous and less strenuous. Following are several of the more vigorous kinds of relays:

Basic Relay Race
8–40 players

This is the most familiar type of relay. Players may divide into as few as two teams with four players each, or as many as six or eight teams; more than this makes the relay difficult to manage. Each team lines up behind a starting line. At a signal, the starting player in each line must run to a turning line about forty feet away, cross it with both feet, and run back to his own team. He touches the hand of

the next runner and goes to the back of his line. The first team to have all runners take a turn and complete the action is the winner. This basic relay race may also be done by having players walk, hop, skip, or use other novel forms of locomotion.

Hobble Relay
8–40 players

Instead of running, the first player lifts his left knee to his chest, holding his left foot firmly with his right hand. On his right foot, he hops forward to the turning line. He changes position there and hops back on his left foot, to touch off the next player in line.

Kangaroo Relay
8–40 players

Instead of running, each player must hold some object (such as a rubber playground ball, beanbag, or block of wood) firmly between his knees. He jumps forward to the turning line without using his hands to hold the object in place. If it drops, he must replace it before continuing. When he reaches the line, he may hold the object in his hand and run directly back to his team.

Over-and-Under Relay
8–40 players

Teams of equal size stand in single file. To begin, the first player in each line holds a rubber playground ball or similar object. At the signal, he passes this object over his head to the player behind him. This player passes it between his legs to the next player and so on—alternating over and under—to the last player in line. He runs with it to the front of the line and begins the action again. The first team to complete the full action is the winner.

Wheelbarrow Relay
12–48 players

In this contest, players take partners on each team and compete as pairs, rather than single individuals. The first two players in each line take a "wheelbarrow" position, one player putting his hands on the floor and stretching his legs out behind him, while his partner, standing between the legs and holding them firmly, raises them to waist height. In this position they race forward. At the turning line they reverse the "wheelbarrow" roles, and return to their team. The first team to have all couples complete the action wins.

Dizzy Izzy Relay
8–40 players

Teams stand in single file behind a starting line. Each first player is given a baseball bat or broom handle at least three feet long. At the signal, he runs to the turning line. There, he places the bat in an upright position on the ground, puts his forehead on its upper end, and runs around the bat three times. He then runs back (usually going around the bat makes him quite dizzy, and he travels an erratic course) to his team, and gives the bat to the next player. The first team to have all players complete the action wins.

Dodge Ball Games

These are an extremely popular form of active games, and stress speed and agility in dodging, as well as throwing skills. For safety's sake, the ball should be a fairly light one, such as a volleyball or rubber playground ball, and only hits below the waist should be permitted. There is little risk of injury when the game is played in this way.

Team Dodge Ball
10–40 players

A center line is drawn, dividing a large play area in half. Players divide into two equal teams, one on each side of the center line. A ball is thrown out. One of the players retrieves it and the action begins. The object of the game is to eliminate players on the opposing team by hitting them below the waist with the ball. Any child hit by the ball below the waist, or stepping across the center line, is eliminated and must go to the side. The game may be scored: (a) by having the team with the most hits after a set period of time declared the winner; or (b) by playing the game until one team is completely eliminated. With a large number of players, more than one ball may be used.

Circle Dodge Ball
12–40 players

Players divide into two equal teams. One forms a single circle with a diameter of about twenty feet, facing in. The other team stands scattered about inside the circle. The outer players are given a ball with which they try to hit the inner players below the waist, thus eliminating them. A hit above the waist does not count. The outer-circle players may retrieve the ball by going into the circle to pick it up, but may not throw it again until they have stepped out of the circle. The time it takes to eliminate all the inner players is recorded by the leader. Then the teams change places and play the game again. The team which took the least time to eliminate its opponents is the winner.

Train Dodge Ball
12–40 players

This is like "Circle Dodge Ball." The players form a single circle, facing in. Four additional players go into the circle and make a *Train* by standing in single file, each player with arms around the waist of the player in front of her. The player in front is the *Engine,* and the last child in line is the *Caboose.* The players in the circle try to hit the *Caboose* below the waist with a volleyball or playground ball. The *Engine* protects the *Caboose* by maneuvering the *Train* to keep in front of her. The *Engine* is also allowed to bat or kick the ball away; other players may not do this. When the *Caboose* is hit by a ball, the player who threw it becomes the new *Engine,* while the others all move back one position, and the old *Caboose* joins the circle. There is no winner or loser in this game—just lively action!

Other Athletic Stunts and Contests

In addition to the active group games just described, there are many athletic individual or dual stunts which children enjoy, and which may be played in recreation programs on playgrounds or in gymnasiums. Here are some good illustrations:

Tailor Stand

Children sit on the floor in a cross-legged position. Arms are folded in front of chests, with elbows held high. At a signal, or in turn, each player must try to rise to a standing position without unfolding arms or changing the crossed position of her feet. If she succeeds, she tries to sit down in the same way.

Coffee Grinder

Each child places her right hand on the floor, keeping the arm as still as possible. Extending both legs out to the left and keeping her body straight, she "walks" around in a circle, using her right arm as a pivot. This can be repeated in the other direction.

Crab Walk

Each child leans back and places her hands flat on the ground, with her feet forward in front of her (back is toward the floor). Keeping

head, neck, and trunk as straight as possible, she scuttles about in a crablike way. This may also be done as a race or relay.

Chinese Get-Up

Two children sit back-to-back on the floor, their arms interlocked. They try to stand up from this position, keeping arms locked. This is not a contest, but a cooperative stunt in which they help each other rise gradually.

Skin the Snake

This stunt is done in teams of equal size, which compete to complete the action first. Each team stands in single file. Each child reaches down between his legs with his right hand and grips the left hand of the child behind him. At a signal, the last youngster in the line lies down on the floor. Without letting go of hands, the other players back up, straddling the child on the floor. As each player reaches the back of the line, he lies down and the others go backward over him. When every player is on his back, the last one to go down stands up again and walks forward, pulling the next child up. This continues, reversing the action until the entire line is standing in the original order.

Back-to-Back

There are many simple combative stunts done between pairs or groups of players. In this one, three parallel lines are marked on the floor at ten-foot intervals. Children stand in pairs on the center line. Back-to-back, they lock elbows with each other. At a signal, each child tries to push her opponent backward across the goal line. The game may be scored by giving one point for each successful crossing. Children may be rotated to compete against each other, although it is a good idea to try to match opponents fairly closely by age and weight.

Cane Battle

Two players face each other, each holding a length of cane or a broomstick about eighteen inches long. They intertwine canes, holding them upright and gripping their own cane at each end. Each player tries to force the opponent to release his or her grip, by twisting, pulling or pushing his own cane. No trip-

ping, shoving, or pushing the opponent's body is permitted. The winner is the first one to force the opponent to let go of either end of the cane; if this does not happen within two or three minutes, the match is called a draw.

Long-Distance Boxing

This is another unusual combative stunt, in which two opponents stand on low wooden boxes or stools about four or five feet apart. Each player holds a broomstick with a boxing glove attached firmly to the end. At the leader's signal, the contestants try to force their opponents off their stools by thrusting and pushing with the glove end of the stick. They may *not* swing the sticks. The first player to force her rival off the stool within two or three minutes is the winner.

Tug of War

This may be played with any age group, but is particularly enjoyed by children and adolescents. The group divides into two equal teams. A line is drawn across the center of the playing area, and a strong rope is laid across this line. Both teams line up on opposite sides of the center line, and grip the rope firmly. At a signal, each team pulls on the rope, trying to pull the entire opposition team across the center line. The first team to do this is the winner.

Other Physical Activities

In addition to the games, modified sports, and stunts just described, what other physical activities are suitable for community recreation? Here are several suggestions:

Volleyball

Volleyball, which many have thought an extremely simple game lacking any real challenge, can be played with great skill and excitement. While it may be enjoyed by the aged or handicapped, it has also been played as a form of international competition before huge audiences throughout the world. In the United States, beach volleyball as played in Southern California attracts thousands of out-

standing players, a number of whom have become national tournament stars. It has been estimated that well over twenty million players take part in volleyball—on beaches and in camps, schools, colleges, and the armed forces. It is a game that can be enjoyably played by those from eight to eighty—and yet too few community recreation departments use this excellent sport.

Skiing

In recent years, we have seen a winter sports boom. In the northern section of the country particularly, there have been many private commercial skiing developments. These have been extremely expensive ventures, including tows, chair lifts, artificial snow machines, and often other elaborate facilities. Can skiing be offered by community recreation departments? As a basic sports activity, a number of departments have already done it.

Some recreation and park departments have set up ski slopes and in some cases installed snow-making machines. They give instruction, offer clinics, and carry on varied skiing activities—close to home. Actually, it is not even necessary to have snow in order to have a skiing program. It is possible to sponsor an indoor ski school, in which many of the basic techniques, safety procedures, and rules of skiing etiquette may be learned and practiced—before the learner ever goes outdoors. Basic conditioning can be carried on. Rules of safety, information, and ski terminology can be taught. In some cases, learners may go so far that they can actually bypass some of the beginning classes on the ski slope later and move into intermediate classes.[3] Recreation departments sometimes use such introductory classes as preliminaries to specially scheduled ski trips.

Since skiing is such a popular activity for young adults in particular, packaged ski trips are often part of the overall program offering for employee recreation departments, campus recreation programs, and armed forces recreation. And, of course, operating ski centers is a widely found form of commercial recreation.

Bowling

Bowling is an activity widely available for youth and adults in commercial bowling centers. However, many young people fail to take part in the activity because of the expense or lack of instruction.

A number of municipal recreation or school-sponsored departments have therefore organized junior bowling programs which include instruction, competition, and the opportunity to engage in a wholesome activity under proper supervision. For example, a Junior-Bowling Program was developed in Westbury, New York, and grew from 50 to 200 participants during a three-year period. Using both volunteer and professional instructors, special tournaments, free bowling clinics, and an annual awards banquet, this program developed into an attractive and successful feature of the total community recreation offering. Recreation administrators have found that, when properly approached, bowling center proprietors have been willing to make their lanes available at reduced rates, or, under some circumstances, without charge, for an introductory period. In other communities, recreation departments have organized housewives' leagues during the morning hours or have established special bowling programs for the physically handicapped or mentally retarded.

Skating

For years skating has been a popular activity carried on informally on streets or frozen ponds—or in commercial rinks or centers.

In more and more communities, artificial ice skating rinks have been built by public recreation departments, particularly when the climate has permitted a skating season of at least four or five months. The activity has proven to be extremely popular—especially when it has been intensively promoted with effective publicity, and with such features as season tickets, instruction classes, special events, and rental to hockey leagues to offset costs. While it may not be a fully self-supporting enterprise, the well-managed and budgeted artificial ice skating rink should come close to paying for itself.

Roller-skating, too, has been effectively sponsored by a number of community recreation departments. In some cases, this has been traditionally presented on outdoor hard-surface areas or paved tennis courts. In others, as in Los Angeles, it has actually been run as a highly successful indoor program in recreation centers. The Los Angeles Recreation and Park Department found that skates with wooden or fiber wheels could be modified so that the nuts on the outside of the wheels were countersunk and did no damage whatsoever to asphalt tile, parquet, or other wood flooring surfaces. In Los Angeles a traveling unit which sets up a "portable" roller skating program has been established. Using special units of skates, musical equipment, and ticket rolls, the programs are run for two-hour afternoon or evening sessions throughout the city.

Recent Programming Trends.

In recent years, racquet sports like badminton, platform tennis, squash, and particularly racquetball have gained popularity—with racquetball being featured in many fitness programs or as a key activity in sports centers and health spas. Another popular vogue has been the growing interest in martial arts, such as judo and karate, particularly in college recreation programs, the armed forces, and voluntary agencies serving young adults. These activities may be approached either from the *self-defense* emphasis, or from a more *philosophical* or *lifestyle* emphasis that links the activity to an interest in Oriental religions as a form of body/mind enrichment.

EMPHASIS ON COMPETITION: "PLAYING TO WIN"

Within most sports activities, the question of competition must be considered. Clearly, "playing to win" represents one of the most appealing and challenging aspects of sports, and is a widely accepted phenomenon in modern society. Many argue that sport teaches important values of self-discipline, team play, and acceptance of positive social values. It is suggested that learning to compete in sports helps to equip youngsters to meet the other challenges they will face throughout life—learning to strive and do one's best in school and college, in the business world, and in other areas of daily life.

At the same time, there is growing agreement by many who are concerned with sports and leisure values, that the emphasis on winning that characterizes many youth sports programs is excessive and must be controlled. Youngsters in particular must learn to both win and lose gracefully, and to enjoy the experience of playing the game for its own sake. One of the most revered coaches of all time, the famous Paul "Bear" Bryant of Alabama, said:

> I personally think that it is important for those coaching youth teams on a volunteer basis to remember that the games should be fun for the youngsters participating. Everyone should get a chance to play, regardless of athletic skills.
>
> The first few years that youngsters participate, they should come away with a feeling that they have enjoyed it. If their team wins, great, but they should always respect the other team and congratulate them for their effort. If their team loses, it isn't the end of the world.
>
> A few years ago, I watched the last inning of a Little League game. One of the teams scored a run in the bottom of the inning to win the game and they were very happy. A few minutes later, as I was walking to my car, I noticed the parents of both teams were opening up coolers and the players from both teams were visiting and drinking soft drinks. They were having fun, both the winners and the near-winners. I think it should be that way on that level of competition.[4]

What is important is that competition does not become the *sole* focus of the recreational sports program. Scheduled games, meets, tournaments, and awards all make sense—provided that they are not utilized at the cost of eliminating less formal, more relaxed forms of competitive or free play. The player with poor or mediocre skills must be given a chance to compete on his or her own level of ability or not to compete at all, as a matter of choice.

Players' Rights and Coaches' Values

The views of many coaches, parents, and other individuals concerned with the well-being of youth are expressed in a recently published *Bill of Rights for Young Athletes* (see Figure 6–6),[5] and a *Code of Ethics for Coaches* (see Figure 6–7).[6] Certainly, there is growing awareness today of the need to keep the competitive elements of sports for children and youth within bounds, and to emphasize their cooperative, "fun" elements as well!

Sometimes, the term "recreational" is used to describe sports programs which are sponsored on a more moderate level of participation and skill. For example, in some communities, Little League or other organized sports programs are presented for highly skilled and motivated young players, while those who are less interested or capable are encouraged to take part in so-called "recreational" games. The coaching principles just presented should apply to all levels of play, and to different age groups as well.

Teaching Sports Skills

Recreation leaders are often responsible for organizing sports tournaments, league play, or other large-scale events. To do so efficiently, they must make up schedules in cooperation with other coaches and officials; arrange for needed facilities for play; and carry out other tasks with respect to public relations, awards and trophies, transportation, safety arrangements, and similar responsibilities.

Another important function of leaders in community sports programs involves the teaching of basic sports skills. While much of this is done in school physical education programs, many municipal, voluntary, or other leisure-service agencies offer sports that are *not* taught in schools, or serve participants who have not learned needed skills at an earlier age. Therefore, it is often necessary to provide basic skills instruction or in some cases more advanced instruction in many areas of sports participation.

Teaching Methods.   Effective teaching in sports is based on a personal knowledge of the skills involved in the activity, combined with an understanding of teaching principles, and the ability to organize logical sequences of instruction and carry them out clearly in a logical sequence of skills. Here are several key principles:

1. To the extent that it is possible, learners should be grouped on appropriate skill and ability levels: beginner, intermediate, and advanced.
2. Learners should be organized most effectively to permit demonstration

FIGURE 6–6

Bill of Rights for Young Athletes~

I Right to participate in sports

II Right to participate at a level commensurate with each child's maturity and ability

III Right to have qualified adult leadership

IV Right to play as a child and not as an adult

V Right of children to share in the leadership and decision-making of their sport participation

VI Right to participate in safe and healthy environments

VII Right to proper preparation for participation in sports

VIII Right to an equal opportunity to strive for success

IX Right to be treated with dignity

X Right to have fun in sports

Reprinted with permission from *Guidelines for Children's Sports,* R. Martens and V. Seefeldt (Eds.). Washington, D.C. American Alliance for Health, Physical Education, Recreation and Dance, 1979.

FIGURE 6–7

Code of Ethics for Coaches

1   I will treat each player, opposing coach, official, parent and administrator with respect and dignity.

2   I will do my best to learn the fundamental skills, teaching and evaluation techniques, and strategies of my sport.

3   I will become thoroughly familiar with the rules of my sport.

4   I will become familiar with the objectives of the youth sports program with which I am affiliated. I will strive to achieve these objectives and communicate them to my players and their parents.

5   I will uphold the authority of officials who are assigned to the contests in which I coach, and I will assist them in every way to conduct fair and impartial competitive contests.

6   I will learn the strengths and weaknesses of my players so that I might place them into situations where they have a maximum opportunity to achieve success.

7   I will conduct my practices and games so that all players have an opportunity to improve their skill level through active participation.

8   I will communicate to my players and their parents the rights and responsibilities of individuals on our team.

9   I will cooperate with the administrator of our organization in the enforcement of rules and regulations, and I will report any irregularities that violate sound competitive practices.

10   I will protect the health and safety of my players by insisting that all of the activities under my control are conducted for their psychological and physiological welfare, rather than for the vicarious interests of adults. Ⓒ

Reprinted, with permission, from an article which appeared in *Spotlight on Youth Sports*, Vol. 2, No. 2, 1979 entitled, ''Young Athletes Have a Bill of Rights: Do We Need a Code of Ethics for Coaches?'' by Vern Seefeldt.

and practice of the skill components of the sport. If at all possible, when working with large numbers of learners, they should be spaced so all of them can be active all the time. Two examples follow:

a. When teaching baseball skills, it is common practice to assign players to groups on the basis of specific skills, such as hitting, pitching, and infield and outfield practice. Working with separate instructors, each player gets instruction and practice for a maximum amount of time.

b. In a sport like tennis, in which only two or four players would ordinarily be on a court at one time, learners should be organized in groups so they practice basic strokes and then rotate rapidly in hitting the ball.

3. Emphasis should be given to learning the correct way to perform each skill, but the instructor should be able to accept each individual's style or movement or unique way of performing. It is not possible in any sport to fit all players to a mold.

4. Periods of demonstration and practice should be followed by periods of actual play in order to keep interest high and to give learners a chance to practice what they have learned. However, the instructor should not hesitate to interrupt such periods of "practice-play," as in the case of a basketball scrimmage, to make teaching points.

5. As basic skills are mastered, the instructor should move players on to more advanced skills and to other areas of learning, such as rules, scoring, and strategy.

6. The leader should seek to encourage learners with praise for their positive achievements, rather than negative criticism that "puts them down" and discourages further effort.

7. Instructors should seek to develop healthy and constructive attitudes toward competition, including such elements as good sportsmanship, accepting the rules of the game, and learning to win *and* lose with grace and good humor.

Organizing Tournaments

Recognizing that competitive events are an important part of sports programming for most participants, leaders are often called upon to organize meets and tournaments. Meets usually involve a single day's competition by a large number of individuals affiliated with teams, in such broad areas as gymnastics or track and field. Individuals compete in varied events, like sprints, hurdles, long-distance runs, and throwing events, and are given points according to their place in the scoring: first, second, or third. At the conclusion of the meet, each team is given the total number of points scored by its members, and the winning order of the teams is determined.

Tournaments on the other hand, usually represent organized competition by individuals or teams in a single type of contest. The effort is to select a winning individual or team, either in a single day's play in which the winner comes to the fore, or in competition spread over a longer period of time. The advantages of such events over informal competitive play are: (a) the place and time of the event are set and publicized; (b) equipment, officials, and supervision are supplied; and (c) play culminates in a championship. There are several types of tournaments. The recreation leader should be familiar with each of these and select the one which is most appropriate for his situation, based on the kind of game to be played, the amount of time allotted, the needed equipment, the available facilities, and the number of participants. It should also be possible to promote evenly matched competition, and to keep the issue of who the winner will be open until the very end of play. The following are examples of three popular types of tournaments.

Elimination Tournaments

These are based on the idea of eliminating all contestants but one through successive stages of play, until only the winner remains. Elimination tournaments are suitable when the players are of equal ability, or when their ability is unknown. It is a speedy way of conducting a tournament, and in many sports and games can be concluded in a single day. Usually, elimination tournaments are based on having numbers of contestants that are multiples of eight: eight, sixteen, or thirty-two entries. These players (individuals or teams)

are placed on a diagram or chart showing when they are to play. If there are more than thirty-two entries, it may be desirable to run preliminary tournaments, to cut down the total number of contestants.

Some familiar terms in tournament play are:

Brackets: pairings that show which players will compete with each other

Round: a vertical row of brackets showing how contests will be scheduled—the first round of play, the second, third, and fourth

FIGURE 6–8   Elimination Tournament

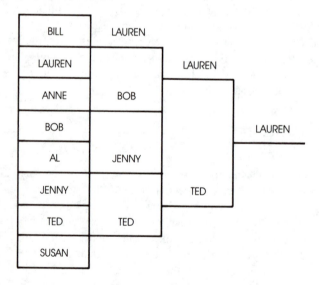

Drawing: starting positions determined by lots

In some tournaments the best players may be "seeded" and spaced out through the brackets so that they do not eliminate each other, and remain in play until the later rounds. The first round of play is held; each player who is defeated drops out, and the winner moves ahead to the next round of play. This is continued through quarterfinals, semifinals, and finals, until the winner is selected.

One weakness is that the elimination tournament gives an individual only one chance to play. If he plays a momentary off-game, he may be quickly and permanently eliminated. Therefore, this type of tournament may be played as a *double elimination,* in which the losers in the first round of play are placed in brackets to the left of the diagram. They play each other to determine a final winner. These winners then play the winners of the regular tournament to determine the final winner.

Round Robin Tournaments

This type of tournament is useful when there is sufficient time and enough facilities available so that every player may meet every other player at least once, thus producing a "true" winner. The ultimate winner is determined on the basis of his games-won-and-lost percentage at the end of the tournament.

No formal diagram is used, since players need not advance against each other. Instead, it is customary in scheduling play to place all contestants or teams in two vertical columns. In the first round, each boy (as an example) plays the boy in the opposite column with whom he is paired. Then, one row would be kept fixed and the other row rotated counterclockwise to obtain subsequent matches. After each boy in Row A had played each boy in Row B, he would then be scheduled against every boy in his own column, and vice versa. Then the player with the best percentage of wins would be declared the tournament victor.[7]

Challenge Tournaments

This is a somewhat freer and more flexible kind of tournament in that no player is actually eliminated. Instead, the goal is to advance by challenging and defeating other players or by the default of a challenged player (failure to accept the challenge). Each player seeks to climb to a higher rank in the pyramid tournament, for example, by defeating a player in the rank above him. In this type of contest, players draw for starting positions on the pyramid. When the play is begun, any player may challenge any other player in his own horizontal row. The winner may then challenge any player in the row above. If he wins, they must

FIGURE 6–9 Pyramid Tournament

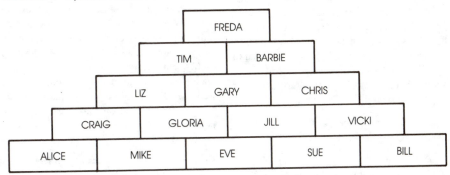

FIGURE 6–10   Ladder Tournament

SARA	PHIL
PAUL	MICHELLE
BART	BOB
JULIE	KEITH
ALISON	SHARI
WOODY	CARL
ANDY	KATHY

then exchange places; thus a player moves up or down in the pyramid according to his record. The player in the topmost position at the end of a set period of time is the tournament winner.

Another type of challenge tournament is the ladder tournament, in which players are listed on a vertical row of names (constructed like a ladder) and may challenge either of the two players directly above in order to move up.

Because challenge tournaments can be conducted over a fairly long period of time, and matches are arranged at the convenience of the contestants, they provide a very flexible kind of competition, useful for situations when all the players may not be available at a given time. Challenge tournaments may also lead to disputes, since some players may disagree about whether a challenge was fairly given or accepted within the stipulated time period.

Planning and Carrying Out Tournaments

A tournament for children on a summer playground or in a community center may be comparatively simple to plan and carry out. However, a community-wide sports tournament which involves many participants, or a large-scale invitational meet, is far more com-plex. As an example of the thorough and creative direction leadership in the area of sports may require, the U.S. Air Force manual dealing with sports programs provides precise guidelines for conducting tournaments and meets. Thirty-three separate steps are indicated, many of them with numerous procedures to be followed. A brief summary of these recommended guidelines includes the following tasks:

Advance Planning and Pre-Tournament Arrangements. Appointing project officer or manager to run tournament; early selection of dates for event; notice sent to participating individuals, teams, or organizations; coordination with appropriate associations; establishing tournament headquarters and mailing address; appointment of tournament committee and outline of its responsibilities; liaison established with relevant officials (medical, food, housing, transportation, security, engineering, etc.).

Detailed Plan of Tournament. Project officer and committee develop plan covering list of personnel needed; time schedule; fuller notification to entries; arrangements for food, housing, etc.; travel arrangements; publicity information; leave arrangements (for armed

forces personnel); seating and handling spectators; obtaining awards; obtaining needed
equipment; program printing; practice schedules for participants; medical personnel;
meeting of coaches and officials to set up
heats, make pairings, brackets, etc.; appointing games committee to handle protests or
appeals, etc.

 Similar detailed guidelines cover the actual

conduct of the tournament itself, and the
posttournament administrative details, such as
presenting awards, forming all-star teams,
paying officials, returning equipment, compiling records, and auditing expenditures. The
key point is that any large-scale tournament
represents a full-fledged administrative operation which must be intelligently planned and
carried out under careful supervision.

National Sports Competitions. Many local recreation and park agencies
enrich their sports programs by conducting local tourneys as part of national competitions sponsored by well-known companies. The Pepsi Challenge/NBA Hotshot program, for example, is a large-scale basketball skills program for boys and girls who are
nine to eighteen years of age. Local recreation and park departments and youth service
organizations carry out competitions on the local level in a basketball speed-shooting
contest with points and bonuses awarded for shooting from different positions on the
court. Winners of these local competitions on three age levels move up to area playoffs
and finals, division championships, conference championships, and ultimately national
championships.

 Another outstanding sports program is Hershey's National Track and Field
Youth Program, which was initiated in Charleston, West Virginia, in 1975, and has
since grown to be the largest and one of the most respected track and field youth
programs in the country.[8] Carried out under the supervision of the National Recreation
and Park Association and in cooperation with the President's Council on Physical
Fitness and Sports, this beginner-oriented program reaches millions of boys and girls
ages nine to fourteen in all fifty states and the District of Columbia. This program seeks
to be more than a track meet, by emphasizing the friendship, sportsmanship, and
physical aspects of track and field as much, if not more, than the competitive element.

OTHER TRENDS IN RECREATIONAL SPORTS

 One of the most important trends in recreation sports during the last fifteen or
twenty years has been the inclusion of larger numbers of participants of differing levels
of skill, as well as special population groups. A key example is the growing effort to
involve the mentally and physically disabled. Such nationally organized programs as
the Special Olympics and the wheelchair games for the physically disabled have been
gaining prominence. Thousands of paraplegics today take part in regional, national,
and even international competition in such activities as wheelchair basketball, weight
lifting, archery, fencing, shot-putting, javelin and discus throwing, and bowling. In
military and Veterans Administration hospitals, as well as in other community
facilities, men and women enjoy wheelchair sports. Even skiing—which one might

think of as demanding especially keen eyesight because of the high-speed risk factor—
is today being enjoyed by more and more blind athletes.

International Games for the Disabled.   As an outstanding example of
sports programming for special populations, the 1984 International Games for the
Disabled, held just before the 1984 Summer Olympics, in Nassau County, New York,
involved:

> . . . 1,850 athletes from 53 countries competing in 14 events, including track and
> field, air rifle and pistol, sitting and standing volleyball, lawn bowling, cycling,
> archery, table tennis, weight lifting, wrestling for the blind, fencing, equestrian
> competition, and swimming.[9]

Host organizations for the event were the United States Amputee Athletic
Association, the National Association of Sport for Cerebral Palsy, and the United
States Association for Blind Athletes. Contestants represented many forms of disability, including dwarfs and those with muscular dystrophy, multiple sclerosis, and
arthrogryposis, a disease of the bones.

Thus, we are dismissing the notion that sports are only for the able-bodied.
Another limiting stereotype—that they are only for the young—is also being undercut.
Today there is a keen awareness of the need for physical activity to maintain maximum
fitness in the middle and later years of life. More and more community programs are
being set up to provide exercise, as well as competition, for older citizens. There are
actually sports leagues—in activities such as softball—which are restricted to those
over sixty-five or seventy. As the senior population grows in the United States and
Canada, this should certainly become an increasingly important part of community
recreation programs.

Guidelines for Working with Special Populations

Particularly in working with special populations, it is necessary to develop
effective methods of teaching, coaching, and organizing sports activities which are
suited to their needs and capabilities. This may range from the extreme of programming for extremely limited populations, capable of participating only at the more
basic level, to the other extreme of programming for groups that are able to carry on the
activity with little modification.

Sports Programming for the Severely Impaired.   Numerous sport and
game programs have been developed for groups with severe physical or mental
limitations. Often, these require ingenious adaptations—such as a ''beeping'' ball—to
permit blind participants to carry on a modified form of baseball. With the severely
mentally retarded, often games or other physical activities are reduced to very simple
developmental tasks, which must be gradually attempted and mastered. These are
illustrated in the following listing of activity objectives of a roller skating program

provided for mentally retarded residents at the Plymouth, Michigan, Center for Human Development.[10]

Roller Skating

Objectives.   Roller skating is used to help develop the balance and motor coordination of the residents. Their sense of accomplishment is increased with mastery of skating skills, and they have a way to use their leisure time constructively. Residents need to learn the following skills:

1. Feeling comfortable with skates on.
2. Standing and moving about with a skate on one foot and the other foot on the floor.
3. Using side rails or rolling stand to initiate movement around the gym or day room.
4. Propelling themselves around the room.
5. Balancing themselves well enough to walk or glide around the room on two skates.
6. Using alternate leg movements to move about on skates.
7. Attempting to skate to music.
8. Participating in a skating party with residents from other buildings.

Structure.   Most ambulatory residents can learn and enjoy skating. From ten to fifteen residents can be in a group for instruction. Fifty to seventy-five residents can participate in a skating party. Instruction is scheduled for twice a week for one hour at a time.

Activity Modification.   To illustrate ways of adapting sports activities for the orthopedically disabled, Pomeroy suggests the following possible modifications for ball games:

1. Walking or wheeling may be substituted for skipping or running, when necessary.
2. A bounced throw or underhand toss may be used to replace a regular throw.
3. Positions such as sitting, kneeling or lying down may be substituted for standing positions.
4. The distances of bases or boundary lines, or of the dimensions of playing areas such as horseshoe courts, volleyball fields or baseball diamonds, may be reduced.
5. Lighter or more easily controlled equipment may be substituted for regular equipment.
6. Players may be restricted to a definite position or area on the playing field.
7. Players may be allowed to hit a ball any number of times, or to hold the ball longer in games like volleyball or basketball.
8. In games like baseball, if a child is unable to run, a runner may be used for him.[11]

In some cases, entirely new games have been devised for the disabled. As an example, one of the events at the International Games for the Disabled mentioned earlier was Goalball, a special contest for the blind. It is played with:

. . . three players on a team, left and right wings and a center, and games are two halves of five minutes each. A soccer-size ball weighted like a medicine ball with bells inside is used.

The ball may be rolled or thrown along the floor—60 feet long—toward a set that is 27 feet wide. Players are on their hands and knees and listen for the sound of the ball, and throw their bodies at it in order to prevent a score.[12]

Special Olympics. In working with groups of disabled participants with higher levels of capability, it is often possible to carry on sports with relatively minor kinds of modifications. The Special Olympics program, for example, sponsors large-scale competitions at a number of levels of disability, including severely and multi-handicapped individuals.

It has developed an extensive instructional and training program, field-tested in the early 1980s by hundreds of teachers and participants in several states. Its sports skills instruction guidelines are presented in detailed handbooks in such sports as skiing, track and field, volleyball, and aquatics. While some of its events are carried on without any form of modification, others may include adapted equipment or rules to permit successful participation by those with auditory or visual impairments, or by those using wheelchairs, walkers, or crutches.

PHYSICAL FITNESS PROGRAMMING

As indicated earlier in this chapter, there is heightened national concern about health and physical fitness-related programs sponsored by leisure-service organizations.

In Canada, this national effort is supported at the highest level by two federal agencies, Fitness Canada and Sport Canada, directed by the Secretary of State and Minister responsible for Fitness and Amateur Sport, and operating under a strong National Advisory Council. These agencies provide substantial support to national organizations designed to increase public awareness of the benefits of fitness and to encourage mass participation in physical activity and sport. In the United States, the primary federal agency in this field has been the President's Council on Physical Fitness and Sport.

Recognizing that the total ''wellness'' concept embraces a range of elements—including emotional or psychological well-being, nutritional concerns, enriched social relationships, freedom from unhealthy dependencies, and even enjoyment and sense of fulfillment in one's work—the view that sport or exercise programs contribute *only* to one's cardiovascular or neuromuscular fitness, is a rather narrow one. Perceived more broadly, sports and exercise activities should also promote a fuller sense of personal well-being, desirable social outlets, a venting of aggressions or tensions, and feelings of accomplishment or competence.

Some recreation agencies have developed extensive fitness programs, incorporating all of these elements, with primary emphasis on the physical-activity and health-related components. As a leading example, New Rochelle, New York, under the direction of Joseph Curtis, initiated a diversified program, with the following goals:

1. To stimulate a greater interest by local citizens in the care and management of their bodies.
2. To teach, in everyday language, basic information about bodies, activity, food, and drink.

3. To encourage self-care.

4. To demonstrate cost-free or low-cost ways to wellness, utilizing existing resources, including those of parks and recreation departments.

5. To use the street-power of parks and recreation departments to reach people.

Twelve different subpopulations were identified as important targets for the City-Fit program within the overall New Rochelle population: (1) young children who were uninterested in athletics or fitness; (2) housewives, confined to household chores; (3) businesspeople who tended to be weekend athletes; (4) "instant arousal" people, such as police, fire, and ambulance staffs; (5) inactive or obese adolescents; (6) unemployed adults; (7) handicapped people; (8) convalescents, recovering from illness or surgery; (9) alcoholics and drug abusers in the rehabilitation process; (10) college-age students; (11) the elderly; and (12) sedentary office workers, such as typists, tellers, or receptionists.

The New Rochelle Bureau of Parks and Recreation used different techniques in approaching these subpopulations. In working with withdrawing drug abusers of alcoholics, for example, a series of low-key "rap" sessions was held at their own counseling center; out of this came a twice-weekly jogging program for five participants—small, but a start.

The City-Fit program tied itself to no single location. It went to where the people were, in shopping malls, churches and synagogues, nursing homes and senior centers, beaches, tennis courts, local banks and businesses, bars, and restaurants. Among its special projects were the following events or programs:

Half-marathon race	Acupuncture, T'ai Chi Ch'uan,
Calisthenics on the street	Shi-Atsu
Jogging groups and classes	Blood-pressure testing and
Yoga	counseling
Massage demonstration and	Cardiopulmonary resuscitation
instruction	(CPR) training
Nutrition workshops	Bicycling
Rope-skipping	Seminars and lunchtime
Hikes and hiking programs	lecture-demonstrations

In addition to such programs, the City-Fit operation included installation of two Parcourses (exercise-and-jogging circuits) at strategic central points in New Rochelle, with more to follow; purchase of several pedalboats for use on two shallow lakes next to the Parcourse, followed by acquisition of several new, untippable canoes and rowboats; and a fitness van, equipped with testing kits, weight-training gear, mats, public address equipment, literature, exercise bicycles, and similar equipment, to carry out on-the-spot workshops and demonstrations. These approaches were invaluable in capturing public attention and involvement, and raising the level of consciousness about health and fitness among many population groups in the city.[13]

Corporate-Sponsored Fitness Programs

Among the most active sponsors of sports and physical fitness programs have been large corporations, which have recognized the importance of maintaining the health of their employees—particularly their key executives—simply from an economic point of view. Maryk points out that in a recent year:

> . . . American business and industry lost an estimated $25 billion in premature deaths and $3 billion in illness of employees, heart attacks alone causing a loss of 132 million workdays. It costs a company $500,000 to replace a key executive of age 50 earning $100,000 a year.[14]

As a result, many of the nation's top companies, including Campbell Soup, Gillette, Johnson and Johnson, Metropolitan Life, the Xerox Corporation, Pepsico, and Prudential Insurance, have established extensive health and fitness programs. Typically, Johnson and Johnson's program is centered around physical fitness, proper nutrition, general health habits, and behavior modification. Known as "Live for Life," it serves several thousand employees at different plant sites, with an activity program that includes aerobic exercise, jogging, team sports, and the use of varied exercise equipment.

In such settings, trained exercise specialists are often employed, with technical skills needed to carry out a medically based program with its roots in sports medicine. For example, Wilson and Hall write, qualified exercise program professionals must be capable of carrying out the following functions:

1. Direct the exercise program, which may be oriented to prevention and/ or rehabilitation.
2. Train and supervise staff.
3. Develop and manage the exercise facility and laboratories.
4. Market the exercise program.
5. Evaluate (in conjunction with a physician) each participant's medical and activity history, a graded exercise test, the pulmonary function tests, and assorted fitness tests.
6. Develop individual exercise prescriptions for participants.
7. Evaluate and/or counsel participants.
8. Accumulate program data for statistical analysis and research.
9. Maintain professional affiliations.
10. Perform other specific program duties.[15]

Such functions require specialized professional training, with a strong base in the physiology of exercise and related courses. However, many other company-sponsored programs are not as deeply rooted in the discipline of sports medicine, and instead seek simply to promote a wide range of appealing physical activities—including exercise programs, individual and team sports, outdoor recreation, and aerobic dance or Jazzercise. Thanks at least in part to such programs and to the nationwide fitness boom, we have recently witnessed a striking decline in the incidence of coronary heart disease and the stroke death rate. Without question, fitness activities will continue to be an important part of recreation programming for many types of leisure-service agencies.

THE ROLE OF RECREATION LEADERS IN PHYSICAL RECREATION PROGRAMMING

Summing up, the sports, active games, and fitness programs sponsored by varied community agencies may range from a traditional concern with typical team and individual games for children and youth, to a much broader involvement of varied population groups on a co-recreational, all-age-levels basis. Similarly, their goals may extend from the familiar, strongly competitive values of the past to a more diversified effort to meet different community interests and needs—including health and fitness concerns.

Within this framework, recreation professionals have a unique opportunity to promote physical recreation activities that meet both leisure-related and significant health needs. From time to time, recreation participation has assumed the character of a "boom-and-bust," fadlike craze, in terms of popular involvement in a new or unique form of activity. It is safe to say, however, that sports and fitness programming will continue to represent a major area of public interest and a continuing responsibility for leisure-service leaders in the years ahead.

NOTES

[1]Keeping in Shape—Everybody's Doing It," *U.S. News & World Report* (13 August 1984): 25.

[2]Bill Gilbert and Nancy Williamson, "Sport is Unfair to Women," *Sports Illustrated* (28 May 1973): 85.

[3]As an example, see Jonathan E. Nelson, "Teaching Cross-Country Skiing," *Journal of Physical Education, Recreation and Dance* (May 1984): 58–64.

[4]From Tara Kost Scanlan, "Motivation and Stress in Competitive Youth Sports," *Journal of Physical Education, Recreation and Dance* (March 1982): 27–28.

[5]*Guidelines for Children's Sports*, R. Martens and V. Seefeldt, Eds. (Washington, D.C.: American Alliance for Health, Physical Education, Recreation and Dance, 1979).

[6]Vern Seefeldt, "Young Athletes Have a Bill of Rights: Do We Need a Code of Ethics for Coaches?" *Spotlight on Youth Sports* (Vol. 2, No. 2, 1979).

[7]Brian E. MacTaggart, "An Effective Round-Robin Schedule," *Journal of Physical Education, Recreation and Dance* (April 1984): 74–75.

[8]"Hershey Track and Field: Ongoing Attention to Fitness," *Parks and Recreation* (June 1984): 46–47; see also Kathi Nyhan, "The Hershey Program—More Than a Track Meet," *Parks and Recreation* (May 1982): 67–70.

[9]"Games to Feature World's Best Disabled Athletes in U.S. Debut," *Dateline, National Recreation and Park Association* (May 1984): 1, 7.

[10]*Activity Therapy Manual*. Plymouth State Home and Training School, Northville, Mich., 1971, 7, 19, 21.

[11]Janet Pomeroy, *Recreation for the Physically Handicapped* (New York: Macmillan, 1964), pp. 306–7.

[12]"Hungary Upsets U.S. in Goalball," *New York Times* (24 June 1984): S-9.

[13]See Richard Kraus and Joseph Curtis, *Creative Management in Recreation and Parks* (St. Louis: C. V. Mosby, 1982), 190–191; also Joseph Curtis, "Effective Communication About Fitness and Welfare," *Parks and Recreation* (December 1983): 29.

[14]Margaretha Maryk, "Corporate Fitness and Sports in a Changing Society," *Journal of Physical Education, Recreation and Dance* (May 1982): 64.

[15]Philip K. Wilson and Linda K. Hall, "Industrial Fitness, Adult Fitness and Cardiac Rehabilitation," *Journal of Physical Education, Recreation and Dance* (March 1984): 40.

STUDENT PROJECTS

1. In class, review the process of teaching sports or game skills. Then have several student volunteers lead the class in active group games, or instruct class members in a basic sports skill. Have members critique their performance, with emphasis on its positive elements, but with suggestions to improve weaknesses.
2. Select a particular sport, such as baseball, softball, or basketball. Show the different forms it might take in a community recreation program, at different levels of ability and interest, and for different age groups.
3. Plan and carry out a tournament in class in an activity that all can take part in, such as table tennis or board games.
4. Hold a debate in class on the proposition that competitive sports programming, with a heavy emphasis on winning, should be stressed in recreational sports activities.

SUGGESTED READINGS

John A. Colgate, *Administration of Intramural and Recreational Activities: Everyone Can Participate* (New York: John Wiley, 1978).

Andrew Fluegelman, ed., *The New Games Book* (Garden City, N.Y.: Doubleday, 1976).

Viola K. Kleindienst and Arthur Weston, *The Recreational Sports Program: Schools, Colleges, Communities* (Englewood Cliffs, N.J.: Prentice-Hall, 1978).

Darwin Hindman, *Handbook of Active Games* (Englewood Cliffs, N.J.: Prentice-Hall, 1955).

CHAPTER 7

Outdoor Recreation and Nature Activities

One of the areas of organized recreation service which has expanded most dramatically over the past three decades has been outdoor recreation. As Chapter 1 points out, the federal, state, provincial, and local governments in the United States and Canada have developed tremendous new resources for meeting growing public interest in travel and tourism. In addition to the expansion of recreation vehicles and other forms of motorized outdoor recreation, millions of enthusiasts have taken up hiking, backpacking, tent camping, and similar pastimes.

MEANING OF OUTDOOR RECREATION

Exactly what *is* outdoor recreation? In the past, it has been defined very loosely or not at all. Some consider that any pastime carried on in an outdoor setting should be considered outdoor recreation. But should a game of checkers on a park bench, basketball played in a schoolyard, or a choral performance in a bandshell be considered outdoor recreation?

The essential point is that outdoor recreation should have a meaningful relationship to the world of the outdoors. It should consist of *those recreational activities that can best be carried on out of doors, which have in some way a direct relationship or dependence on nature, and that place the participant in direct contact with the elements.* Seen in this light, such activities as hunting, fishing, hiking, camping, water-skiing, skiing, scuba diving, picnicking, pleasure driving, horseback riding, archery in the natural setting, and bicycling along trails are all clearly outdoor recreation.

Certain activities may be more difficult to differentiate. Tennis probably should not be considered outdoor recreation, although it may be part of a multiuse outdoor recreation facility. Golf, on the other hand, because it involves tramping over fairways and roughs and, to a degree, combatting nature, may fairly be called outdoor recreation. Swimming in an indoor pool does not deserve the name, but swimming in an outdoor pool, a mountain lake, or an ocean beach facility does.

Why has outdoor recreation become so popular? One reason is that Americans and Canadians have always viewed themselves as "outdoors" people. Our tradition includes many legends and tales of the pioneers along our Western frontiers, of loggers, cowboys, and explorers. Small wonder that camping, backpacking, and related outdoor pursuits have been popular for many years.

A second reason is that our lives have become so sedentary and mechanized that we need more vigorous physical activity—such as the kind that can be found in canoeing, hiking, swimming, biking, hunting, fishing, climbing, and skiing. Modern urban living is often so noisy, competitive, and stressful that there is a need to get away from the hubbub of the city and industrial life and come in contact with the world of nature. In fields, forests, mountains, streams, and lakes, campers and hikers see order and beauty in the world, and perceive the complex intricacies of animal or vegetable life.

For some, the outdoor environment provides the opportunity for daring risks and meeting challenges. For such individuals, outdoor recreation offers excitement and a sense of personal accomplishment not found in their daily lives.

TYPES OF OUTDOOR RECREATION ACTIVITIES

Outdoor recreation programs tend to be provided chiefly by public agencies, although some facilities are offered by voluntary, commercial, or other sponsors. They take two broad forms: The first is the provision of facilities that include forest camping areas, ski centers, scenic overlooks, fishing streams, geysers and other unusual natural phenomena, historical monuments, and mountain trails. For the most part, these do not involve direct instruction, leadership, or supervision of activities. The participant is generally free to carry on by himself or herself, although in some programs there may be instruction, interpretive lectures, or guided tours.

The second type of outdoor recreation program consists of activities that require direct leadership. These may involve interpretive services, providing guides, instructors, or other organized forms of leadership or assistance.

This chapter describes the role of governmental and other types of leisure-service agencies in providing outdoor recreation opportunity, as well as specific examples of various kinds of nature-oriented programs and services.

Federal Role. The federal governments in both the United States and Canada play an important role in managing outdoor recreation resources, such as major parks, forests, lakes and reservoirs, seashores, and other facilities. In addition, they promote conservation and resource reclamation, assist open-space and park development programs, provide funding assistance to states and local municipalities, offer technical assistance and enact regulations and standards with respect to watershed production, environmental quality, or access to facilities for the disabled. To illustrate, Table 7–1 shows the specific activities engaged in by visitors to areas operated by the United States Forest Service in a recent year.

In Canada, the major federal agency concerned with providing outdoor recreation opportunities for Canadians and the millions of tourists who visit the country each year is Parks Canada, part of the Conservation Program of the Department of Indian and Northern Affairs. Its National Parks Branch operates twenty-eight major parks totaling over 50,000 square miles, and also manages a number of National Marine Parks, National Landmarks, Wild Rivers, Historical Trails, and Parkways, as part of a total opportunity system for outdoor recreation.

State and Provincial Programs. Each of the fifty states in the United States, and each of the twelve Canadian provinces provides a wide range of outdoor recreation facilities, programs and services, both for its own residents and to encourage tourism. To illustrate, one of the most active states in this area has been New York, which is blessed by a wealth of natural resources and recreational facilities. These include a wide variety of scenic views, historical sites, fishing streams, reservoirs, resort areas, boat basins and marinas, summer colonies, waterfalls, underground caverns, battlefields, chasms, ski centers, gliding centers, motor racing tracks, arts

TABLE 7–1   Summary of National Forest Recreation Uses (1981)[1]

Activities	Visitor-days (1,000)	Percent
Camping	59,628	25.3
Picnicking	9,707	4.1
Recreation travel (mechanized)	55,198	23.4
Water travel	8,132	3.5
Games and team sports	1,033	.4
Water skiing, other water sports	983	.4
Swimming and scuba diving	5,334	2.3
Winter sports	11,262	4.8
Fishing	16,973	7.2
Hunting	16,413	7.0
Hiking and mountain climbing	12,791	5.4
Horseback riding	3,651	1.5
Resort use	4,429	1.9
Organization camp use	3,936	1.7
Recreation cabin use	6,400	2.7
Gathering forest products	5,056	2.1
Nature study	2,019	.9
Viewing scenery, sports, environment	8,525	3.6
Visitor information (exhibits, talks, etc.)	4,239	1.8
Total	235,709	100.0

festivals, canals, and fish hatcheries—all of which attract huge numbers of residents and tourists.

In addition to providing outdoor facilities, many states have assumed the responsibility for educating their citizens (chiefly the young) in the most intelligent, environmentally sound, and enjoyable use of outdoor recreation resources. Three major elements of such instruction in New York State include required courses in hunter safety, young boatman's safety courses, and an extensive program in conservation education.

As an example of how states and provinces may assist local programs, the Province of Alberta, Canada, has financially assisted local school districts in the development of outdoor recreation and environmental education programs.

Alberta also operates a leadership training center in outdoor education and recreation skills. This center, Blue Lake, provides a variety of courses for adults in such areas as cross-country skiing at several levels of proficiency, ski-touring, canoe building, and winter camping and survival. Other Canadian provinces offer similar programs.

County Outdoor Recreation Activities. Many county recreation and park departments have also developed outstanding outdoor recreation programs.

Because county governments often embrace fairly large geographical areas, including land beyond metropolitan or municipal boundaries, they are in an advantageous position to develop major outdoor recreation facilities sited to meet a variety of different needs.

Municipal Outdoor Recreation Programs. Several examples of outdoor recreation programs provided by municipal recreation and park departments are presented in this section. They place heavy emphasis both on educating participants in outdoor recreation skills and values, and on providing facilities and leadership that facilitate varied forms of outdoor recreation involvement.

Pasadena, California. In Pasadena, the Nature and Outing Division of the city's municipal Department of Recreation offers many year-round outdoor recreation programs for all age groups. One of the major features is an annual family camping course, consisting of six lecture and demonstration sessions and one weekend camping trip.

The Pasadena Recreation Department also sponsors an elementary school nature science excursion program, an outdoor education and conservation program for fifth and sixth graders. The nature specialist visits the classroom in advance to prepare the children, and then an all-day trip is made to the primitive Arroyo Seco Park area. There, children engage in a two-hour exploration hike, visiting a flood-control dam, a water channel, a settling basin, a nature trail, and a sand and gravel plant. Students build an open fire, cook lunch, collect nature specimens for their classroom, and visit a U.S. Forest Service station. Special excursions of this type are also provided for physically or mentally handicapped children in the school system.

The Nature and Outing Division also sponsors the following: (a) fly-tying classes; (b) introduction to fishing classes (both fresh water and salt); (c) ski shows; (d) dry land ski schools; (e) hunter safety and gun safety programs; and (f) a youth camp site which is made available to many youth groups in the community, who provide their own leadership.

Milwaukee, Wisconsin. In Milwaukee, the Public School's Department of Municipal Recreation and Adult Education sponsors many activities relating to outdoor recreation, including trips to wilderness areas in county park systems, exploration hikes in state forests, and a gardening program for younger children.

Week-long day camps are held in Kettle Moraine State Forest for children between eight and twelve. They are picked up at neighborhood playgrounds in the morning and returned to them around 5:00 P.M. In these day camps, nature hikes, cookouts, campfires, woodland crafts, and nature lore comprise the program. Trips to nearby places of interest include a dairy farm, fish hatchery, conservation planting area, and lookout peak.

Other activities include junior and senior conservation clubs; astronomy and 4-H clubs; a Junior Audubon program; gun, boating, and water safety clinics; fishing trips; and hiking programs. Other age groups are served through a citywide adult hiking club and a family camping association involving over 1,000 families.

Phoenix, Arizona. This city's Parks and Recreation Department serves all age groups, with numerous outdoor recreation activities designed primarily for adults, including archery clubs and ranges; regularly scheduled bird walks; weekly bicycling excursions; extensive bridle paths; canoeing facilities; a city-owned mountain campground for residents to use, over 90 miles from Phoenix in the Bradshaw Mountains; fishing and casting clinics; hiking events; horseshoes competition; museums; nature study; picnic grounds; rockhounding hobby activities; dry-land skiing; and an attractive zoo.

Instructional Programs

Many municipal recreation and park departments provide instructional programs which educate participants in varied forms of outdoor recreation: (a) motor boating and boating safety classes; sailing classes and clubs; (c) hunter safety and community shooting programs; (d) family camping clubs and courses; (e) day camping programs; (f) outdoor recreation for the disabled; (g) nature activities, projects, and games; and (h) other miscellaneous programs.

Motorboating and Boating Safety. It was reported in the mid-1970s that over 700 people each year lost their lives in boating accidents, and thousands of others were seriously injured. Research has shown that the greatest number of fatalities occurred in the use of outboard motorboats, rowboats, and canoes, all of less than sixteen feet, in a cruising situation. A common cause was "fault of the operator"— meaning speeding, overloading, improper loading, no proper lookout, carelessness, or bad judgment. While many states have licensing requirements for powered pleasure craft, they do not have them for their pilots. Therefore, courses in small craft operation are becoming more and more common, offered by schools, colleges, boating organizations, or public recreation and park departments.

Such small craft courses usually give attention to the following aspects of boating safety: registration, safety certificates, and safety patrols; required safety equipment on all motor boats; meaning of signals on boats; safe fueling procedures; boarding; loading; safety checks; rules of the road; piloting; buoys and lights; use of compass; speed, winds and currents, and charts; docking and mooring; water skiing; fishing; meaning of skin diver's flag; swimming away from boat; cruising; procedures for accidents; rescue breathing; drowning, shock, and sunburn.

An increasing number of community recreation and park departments now offer courses of this type. Even when boating waterways may not be immediately accessible, so widespread is the interest in this sport that it has become an important and highly valued program feature.

Sailing Classes and Clubs.   Another popular aquatic sport is sailing. Far from being the exclusive pastime of the wealthy elite as it was years ago, today sailing appeals to millions of people of all ages and social classes. An example of how sailing may be developed as a community recreation activity is found in Quincy, Massachusetts. Quincy, a city with twenty-seven miles of shoreline and a population of about 88,000, has traditionally had a strong interest in sailing, both as a livelihood and a sport. The city's recreation department staff includes a supervisor of boating and sailing, whose major task has been to introduce Quincy's youngsters to boating. His program involves a fleet of twenty-eight boats and, in a recent summer, a staff of seven and over 400 young participants.

Hunter Safety and Community Shooting Programs.   Hunting has traditionally been an extremely popular activity throughout the United States and Canada. However, it is viewed as having a high danger potential, with guns annually causing a significant number of tragic accidents and deaths. To some extent, this danger is exaggerated. A five-year insurance company study of claims paid for sports accidents found that hunting and shooting rated sixteenth, far below baseball and football. One good reason for this has been that many states require that novice hunters take courses in the use of firearms and qualifying tests before being given licenses. Many municipal recreation and park departments give such courses, with the assistance of volunteer National Rifle Association instructors.

In some communities, school physical education classes have sponsored gun safety courses to promote safe hunting and shooting recreation. In Little Rock, Arkansas, every junior high school boy and girl receives instruction in gun handling and firing in a two-week physical education class unit. The need for this program was based on findings that the majority of boys and girls were already hunting or target shooting, and that most student gun accidents were statistically shown to occur at the junior high school age level.

In other communities, shooting has become a popular recreation activity in a variety of facilities. Shooting ranges, both indoor and outdoor, may range from the very simple and functional to highly elaborate and expensive areas. Their objectives may be purely social or may include hunter safety and competitive shooting.

Family Camping Clubs and Courses.   Since World War II, family camping has become increasingly popular as an inexpensive form of family fun and travel, as shown in the greatly increased statistics of overnight camping in federal and state campgrounds. Equipment varies greatly, from simple mountaineer tents, or sleeping bags and ponchos (for the hardy), to elaborate and expensive trailer hookups. Some camping families go to primitive areas and live on dehydrated foods, which they must pack in over mountain trails or carry through rough water by canoe. Others live as luxuriously as if they were at home. But whatever the details, this is certainly one of the most popular forms of outdoor recreation for millions of Americans.

The very idea of camping implies that ones goes to a wilderness or forest site away from home. How then can most community recreation departments realistically offer camping programs?

The answer is that local recreation and park departments may stimulate interest in this activity, offer courses in family camping, and sponsor clubs or organizations based on it. For example, in Moline, Illinois, the public recreation department has sponsored a family camping club with several hundred members. This group has held monthly meetings devoted to camping clinics and special activities, and plans mass trips to distant parks. Similarly, the Linden, New Jersey, recreation department has sponsored a family camping club including both travel trailer and tent camping enthusiasts. Club members hold rallies at various campgrounds throughout the year and work with state agencies to expand camping opportunities and facilities.

Day Camping Programs.   Another outdoor recreation program feature sponsored by many municipal recreation and park departments has been day camping. Such camps usually differ from ordinary playground activities in that children are signed up for regular participation over a period of time. This may be the entire summer, or may involve only a week or two, with the membership being rotated to give as many as possible a chance to participate. Day camping should involve transportation to a wooded or natural site away from the regular neighborhood playground and should also include the serving of at least one meal to the children.

Customarily a full schedule of activities is planned, with a strong emphasis on nature activities, games, and crafts. Children are usually divided into small groups under competent leadership, in a decentralized type of program operation.

Some communities have actually established campsites at a considerable distance from their home base. The citizens of Hawthorne, California, for example, joined together to purchase and develop a twenty-acre all-year mountain camp, 100 miles northeast of their city. Located in the San Gabriel Mountains near the 6,000-foot level of the Angeles National Forest, the camp provides a varied program for children in eight-day sessions from June through August, and a school outdoor education experience for classes from the elementary school district during the winter. Winter weekends are scheduled for family units. Believing strongly in the need for this type of outdoor recreation experience for all ages, the residents of Hawthorne have cooperated fully to make the experience possible for all, providing financial aid to youngsters when needed. The summer eight-day session includes such activities as: fishing, horseback riding, wildlife study, forest lore, geology, panning for gold, weather forecasting, and astronomy.

Outdoor Recreation and Camping for the Disabled.   Another important trend in the outdoor recreation field has been to provide outdoor experiences and camping opportunities for disabled individuals and groups. These have ranged from day camping programs for physically disabled children and youth, to wilderness camping experiences or survival programming for emotionally disturbed or mentally ill adolescents and adults. Several examples follow:

Cerebral Palsy Day Camp. In Nassau County, New York, there is a playground specifically designed to meet the needs of physically handicapped children. On the grounds of the Nassau County Cerebral Palsy Association, in Roosevelt, Long Island, New York, the area is composed of several large (fifty feet in diameter) circular sections, connected to each other by wide, semipaved paths.

Each area is equipped with slides with graduated approach ramps, wide bicycle paths, a maze that can be explored by youngsters in wheelchairs, and a water-and-sand play area designed to be used by children in wheelchairs or on crutches. The whole purpose of the playground is to modify activities and facilities so that they can be used successfully by children with cerebral palsy—and so that the youngsters can be encouraged to dare new adventures and learn new skills.

In addition, a day campsite, placed in the woods next to the playground, offers large tents placed on wood platforms flush with the ground, a crafts area and storage house, a swimming pool, and a fishing hole (made from an old concrete foundation) where children may sit in their wheelchairs and fish through a screened opening for safety. There are also paved paths throughout the woods, used by the children for hiking and for group nature activities.

Daniel Boone Camp. The St. Louis Society for Crippled Children has been active for many years in helping sponsor and arrange the admission of disabled children in regular residential summer camps in its area. A number of private or agency camps have cooperated quite effectively in this effort. However, it was found that a number of children were so severely handicapped that they could not function adequately in regular camp programs. Therefore the Society built a special camp in St. Charles County, called the Daniel Boone Camp, which is used by the most severely disabled youngsters, including children with cerebral palsy, hydrocephalus, spina bifida, and epilepsy, as well as blind children and children recovering from encephalitis and brain surgery.

Campers are treated basically the same as normal children, without any emphasis on their disability—although they have been admitted under careful medical clearance and guidance, and a trained social worker supervises the camp activities. It has been found possible to integrate children with many different types of disabilities, providing that the groups are kept small, the program flexible, and the staff capable and well-oriented.

One of Daniel Boone Camp's main concerns has been to motivate children to try *new* skills and experiences. Many of them, with severe disabilities, have been so overprotected that they have failed to live up to their full potential of physical performance. As they have gained confidence, a number of severely handicapped youngsters have moved from a summer at Daniel Boone to the point where they were capable of being admitted to a regular camp, for an integrated experience with nondisabled children.

"Risk" Programming for Disabled.   A special form of outdoor recreation is found in "challenge" or "risk" programming for the mentally or physically disabled. For example, the Northwest Outward Bound School in Eugene, Oregon, has sponsored a pilot course for adults with such varied disabilities as cerebral palsy, vision impairment, epilepsy, or spinal cord injury. Among the challenges met by these disabled individuals during a seven-day course were: descending a steep mountain trail; crossing a river hand-over-hand on a rope traverse (a rope sling had to be used for some participants); preparing food under primitive circumstances; and climbing and rappeling rocks.

Outdoor recreation can be a vital tool in helping disabled children, youth, and adults gain confidence and overcome the limitations that have often been arbitrarily imposed on them. However, it is essential to be realistic about the limitations that clients' impairments may cause—both psychologically and physically. Malone and Mashek comment:

> Participants from disabled populations must feel safe while still being challenged. Leaders should know the participants' limitations and determine how to exceed them safely. Appropriate stress levels are beneficial and should not be avoided [but] leaders must identify the fine line between beneficial challenge and unnecessary risk.[2]

Another organization, the Community Council for the Exceptional Person, in Paoli, Pennsylvania, has taken hundreds of disabled youth and adults on two-week trips into wilderness areas, or on canoeing or sail camping expeditions.

GENERAL CONCERN WITH HIGH-RISK PROGRAMMING

Throughout *all* forms of outdoor recreation, the problem of safety hazards and the risk of serious injury must be carefully considered. This has become particularly evident because of the growth of popular interest in hang-gliding, sky-diving, rock-climbing, dirt-biking, scuba-diving, and cave-exploration, in addition to such familiar activities as horseback riding, hunting, or boating which have a degree of physical risk. The possibility of accidents in such activities which might lead to costly lawsuits has inhibited some recreation agencies from sponsoring them actively. However, with appropriate safeguards and skilled leadership, as well as the use of waiver forms or other techniques that ensure participants' awareness of risk factors and compliance with safety guidelines, the problem can be minimized.

Based on a careful analysis of the actual frequency of accidents in high-risk recreation, Allen and Meier write:

> The purpose of any recreation agency is to provide opportunities for people to engage in need-satisfying leisure behavior, whatever those needs might be. Although more

dangerous (in some cases, perhaps) than moderate forms of recreation, risk recreation is certainly preferable to inactivity, nonparticipation, and boredom. The values and benefits of risk recreation usually outweigh any risks involved.[3]

As a single example of how a municipal leisure-service agency may choose to move vigorously into this field, the Portsmouth, Virginia, Park and Recreation Department has initiated a family-oriented "Hi-Adventure" program consisting of activities using air, land, and water. The overall list of workshops, classes, trips, and other experiences co-sponsored with other public, private, or commercial agencies in Portsmouth, includes: hang-gliding outings and lessons; hiking seminars and guided outings; horseback riding lessons; grass skiing; cave exploring; canoe lessons and trips; white-water rafting and camping; and deep-sea fishing and shark fishing.

Nature Activities

In addition to the kinds of outdoor recreation programs described earlier in this chapter, there are many other activities which are based on the natural environment which may be used as part of playground, camping, or other structured recreation sessions. Examples of these are presented under the following headings: (1) nature games; (2) nature study activities; and (3) campcraft activities.

Nature Games

Some of these games are best played while on a hike through natural terrain. Others may be played anywhere. They involve certain specific kinds of skills: identification and knowledge of natural objects, trailing skills, alertness, and awareness of the natural world.

Sniff

Players are blindfolded and, one by one, are allowed to smell certain common objects which have been gathered in advance. These should have strong and recognizable odors like cedar, apple, cucumber, mold, tomato, skunk cabbage, balsam, mint, black birch, onion, and fish. The player who can correctly identify the largest number of objects is the winner.

Nature Sounds

The group sits quietly in a clearing in the woods. Each person listens, writing down all of the nature sounds he hears—the wind, birds, insects, leaves rustling, etc. (each sound must be specifically identified). After a five- or ten-minute limit, each player reads his list. The longest correct list wins the game.

Feel

The same game may be played by having each child in turn feel certain objects, like shells, stones of various types, flowers, leaves, bark, and whatever can be gathered in the vicinity. Each object should have a very distinctive texture or shape, and must be exactly identified. The player with the highest score of correct answers is the winner.

Nature Treasure Hunt

The players are divided into several teams. Each team is given a map which leads them, by a different route, to the same "treasure." On the map are directions and clues using natural objects, rocks, trees, flowers, etc.; at each clue, directions to the next clue are found. The first team to reach the "treasure" is the winner.

Retrieving

This game is somewhat similar to "Nature Relay." Players are divided into several teams. One player from each team is active. The leader holds up some object or nature specimen—a leaf, twig, flower, or feather. At the signal, "Go!" the active player on each team must run to find and bring back a similar object. The first player to do so wins one point for his team. Each player is active in turn, and the first team to accumulate a given number of points is the winner.

Nature Artists

Players divide into teams. Each team sends an "artist" to the leader. When they are all together, the leader shows them the name of a natural object (bird, animal, tree, or plant) he has written down. They run back to their groups and draw the object, until it is correctly named by a member of the group. The first team to guess correctly wins one point. So the game goes until each child has had a chance to be the "artist."

Nature Alphabet

This game is played with two teams facing each other in lines. The leader names a category, such as birds, flowers, trees, or animals. Then he names a letter of the alphabet. In turn, the first player in Team A and then the first player in Team B must name something in the correct category starting with that letter—within five or ten seconds. If he cannot, the other team wins a point. The game is repeated with the next player in the line and with a new letter each time. If the same letter is used again, players may not name the same object as before. The team with the highest total of points at the end is the winner.

In playing such games as Nature Treasure Hunt, care must be taken not to have the players "collect" objects in a way that might damage the natural environment.

Nature Study

Nature study is not just a matter of memorizing the characteristics of wildlife or vegetation, or having a number of practical projects to carry out. Instead, it involves seeing nature as something exciting and meaningful, even in its tiniest or least significant aspects. Children are usually eager for adventure and exploration, and recreation leaders and camp counselors must join them in this spirit as they approach nature involvement.

It is not essential that the nature specialist in a camp or outdoor recreation program have a specialized degree in botany or life sciences. However, he or she should have a rich store of nature lore, and an understanding of the interrelationships of living things in the natural setting. Equally important, the nature specialist should be resourceful in exploring the playground, park, pond, and forest to uncover the many possibilities for nature discovery that lie close by. This means viewing each plant, each insect, each water creature, leaf, bird, or twig as a source of wonder and interest. The leader who brings along a magnifying glass, or a pocket book to help in identifying nature objects is on his or her way!

What are some specific activities that children enjoy in a camp or recreation setting?

Gardening

This is a particulary useful hobby even for comparatively limited areas, and sustains interest through an entire playground season as different flowers and vegetables are planted and grow. Children may cultivate their own small plots, may do landscaping or transplanting, and even—with adult direction—carry out more ambitious projects, such as developing rock gardens, growing miniature or dwarf plants, and propagating plants and shrubs. In many communities there are garden clubs with interested adults who will be glad to volunteer as instructors for gardening programs on summer playgrounds.

Weather Study

Again, under competent guidance, children may carry out a variety of activities related to weather study. They may learn basic facts about climate, to make and read barometers, to use weather forecasting instruments, and to record, chart, and interpret data. A study of astronomy may be closely linked to such projects.

Terrariums

Children may construct simple, miniature terrariums, using mosses, small plants, bright stones, and berries to make colorful displays. These may be used to house salamanders or small turtles, although care must be taken to provide sufficient food for these small pets, since the terrarium itself does not provide natural food for them.

Nature Crafts

Among the many craft activities based on nature are: photography, making plaster mold prints of nature objects, whittling or wood carving, or making prints of leaves (using a spattering or ink-rolling method). Other activities may involve fly tying, weaving or making displays with cattails, constructing models using "lashing" techniques, and making decorations, bookends, centerpieces, or lamp bases with driftwood. Children may do block printing using cut potatoes or apples, make tiny decorative trees from pods and cones, or construct nature jewelry.

Marine Studies

In some cases, outdoor recreation and education programs may be able to use the special resources and leadership provided by other agencies. For example, the Sandy Hook, New Jersey, State Park operates a "Shore and Marine Environmental Program" at the Spermaceti Cove Interpretive Center, which is made available to school and other community groups for special courses or outdoor learning experiences. Other state, provincial, or federal agencies provide similar special programs and services in environmental education throughout the United States and Canada.

Campcraft Activities

Closely allied to these activities are the skills that are needed for survival in the woods, or simply for comfortable and enjoyable camping. More than ever, it is essential that such activities be carried out with a full awareness of their possible environmental impact—and that no projects be led that might harm the natural setting in any way.

Knotcraft

As part of a sailing program or simply as an aid to making camp in the woods, it is essential to be able to make a number of useful knots that can be tied easily, will hold fast, and can be untied without difficulty. Several of these include the square knot (or reef knot), the close hitch, the bowline knot, the sheet bend, and the half-hitch knot.

Compass

Children enjoy learning to read, understand, and use the compass. They may under-

take special problems involving finding their way to certain spots by compass, or may play the Swedish game "Orienteering," which tests several kinds of compass skills.[13] Similarly, they may learn to read maps and to understand contour lines, and gain practice in making their own maps.

Measurements

Part of outdoor living involves learning to measure distances and dimensions. Children may learn to measure distance, first by estimating it roughly and then (having determined the length of their individual pace) by pacing it off. They may also learn to quickly measure things by using their own personal dimensions (hand span, length of index finger, length of foot, height, eye level, or upward stretch).

Morse Code

Children are always fascinated by the universal language of dots and dashes. Once they have learned to send it and to receive it, however slowly, they may experiment with different ways of signaling. These may include the use of flags, smoke, arms, whistles, buzzers, or, at night, fire, lantern, or flashlight.

Skills Tournament

At the end of a summer season, children may participate in a tournament where they compete in performing the various campcraft skills they have learned. They should be divided into teams, with each youngster having a chance to compete in one or more events, while his teammates "root" for him. Activities include the following: (a) pitching a tent; (b) making a tripod basin rack or other lashed construction; (c) building a fire (sometimes done so the first child who has a pot of water boiling is the winner); (d) driving nails into a log; (e) making a pile of shavings with a jack-knife; (f) making knots; and (g) giving signal messages. Each event is scored for speed, with the first to complete it given three points, the next two, and the next one, so that players are encouraged to keep going even if they are not the first.

Other Community Nature Projects

In addition to such activities, many community recreation and park agencies sponsor varied nature projects or educational programs, such as the following:

Austin, Texas, Nature Center. The Austin Recreation Department sponsors a city-wide Nature Center, which includes clubs and classes that meet weekly in such areas as astronomy, archaeology, plant and animal life, earth sciences, and meteorology. Participants meet with advisors and teachers from such organizations as the Travis Audubon Society, the Austin Gem and Mineral Society, the Forty Acres Astronomy Club, and various science departments of the University of Texas. They carry out field trips, develop science and nature projects, and have received considerable assistance from the national organization, Nature Centers for Young America.

Milwaukee "Starwagon." Another example of science interests being promoted by a municipal recreation department is the traveling observatory and planetarium operated on playgrounds in Milwaukee, Wisconsin. Most of the funds required for the "Star-wagon's" construction were raised from private sources, although the Milwaukee Astronomical Society assisted in designing it, and it was actually built by the recreation division's service and maintenance department. The mobile unit itself is 21 feet in length and has a 15-foot diameter collapsible dome with a colorful rainbow steel arch. Its equipment includes a 3½-inch refractor telescope and a 6-inch reflector telescope, a planetarium projector, charts, space-interpretation globes, satellite-tracking telescopes, and similar devices necessary for a space program. The entire unit is attached to a department truck or jeep and can readily be taken to any section of the city.

Animal and Pet Activities. A popular form of nature activity in community recreation involves the sponsorship of pet owners' clubs and of other hobbies or activities dealing with animals. This may include workshops on the proper care and training of animals, in which veterinarians discuss animal nutrition, diseases, and medicine, and kits or other materials from dog food companies are displayed.

It may include dog obedience classes meeting for ten or fifteen sessions at several levels of training. Often the final sessions of such courses involve demonstrations, contests, and the judging of special events and performances. One such club, in Reading, Pennsylvania, the Berks County Dog Training Club, has compiled an enviable record of public service through entertainment given to hospitals, and through cooperation with city police in solving problems caused by unruly pets.

On summer playgrounds, pet shows may include a wide variety of events and categories, some of them humorous. All, however, should be aimed at developing sound attitudes regarding pet owner responsibilities, plus effective skills in actually caring for pets.

Nature Festivals. Finally, a number of recreation departments have sponsored nature festivals on a community-wide basis as important special events. In Richmond, Virginia, for example, the department of recreation and parks has presented a large outdoor nature show, including two elements: (a) a cross-section of the city playgrounds' organized nature programs; and (b) displays by organized groups, including astronomy, mineralogy, and garden clubs. The festival was housed under a large tent, and had such features as: playground collections of rocks, reptiles, and butterflies; arts and crafts displays; birdhouses and gardens; an azalea exhibit; a Boy Scout exhibit on erosion control; a private collection of South American iguanas, lizards, turtles, and quail; Indian dances; and displays by the Virginia State Commission of Game and Fisheries and State Park Service.

In addition to such publicly sponsored programs, many voluntary organizations, such as the Boy Scouts, Girl Scouts, and 4-H clubs, as well as such conservationist groups as the Sierra Club carry out special programs in environmental education and outdoor recreation.

In some cases, even private or commercially operated recreation programs may provide environmental programs or other unique outdoor recreation opportunities. For example, Kiawah Island is a spectacular seaside resort community nestled within 10,000 acres of primitive, semitropical wilderness south of historic Charleston, South Carolina. Among the numerous activities planned by the Island's recreation staff for children, youth, and family groups are jeep safaris along the Island's beaches and in its palmetto forests; marsh creek canoeing; nature walks; a physical fitness trail; beachcombing; sailing; fishing; crabbing and numerous other pursuits utilizing the Island's unique natural setting.

IMPLICATIONS FOR LEADERSHIP

This presentation of outdoor recreation program trends and activities has several implications for those who are preparing for leisure-service careers. First, it is obvious that *all* leaders should be fully aware of the potential appeal that varied outdoor recreation activities may have for their participants. Many public, voluntary, therapeutic, and other recreation organizations sponsor camping trips and outings, nature-study or other environmental projects, ski trips, and other enjoyable outdoor recreation programs.

At the same time, outdoor recreation itself offers the possibility of a specialized career for young professionals. Those with a special interest in environmental studies may find positions as naturalists, outdoor educators, directors of nature centers, and similar roles. Others who have a high degree of competence in specific areas of outdoor recreation, such as boating, marksmanship, skiing, scuba diving, or horsemanship may build careers in these activity areas.

In some cases, leaders who have difficulty in finding full-time employment as environmental recreation specialists may be able to build a cluster of part-time assignments throughout the year, working for schools, camps, recreation and park departments, and other organizations. It is certainly possible to support oneself comfortably through a combination of such positions; in time, one of them is likely to expand into a single full-time career role.

As in any field of specialized preparation, however, outdoor recreation demands a high degree of both theoretical and practical knowledge. Those who plan to work in this field should take as many courses in related science areas as possible, should gain varied experience in outdoor recreation activities and leadership methods, and should qualify for certification as instructors with the leading organizations in the field.

NOTES

[1]*Statistical Abstract of the United States, 1984* (Washington, D.C.: U.S. Dept. of Commerce, Bureau of the Census, 1984), p. 233.

[2]Gregory A. Malone and Bill Mashek, ''Planning Therapeutic Outdoor Programs,'' *Parks and Recreation* (September 1983): 48.

[3]Stewart Allen and Joel F. Meier, ''Let's Take a Risk with Adventure Recreation,'' *Parks and Recreation* (February 1982): 50.

STUDENT PROJECTS

1. Develop a plan for a college outing club, including various outdoor skills classes or clinics, trips, and other special programs. If there already is such an organization in your college, review its program and recommend possible new activities.
2. Select a single outdoor recreation or nature-oriented activity, such as backpacking, fishing, or sailing. Develop a manual for leading an instructional program in this activity, including skills development, safety and accident-prevention, and other leadership functions, making use of materials found in the literature or published by national organizations involved in outdoor activities.
3. Have students conduct workshop sessions in specific outdoor recreation activities in class or in nearby outdoor sites, including the use of such equipment as tents or cooking gear.
4. Plan and carry out a class camping trip on an overnight or weekend basis, or an outdoor education field-study trip.

SUGGESTED READINGS

Phyllis M. Ford, *Principles and Practices of Outdoor Environmental Education* (New York: John Wiley, 1981).

Catherine T. Hammett, *The Campercraft Book* (Bradford Woods, Ind.: American Camping Association, 1981).

Richard G. Kraus and Margery M. Scanlin, *Introduction to Camp Counseling* (Englewood Cliffs, N.J.: Prentice-Hall, 1983).

Michael Link, *Outdoor Education: A Manual for Teaching in Nature's Classroom* (Englewood Cliffs, N.J.: Prentice-Hall, 1981).

George S. Wells, *Guide to Family Camping* (Harrisburg, Pa.: Stackpole, 1973).

CHAPTER 8

Recreational
Arts and Crafts

One of the most useful and enjoyable forms of recreation is arts and crafts. The customary separation of such activities into two categories—"arts" and "crafts"—is somewhat arbitrary. All true art processes must have a degree of craft or skilled technique, and good craft products obviously have elements of art in their design.

MAJOR CATEGORIES OF ACTIVITIES

Instead, it is possible to identify four major categories of activities which fit under the general heading of arts and crafts.

1. The first consists of those graphic and plastic forms which are commonly referred to as art, including painting (oil, watercolor, or tempera), drawing, printmaking (wood block, etching, or lithography), and sculpture. These are generally nonutilitarian except for serving as decoration. They stress personal expression, and are sometimes referred to as "visual arts."
2. The second category includes those activities which stress mastery of a given craft or technical skill, and which produce objects that are customarily seen as having functional value: carving, leather work, woodworking, ceramics, weaving, jewelry making, and similar crafts. Again, in the hands of an imaginative and gifted performer, these "crafts" have high aesthetic value.
3. The third category includes a wide variety of projects such as paper

crafts, wire or soap sculpture, simple puppetry, model making, and nature crafts, which do not require considerable talent or technical skill but which nonetheless provide the opportunity for individual creative expression. Such activities are used very widely in arts and crafts programs for children, the aging, and the disabled.

4. Last are those forms of activity which have no pretension to being original or creative in the true sense, either as art or craft. These employ a mechanical approach to drawing or painting, including "painting by the numbers" (filling in designated areas with numbered colors), assembling mosaic pictures in the same fashion, using molds to make ceramics, or carrying out any of hundreds of mechanical manipulative processes using "kits" or prestructured materials.

All of these activities provide certain forms of enjoyment and personal satisfaction as part of recreational participation. Obviously, however, the greatest values come from those activities in which the performer is most fully involved in a creative way, rather than simply carrying out a mechanical or predesigned procedure.

THE CREATIVE APPROACH TO RECREATIONAL ARTS AND CRAFTS

What are the significant values of artistic involvement by individuals of any age or background? They fall into two categories: (a) personal values for the participant; and (b) administrative values, in terms of the special contributions of such creative activity within leisure programs.

Personal Values. Arts and crafts activities fill the important need of all human beings to explore their own resources, to manipulate the environment, and to create something that is beautiful, personally expressive, decorative, or useful. While every individual certainly does not have the capacity to become an *artist* in the sense of becoming a highly professional and technically skilled creator of outstanding art products, he or she can certainly make valid personal expressions and can uncover heretofore untapped talents and abilities.

Administrative Values. There are several significant advantages to arts and crafts activities for the administrator of organized recreation programs. They appeal to many persons who are not interested in sports and games, outdoor recreation, or similar physically or competitively oriented programs. They may be carried on indoors or out, at all seasons of the year, and by persons of any age or physical condition. In addition, they may be carried out in all sorts of groupings, with people working on common projects or by individuals working completely on their own. Thus they are extremely flexible elements in program organization.

In another more practical sense, arts and crafts groups may provide a unique means of raising money or contributing to the success of other programs by sponsoring arts and crafts sales or by designing publicity posters, theater sets, or other needed program elements. Hanners, for example, describes the fund-raising efforts of a high-school art club which has designed and built floats for local parades:

> . . . float building can be a motivational tool. The basic idea that art is useful is emphasized in planning and construction. The students utilize every design element and principle. Different areas of art are used, from sculpture to painting. And it is a fantastic way to introduce a galaxy of media. . . . Our club is able to build a creative and impressive work of art and subsidize its treasury while doing the project.[1]

In numerous other ways, arts and crafts may be employed to support other recreation programs and projects. However, such purposes should not be the *primary* thrust of the activity. Instead, the creative growth and enrichment of the participants should be stressed throughout.

Leadership Methods in Arts and Crafts

The creative approach to arts and crafts leadership involves far more than just letting participants do what they please. Instead, it requires careful guidance and direction, which introduces skills, concepts, and the opportunity for creative expression, while at the same time not dominating the learner, or forcing his or her development into a single mold. For example, in presenting art experiences to partici-pants, the leader does the following:

1. He or she introduces the medium to the participants, initially selecting it on the basis of what is known to be appropriate for their age level or stage of artistic development. Thus, in working with younger children, fingerpainting or tempera might be used, while teenagers or adults might begin with oil or watercolor painting.
2. The leader gives initial instruction in the use of the medium—how paper or canvas surfaces should be prepared, how pigments are to be applied, how brushes may be used. This does not imply a rigid, set method which must be followed, but rather a helpful introduction to the technique. In the case of crafts activities, obviously a more detailed presentation of the technical process is needed before participants can become involved creatively.
3. The leader may help participants get under way in their exploration of the medium by structuring projects. Thus, he or she may help them decide on subjects they wish to draw or paint. They should be free to work on their own problems, although sometimes it is helpful for all of the members of a drawing class or group to work on the same problem. The leader may also introduce certain ideas of design, composition, use of line, masses of color, textures, or rhythms, which members of the group may explore in their drawings or paintings.
4. Without imposing his or her own critical judgment (and thus giving participants the idea that they must satisfy *his* or *her* standards), the

leader helps the members of the group know *how* to look at or think about a drawing or painting. In other words, they begin to develop their own critical judgment, both in examining their own work and that of other members of the group.

5. The leader may introduce certain concepts of drawing—the structure and proportions of the human body, the physical forces underlying movement, the use of geometric forms in blocking out figures, or even the rudiments of perspective drawing. The purpose of this is not to turn out individuals who can draw accurately in a photographic sense, but rather to help them understand the basis of valid draughtsmanship that underlies even highly abstract work.

6. The leader should stress the growing ability of the participant to judge what is genuine, creative, and expressive in his or her own work, as well as what is superficial or artificial. Thus, participants begin to understand the value of art as a form of personal expression and to look in a sophisticated way at other drawings, paintings, and art forms.

7. Finally, the leader promotes a general interest in the arts. Paintings and drawings are exhibited, children and adults are encouraged to bring in reproductions for display, and trips to museums, exhibitions, and other art events are arranged.

RECREATION PROGRAMS IN THE ARTS

What should the role of an organized recreation program be, with respect to the graphic and plastic arts, and to craft activity? Five functions may be defined:

1. These activities should comprise an important part of the recreation program for children throughout the year on playgrounds and in indoor centers. This suggests that all recreation participants should have a minimal exposure to satisfying activities in arts and crafts, whether or not they have a special interest in the field.

2. They should also be presented to adults, in the form of special recreation or adult education classes which are scheduled (usually on a weekly basis) along with many other recreational choices.

3. In recreation programs that are designed to meet the needs of certain special groups (the physically handicapped, the mentally ill, or the aged), in institutions or in the community at large, arts and crafts are extremely useful. They are highly adaptable for those with physical functioning, and provide emotional outlets for persons who need them or cannot express themselves effectively in other ways.

4. On a somewhat more advanced level, a recreation agency or department may develop an intensive program in the arts which stresses variety and depth—serving children and adults with *many* types of arts and crafts experiences in a special setting. Teachers who are themselves outstand-

ing artists may be employed, and students with special talents are given the opportunity to develop a high level of proficiency.

5. Finally, the recreation department within a community may assist and promote the work of other organizations (schools, clubs, civic art associations) by arranging or coordinating shows, art festivals, workshops, and exhibits—thus acting as a strong force for community culture.

Arts and Crafts for Children

The projects listed below are useful examples of arts and crafts activities for children in playground settings:

1. Take a group on a ''sketching'' tour around the park or the neighborhood. Tell the children to draw what they see. They can make sketches of the activities in the park, the scenery, the nearby houses, cars, other children, or whatever else that can be seen. Some of these sketches can be used in larger paintings.
2. Use ''Suggestion Cards.'' For example: A Rainy Day; A Trip to the Store; The Circus; My Pets; A Trip to the Moon; Sea Creatures; A Dream; What Scared Me Most; Cowboys; On the Farm; Fighting Animals; Strange Birds; My Favorite Sport.
3. Have different children pose for the group. Drawing from a model is the best way for children to learn to draw people. Change the pose about every ten minutes in order that the children may learn to draw people in many different positions. These sketches can be done in a few quick lines with a soft pencil or crayon.
4. Suggest that each one in the class draw a picture about the thing he or she likes to do best. Have a discussion before beginning.
5. Read an imaginative story to the class. Let the children illustrate the story in the way they visualize it, or draw the part of the story that was most interesting to them. Songs and poems can be illustrated in the same way.
6. Have an art exhibit on your playground. Children feel proud and encouraged to see their paintings displayed: an exhibit will help to arouse interest in art for others.
7. Have the children make ''scribble drawings,'' and from these obtain ideas for shapes and forms to be developed further as drawings or paintings.[2]

Leadership Guidelines for Organizing Activities

Other public or voluntary leisure-service agencies publish useful arts and crafts manuals. One such manual suggests the following programming methods:

1. Schedule arts and crafts at least twice weekly, in playground or community center programs.
2. Know definitely the projects you intend to offer, planning activities well in advance. Post a display model of a finished craft one week in advance, to encourage interest.
3. Be sure you have all supplies and materials necessary to make the project, and that these are set out and ready to go.
4. Explain each step clearly and concisely as you progress. Let children use their creative ability, but keep group closely supervised, giving suggestions and help as needed.
5. Encourage children to be orderly, and to have respect for the proper use of tools.
6. Allow enough time; rushing produces careless work, mistakes, spilling of materials, and even injuries.
7. Encourage children to finish every project they start. If a child cannot finish an article in the regular crafts session, set aside a special time for this.
8. Allow enough time for cleanup and storing supplies and unfinished projects properly, and expect all children to take part in cleaning up.
9. Encourage and praise children as much as possible, without being insincere.
10. Display finished projects. Children are proud of a job well done, and you should be too.[3]

Examples of Crafts Projects

There are hundreds of crafts projects, including not only the familiar activities of weaving, ceramics, modeling and sculpture, leatherworking, and jewelry making, but also a great variety of simple projects using paper, plastic, cardboard, scraps of materials, bottles, tiles, clothes hangers, beads, shells, boxes, cartons, styrofoam, fabric, and a host of other ''scrap'' materials. While it is not possible to illustrate *all* of these different types of projects, ten different examples of useful activities are given in this chapter. These are projects which can be undertaken with a minimum of special materials or skills, and yet which result in creative discovery, interest, and decorative and useful products.

Project 1
Clay Pot (Coil Method)

Here is a simple method that most pottery teachers use to teach beginners how to make a pot. It is used with regular clay that will dry and can be fired, rather than the plasticine that comes in clay modeling kits for children.

On a flat surface covered with linoleum or oilcloth (so the clay won't stick), use a rolling pin to make a slab of even thickness. From this slab cut a base for your pot. Next, place some clay on the table and roll it back and forth with the palms of your hands to make a coil (Figure 8–1a). Try to keep the diameter of the coil even all along its length.

Now make a slight impression around the rim of the base and cover this generously with slip (a thick glue of clay mixed with water).

Set the coil in place, cut ends to fit, and seal with more slip. Press coil firmly onto the base and smooth out the sides with your fingers or a modeling tool. Continue adding coils in this way, building straight up (Figure 8–1b and Figure 8–1c), or flaring the walls in or out.

When pot is built, sides may be smoothed for finished effect. Coils can also be pressed onto a slab to make a decorative trivet (Figure 8–1d). Firing in an electric or gas kiln will harden the clay so the pot or trivet can be used.

FIGURE 8–1

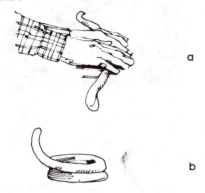

a

b

c

d

Project 2
Soap Sculpture

Most people are familiar with the kind of soap sculpture in which you carve an animal or other object out of a cake of soap, using a sharp knife or other cutting instrument. Here's a somewhat different project.

Decide what kind of animal or other creature you want to make. Now imagine that a bar of Ivory soap is the animal's body. What kind of shapes do you need to add—wings, a tail,

feet? Draw these shapes on an empty Clorox or other sturdy plastic bottle. Add pointed wedge shapes, to push into the soap.

Now cut the shapes out with sharp scissors (Figure 8–2a). Press them firmly into the soap (if it is fresh, it will be soft enough to do this) and there's your soap sculpture! It will float in the bathtub (Figure 8–2b).

FIGURE 8–2

a

b

Project 3
Tie-Dyeing

An unusual way to make colorful and interesting designs! You will need the following materials:

powdered dye, of at least three or four different colors

1 cup salt
water
cloth (preferably white cotton fabric which has been washed; *not* permanent press or synthetic fabrics)

FIGURE 8–3a

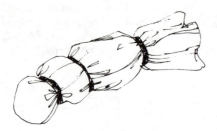

FIGURE 8–3b

other equipment: string or rubber bands, scissors, old pans or dishes to mix dye in, and stove or hot plate

Mix the dye (following directions on package) and keep hot, but not boiling, on stove or hot plate. Test dye in advance on a strip of cloth to see if colors are as bright as you would like.

To dye fabric with a "sunburst" effect, dampen a piece of cloth, hold it by the center, and bring corners together evenly. Then tie strings or rubber bands around the cloth, as in Figure 8–3a.

Dip the cloth in the lightest color of dye for a minute or two. Take it out of the dye, and rinse in cold water.

Then take off one or two strings or rubber bands where you want the next color to be, keeping strings wherever you want the cloth to keep the first color. Dip again, in slightly darker dye, and rinse with cold water. Always make sure strings are very tight.

Continue this, each time using a darker dye. Rinse fabric with cold water until dye is fixed, and water runs clear. Then undo the strings, open up the cloth—and you should have a *sunburst* (Figure 8–3b).

You may do this with white T-shirts, but remember, only wash tie-dyed fabrics in cold water!

Project 4
Paper Beads

Magazines, newspapers, construction paper—almost *any* kind of paper is suitable for this project.

Cut several long isosceles triangles. Take the wide end of a triangle, and wrap it around a nail (Figure 8–4). Continue winding it up tightly, and attach the end with a dab of glue. Slide it off the nail to dry.

These long beads can be shellacked or painted with acrylics, or may have their own interesting colors if they are cut from full-color magazine pictures. They are extremely durable and can be strung to make necklaces, room dividers, or whatever you fancy.

FIGURE 8–4

Project 5
Finger Painting

One of the most familiar and enjoyable art activities—particularly for younger children. You can buy ready-made finger paint supplies, or make your own, using this formula:

1 cup corn starch
½ cup soap flakes
1 quart boiling water

Mix these ingredients together. Then separate into several batches, and mix each batch with a different color of powdered paint from an art supply store.

For best results, paint on slippery shelf paper. Try using hands different ways—fingertips, palm or heel of hand, or knuckles with different pressures and rhythms (Figure 8–5a).

Try making finger paint prints! Lay a sheet of paper over your wet painting, rub gently, then lift off carefully (Figure 8–5b).

FIGURE 8–5a

FIGURE 8–5b

Project 6
Feather Jewelry

Cut a thin piece of leather into a rectangle, diamond shape, or circle that is slightly smaller than you want the finished piece to be. Attach the ribbon or ribbons or a neck chain to the back with glue, or cut two slits and run the ribbon or chain through the leather.

Beginning at the outer edges of the leather, glue down feathers one at a time, using small dabs of glue. Working symmetrically gives the most pleasing results. Use your most striking feathers in strategic places. Keep working toward the center, shaping feathers to desired sizes with small scissors.

When you reach the center, glue down the feathers very carefully so that all the ends meet, and the center ribs of the feathers radiate out like the spokes of a wheel (Figure 8–6).

You can make necklaces, bracelets, or pins using this method. A simple macramé cord can be substituted for the ribbon or neck chain.

FIGURE 8–6

Project 7
Candle Making

Another craft that has become extremely popular with those of all ages in recent years.

Melt paraffin mixed with beeswax (if you have it) in a double boiler or in tin cans set in a pan of boiling water (paraffin is flammable and should never be directly heated). Add coloring made from shaved crayons or standard candle coloring.

Prepare the mold by making a hole in the bottom and stringing a wick through it. Many things make good candle molds: cut-off milk cartons, flat-sided (no ridges) tin cans, or aluminum foil. You must use real candle wicking, which is specially treated string. Seal with a small screw. Place a stick across the top of the mold and center the wick. Tie wick securely to stick (Figure 8–7a).

Now you're ready to pour in the wax. Make sure it's very hot. Wax takes several hours to harden, so if you're adding it in layers, be patient. Also the wax will shrink, so the top of candle will be concave. Just add more hot wax to flatten it. When hard, unmold. If you're using a tin can, just remove the bottom and slide out.

Some things to try:

Add wax in stages; each time a new color is added, tip mold in a different direction to harden.

Use a kitchen knife to carve decorations on finished candles.

FIGURE 8–7a

FIGURE 8–7b

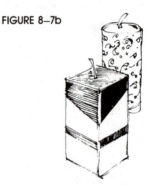

Put ice into mold just before adding wax. Result: a lacy candle. For different effects, see Figure 8–7b.

If you live near the seashore, you can make wax from bayberries. Gather a large number and boil them in a pot of water. A light green wax will rise to the surface.

Let cool; then skim off wax to use by itself or in combination with paraffin.

Project 8
Flower Pressing

Another enjoyable nature craft project. For a simple flower or leaf press to take along on hikes, use two equal-sized rectangles of stiff cardboard. Make slits in them and thread ribbon through as shown in figure 8–8a.

To use the press, place flowers on blotter paper and cover with several sheets of newspaper. Continue making layers of flowers and newspaper. Always place flowers of equal thickness together. Put layers into press, draw the ribbons tight, and tie. When you get home,

FIGURE 8–8a

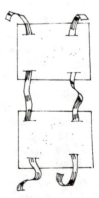

FIGURE 8–8b

place the press under some heavy books or similar even weight. The flowers should be dry in a few days, and can then be mounted on cardboard, using small drops of glue. For an example of a pressed flower collage, see Figure 8–8b.

You can paint faded flowers with watercolor mixed with detergent to make it adhere.

Project 9
Nature Mobile

Use whatever nature objects are available in your area: pine cones, seed pods, shells, mica. The first step is to make a frame from which to hang the objects. Bent coat hangers, dowels, driftwood, or sturdy sticks will work well. The frame can be of just one piece with a piece of string or fishline tied to the center, or can be several pieces crossed to make a star shape.

Next, make small holes in all your objects (using a heated needle helps with shells) and string them, knotting them securely so they won't slip. Attach them to the frame, designing as you go so that the whole balances. You can work symmetrically or not, as you choose. Leave enough space between objects so that each will really show. You can make a simple mobile, and then keep adding to it as you find more good objects (see Figure 8–9). Hang it someplace where the wind will make it move.

FIGURE 8–9

Project 10
Tote Bag

Select two durable fabrics (½ yard of each), one for the outside of the bag and one for the lining. Cut one rectangle from each piece of fabric, fourteen inches by thirty inches.

FIGURE 8–10

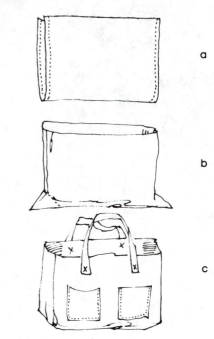

Place the pieces right side together, and sew around three sides. Turn right side out and press. Turn under the fourth side and stitch it shut, using thread that matches outside fabric. Now is the time to add pockets, embroidery, or any decoration you choose. Next, fold in half, lining fabric on the outside. Stitch up the two sides (Figure 8–10a). Sew across the lower two corners (Figure 8–10b) to give the bag fullness. Turn right side out.

To make handles, cut two strips four inches wide and fourteen inches long. Fold in half lengthwise, wrong side out, and stitch up the long side. Turn right side out, using a safety pin to pull the fabric through itself. Press. Tuck the ends in and stitch them shut. Pin the handles in place and sew them on, using the X design for strength (Figure 8–10c).

This process makes a bag with no raw edges. You can omit the lining and have seams show on the inside.

Arts and Crafts for Adults

Many of the projects just described can be used with adults as well as with children. However, a typical pattern is for adult arts and crafts programs to consist of courses or workshops in a single creative activity which is approached in depth—rather than a series of simple craft projects. Often these may be carried on during the school year, in a series of sessions that are ten or fifteen weeks each. For example, many public recreation agencies, school-sponsored adult education programs, or voluntary organizations like the YWCA offer courses in such activities as the following:

Woodworking and Cabinet Making
Oil Painting
Sculpture
Portrait Painting
Life Painting and Sketching
Elementary and Advanced
    Ceramics
Painting and Sketching
Dressmaking
Sewing

Millinery
Tailoring
Watercolor Painting
Drawing and Painting for Beginners
Color Photography
Enameling on Copper
Arts and Crafts for Counselors and
    Leaders

Usually such classes are offered with a minimal fee charged each participant, and with the understanding that if there is insufficient enrollment (between ten and fifteen students are usually required to justify giving a course), the class will be canceled.

Programs for Special Groups

Arts and crafts are extremely useful in meeting the needs of special groups. They are one of the most popular activities with older citizens, although aging persons may be hesitant about beginning creative activities of this type if they have never engaged in them before. Their fear of possible failure or ridicule needs to be reduced by the warmth and encouragement of the instructor. If their first projects are extremely simple, they will be encouraged and ready to try more difficult tasks.

Art as Therapy.   Although art may be used with many special populations, a distinction should be made between its use as a general recreational activity adapted for the disabled, and its use as a specific form of therapy.

In the former case, it may simply represent a valuable channel for personal expression and a means of creative involvement when few other recreative opportunities are possible. For example, Rosner points out that, to overcome the sense of loss and uselessness that many medical patients experience, it is helpful for them to be able to produce personally meaningful art works. Sometimes, she writes, even very limited forms of art expression can give the disabled artist a strong sense of personal accomplishment:

> Where physical disability is extreme, making art may still be possible but sometimes the art must be made in unusual ways. Adaptive measures may include taping implements into the hand, placing them in the mouth, taping paper down to offset poor motor control, moving the paper around—in general, maneuvering the materials and even oneself into various positions to ensure that the patient can reach the paper and apply sufficient pressure.[4]

When approached as therapy, particularly with emotionally ill patients, art may be used as a helpful technique in diagnosis, assisting communication, and fostering the development of a therapeutic relationship. For example, Greenspoon describes the use of art with a severely disturbed adolescent:

> This adolescent's sense of self was so poorly developed that self-expression was difficult if not impossible. Gradually she began to permit herself to become aware of her affective life as she found a means of self-understanding and communication through her art work. Her expressive capacity developed, permitting in turn the establishment of a relationship with me, her art therapist. In time, her sense of isolation decreased, and her ability to reflect and gain insight improved.[5]

Frequently, art expression—particularly graphic art—may be extremely helpful to the patient in expressing his or her self-image; a commonly used technique is to have individuals paint or draw themselves, sometimes within their family constellation. The rationale for the therapeutic use of graphic arts includes six advantages of art therapy over the free association verbal approach often used in psychotherapy. These may be briefly summarized in the following manner:

1. It is more difficult for the patient to be evasive graphically than verbally. His or her attitudes toward the object depicted are revealed, intentionally or not, in the manner of drawing, application of color, style, and focus on detail.

2. Personality traits are more readily and more clearly displayed in creative work than in unchallenging, routine work.

3. Anxiety is much less likely to be aroused during painting than during conversation, because the patient may not be aware of the symbols he or she uses to the same extent of being conscious of them in his or her speech.

4. The need for consistency, objectivity, and rationality is much less obvious in free art work than in speech, because nonverbal symbols, being less frequently employed for social communication, are less standardized.

5. There is greater freedom for the free flow of the patient's imagination in painting than in conversation. During the creative process, the patient works uninterruptedly, without any interference from the therapist.

6. In painting, the patient is involved neuromuscularly and physiologically more than in talking. For literate and highly educated adults, this fact indicates that eye-hand-motor coordination seen in graphic imagery might be nearer the unconscious than is the producing of words.[6]

Art Centers

A number of municipal and county recreation departments have taken the lead in establishing special buildings where intensive programs of arts and crafts are provided. An excellent example is the Adult Arts and Crafts Center established in 1952 by the St. Petersburg, Florida, Recreation Department. Serving many hundreds of men and women, including large numbers of retired residents of the city, this center has been housed in recent years in the Maritime Base, formerly a Marine training station in Tampa Bay. The scenic surroundings (boats, docks, and colorful waterfront activities) provide interesting subjects for painting, oils, watercolor, and pastel classes. Other activities include sculpture and such crafts classes as loom weaving, woodworking, basketry, ceramics and pottery, metal art, enamel on copper, leather work, puppets and marionettes, and doll making.

It is important to recognize that, in some communities, arts and crafts may not be presented as a separate area of activity, but may be linked to the performing arts within a total program of cultural and creative involvement. For example, in Rocky Mount, North Carolina, there is a unique arts and crafts center. This began in 1957 as a community arts center, supported heavily by small, voluntary contributions from interested citizens. A large house was rented, and classes were offered in drawing, painting, ballet, music, and art appreciation, taught by qualified instructors from neighboring colleges. Activities also included lectures, exhibits, sidewalk art shows, concerts, ballets, and theater performances.

PROMOTION OF COMMUNITY-WIDE ARTS ACTIVITIES

An important function of many public recreation departments is to assist and promote the work of other organizations in the cultural field, through community-wide efforts. To illustrate, the Ottawa, Canada, Department of Recreation and Parks has sponsored a successful annual summer arts festival over the past three decades. With the assistance of numerous community arts organizations, it has presented as many as forty different music, art, drama, and film events in a single summer.

The emphasis in Ottawa has been on presenting the work of local or regional artists, and on gradually raising the artistic standards and tastes of the community at large. Gradually, through these festivals, the Department of Recreation and Parks has developed strong relationships with many cultural groups in the community and surrounding area, and has succeeded in bringing the artist and his public closer to a common level of understanding and appreciation.

Other Community Programs

Sometimes a community's interest in the arts will take a unique and special-ized form, related to social trends and needs. For example, the Cultural Affairs Division of the Los Angeles City Department of Parks and Recreation, and the Street Mural Project of the Los Angeles County Department of Parks and Recreation have been responsible for a number of major murals throughout the city. The renewed interest in public painting began in the early 1970s, with street murals painted by young participants in the south-central community of Watts, in East Los Angeles, and in Venice. Its purpose was to contribute to the city landscape, to encourage neighbor-hood pride, and to stimulate both individual and group creativity.

Particularly in the Chicano neighborhoods of East Los Angeles, intense mural production got under way, much of it based on ethnic themes. Young Mexican-American artists dealt with the Chicano heritage and culture, with scenes from history and current social struggles. Thus art, when sponsored by public recreation and park departments, can become a vital community process and contribute to the image and spirit of the city.

IMPLICATIONS FOR LEADERSHIP

This chapter has demonstrated a number of ways in which recreation agencies may serve the needs of children, youth, and adults, as well as special groups, in the area of arts and crafts. Various examples of programming are described, and a number of activities and leadership guides are briefly cited. More detailed descriptions of arts and crafts projects and instructional techniques may be found in the handbooks and texts listed in the bibliography.

It should be emphasized that the arts appeal to all ages, both sexes, and to a range of cultural interests that help to make the leisure-service program a truly diversified and well-balanced offering.

Leaders should therefore be alert to the possibilities for including varied forms of arts and crafts within their programs, both as independent forms of activity and in cooperation with other program elements. Although they may feel that they do not have sufficient "talent" in drawing or painting—and that they therefore cannot lead arts and crafts activities themselves—many crafts projects do not require any special artistic ability. Instead, simply by learning some basic techniques or projects any leader should find it possible to gain the basic skill needed to present such activities successfully.

Beyond this, if it is not possible to obtain part-time paid specialists in arts and crafts activities who can instruct classes on a more advanced level, the ingenious leader may be able to find gifted volunteers who will be willing to provide instruction because of their enthusiasm about the activity. Without question, given the proper administrative support, arts and crafts can become one of the most attractive and rewarding program elements in any recreational setting.

NOTES

[1]Kathleen Hanners, "Learning and Earning," *Arts and Activities* (November 1983).

[2]*Summer Staff Manual* (Louisville, Kentucky, Parks and Recreation Department, n.d.)

[3]*Arts and Crafts Manual* (Ft. Lauderdale, Florida, Recreation Department, n.d.)

[4]Irene Rosner, "Art Therapy and Two Quadriplegic Patients," *American Journal of Art Therapy* (July 1983): 115.

[5]Debra B. Greenspoon, "The Development of Self-Expression in a Severely Disturbed Adolescent," *American Journal of Art Therapy* (October 1982): 17.

[6]See Elizabeth Rosen, *Dance in Psychotherapy* (New York: Teachers College, Columbia University, 1957), p. 33.

STUDENT PROJECTS

1. Develop a plan for arts and crafts programming in a community center operated by a public or voluntary agency, including activities of several different types, geared for different age levels.
2. Plan and carry out an arts and crafts workshop in class, with several students who are experienced in this area demonstrating skills in such activities as papercraft, simple puppetry, leatherworking, or ceramics. Class members take part in the activity and then evaluate the leadership techniques shown by the workshop team.
3. Have a team of students examine the various uses of arts and crafts with special populations, both as a form of recreational interest and art therpy. This should be done both through research in the literature and through field observations, where possible. They then form a panel and present their findings and guidelines to the class.

SUGGESTED READINGS——————————————————————————————

Kenneth R. Benson and Carl E. Frankson, *Arts and Crafts for Home, School and Community* (St. Louis: C. V. Mosby, 1975).

Louis B. Hellegers and Anne E. Kallen, *The Family Book of Crafts* (New York: Sterling, 1973).

Jay S. Shivers and Clarence R. Calder, *Recreational Crafts: Programming and Instructional Techniques* (New York: McGraw-Hill, 1974).

John Squires, *Fun Crafts for Children* (Englewood Cliffs, N.J.: Prentice-Hall, 1964).

CHAPTER 9

Music, Drama, and Dance in Recreation

One of the most exciting aspects of the present leisure scene in the United States and Canada has been the growth of cultural programming—particularly music, drama, and dance activities—in communities large and small. Orchestras, choral groups, bands, modern dance and ballet companies, dance classes, little theater groups, drama workshops, and a host of similar enterprises are to be found springing up like mushrooms.

As indicated in Chapter 8, many public recreation departments have been active in promoting the arts, often in cooperation with nonprofit cultural arts organizations. Sometimes this is done through a community arts council, as in Vancouver, British Columbia, where such a council, the first in North America, was instrumental in creating a major civic theater complex and promoting all forms of arts in the region.

Recently, the National Recreation and Park Association established a National Task Force on the Arts, with the following major objectives:

1. To develop avenues of communication and cooperation with national arts organizations and work to develop cooperative recreation and arts programming at the national level.
2. To develop an awareness of the potential for the arts in park and recreation settings at the state and local levels.
3. To promote regular arts programming within city, county, state, and federal park and recreation agencies, in part by developing a national position paper on the arts in recreation for the 1980s.
4. To explore the funding and legislative impact of arts programs on park and recreation agencies.
5. To plan arts institutes and other art programs as part of National Recreation and Park Congresses.[1]

TYPES OF ARTISTIC EXPERIENCE IN RECREATION

Although there is considerable overlapping among the arts, they are usually divided into two broad categories: *applied* and *performing* arts. Chapter 8 presented examples of applied recreation projects, in which the experience yields a tangible product, such as a painting or piece of sculpture. This chapter is concerned with music, drama, and dance, as forms of performing arts involvement.

Levels of Artistic Involvement

It should be understood that creative activities like music and dance may be carried on at different levels of creative worth or seriousness. For example, dance may be regarded as a serious art form, as in ballet or modern dance, or as a form of casual social fun, as in a teenage dance party. Similarly, music programs may include the serious performance of classical works, or may consist of informal community singing or rhythm band activities.

Kelly points out that in general, the so-called "fine arts" are being broadened by the addition of other forms of creative expression that are being accepted as having serious artistic worth. He writes:

> Since folk melodies have been incorporated in music by the greatest composers for centuries, it is not that radical to accept some folk music—both recently composed and historically authentic—as significant in the whole spectrum of music. And even the classic ballet companies have incorporated many folk and jazz elements into their repertoire. The trend in the arts is toward inclusion rather than toward narrowing.[2]

For this reason, recreation leaders would be making a mistake to accept too seriously a distinction between "highbrow" and "lowbrow" forms of artistic experience, or to assign a higher status to the former. All forms of artistic and expressive activity add to the cultural richness of a community, and all should be encouraged.

Recreational Values of Music, Drama, and Dance

Like arts and crafts and other creative activities, music, drama, and dance have important personal and administrative values as part of organized recreation programs.

Personal Values. Through participation in the performing arts, participants discover their own creative talents and give voice to ideas, shapes, sounds, or movements that are theirs alone.

Instead of simply being entertained by the efforts of others, participants in creative forms of recreation make their own fun. They are "doers," and not just passive recipients of the creative work of others.

An important value of recreational experience in the arts is that it helps to enrich the level of cultural taste in the community at large. While some may scoff at the quality or significance of "amateur" performance or imply that it has little aesthetic worth, the fact is that, through mass participation in the arts, we are building a huge audience for professional performance. This is not a matter of numbers alone; the Sunday painter is likely to be a more intelligent, sensitive, and discriminating audience than the individual who has never held a brush in his or her hand.

Administrative Values. In addition to these personal values, the performing arts have certain special benefits as elements in community or agency recreation programs:

1. They appeal to many individuals who, by temperament and personality, may be not at all interested in programs of sports or games. Unlike the latter forms of activity, they stress cooperation rather than competition, the intellectual rather than the physical, and thus diversify the attraction of the recreation program for different groups.
2. They extend and continue school learning. Too often, individuals who have learned to play a musical instrument, to sing as part of a chorus, or to enjoy a certain form of craft activity, would have no encouragement or opportunity to continue this hobby if it were not for an organized recreation program.
3. The arts may be enjoyed on many levels of skill and are equally appropriate for little children and older persons. They can be carried on indoors and in all seasons. In regions where the climate limits outdoor play during a good part of the year, the arts are particularly useful.
4. The arts have a unique capacity for enhancing desirable social relationships. In them, the friendly camaraderie of the barbershop quartet or Little Theater group, the intense cooperation and discipline required by the orchestra or performing dance group, invariably result in a level of friendly cooperation and responsible citizenship that does much to improve social interaction within a community or neighborhood.

INTERRELATIONSHIP OF THE ARTS

Although each of the performing arts is dealt with separately in this chapter, it should be pointed out that they all have strong ties with each other. Not only do they share certain common elements such as rhythm, balance, color, contrast, and design, but they are often closely related in actual performance.

Nonetheless, in order to provide focus to different kinds of creative programs within public or other recreational agencies, they are usually categorized under specific headings. Within this chapter, the three major types of performing arts that appear in community recreation programs—music, drama, and dance—are described and analyzed. Guidelines for presenting such activities in community recreation programs are offered, accompanied by examples of simple activities that may be used in leadership practice experiences in a classroom setting.

MUSIC IN COMMUNITY RECREATION

Music is one of the most appealing and adaptable forms of community recreation activity. It can suit any age, sex, taste, mood, or level of ability. It may be used with other activities such as dance or drama, and is frequently a major program element in civic pageants or celebrations, sports events, therapeutic programs, and recreational events of all kinds.

Studies have revealed that there are many thousands of orchestras, bands, and choruses in schools, colleges, and other educational settings throughout the United States and Canada. Similarly, music has become a major factor in voluntary, employee, and other community recreation programs, with activities ranging from ''kazoo bands to symphony orchestras—from musical games to opera.''

In general, community recreation departments promote musical participation in the following ways:

1. They offer instruction, primarily to children's groups, throughout the year but most intensively in the summertime. In this, they often relate their activities closely to those provided by the school system; frequently the school music specialist is given an opportunity to work more intensively with children through the recreation program.

2. They provide facilities, in the form of auditoriums, outdoor theaters or bandshells, rehearsal or practice rooms and storage areas. Some recreation departments with highly developed music programs may also provide equipment, such as instruments, music libraries, costumes, recordings, tape recorders, and similar needed materials.

3. They cooperate with other agencies in helping to organize and promote community-wide musical events, such as festivals, clinics, concert series, and children's programs.

4. In collaboration with musical organizations, or with the schools, recreation departments may help train leaders in this field by sponsoring institutes, workshops, courses, and similar sessions.

5. They may actually sponsor musical groups themselves, such as dance bands which play at events in local communities, pop bands, accordion bands, choral groups, symphony orchestras, and smaller units.

6. Many public recreation departments sponsor mobile units, which travel throughout the community, staging musical performances of all kinds, or providing music lessons or informal participation programs.

7. Some departments provide the opportunity for talented instrumentalists, singers, or groups to perform, either through ''talent showcases'' which

schedule their appearances throughout the community, or through competitions in classical, popular, or rock performance.

As an example of such program efforts, for a number of years, the Portland, Oregon, Department of Parks and Recreation has operated a highly successful Community Music Center. This program began when an amateur adult orchestra was founded in Portland. Shortly after, the Children's Conservatory was begun, offering a program of private lessons, theory, chamber music, and orchestra. This was made available to young people over a twelve-year span (ages six to eighteen) at minimum cost, and succeeded in providing numbers of excellent instrumentalists, who have joined the adult orchestra.

The Community Music Center developed, in time, two string orchestras, advanced and intermediate; these perform frequently at art festivals, museums, and other civic or cultural events. The conservatory also sponsors monthly recitals, at which children may perform their original works.

In many communities, recreation and park departments sponsor special summer music schools or workshops, usually in close collaboration with the schools. Often school facilities are used, and those in charge of instruction are the regular school music specialists, although other talented teachers may be used, since certification is not required in such settings. These summer schools have certain advantages in the intensive enrichment of the child's musical education: (a) there is no competition from academic subjects; therefore children have more time for practicing and make greater progress; (b) because the music program usually takes the entire morning, five days a week, there is sufficient time to give each child solo instruction two or three days a week, if not daily; (c) with large groups of youngsters participating, it is possible to group them according to ability; and (d) because each child is present due to his or her ability and interest, and on a voluntary basis, morale is high.

Music as a Playground Activity

Of course, not all recreational music is as ambitious as the programs just described. Instead, a good deal of programming in this area consists of presenting music as an informal playground or community center activity. In such settings, it typically involves singing, creative rhythmic movement, or playing rhythm instruments.

Singing for Young Children.
When songs are introduced in recreational programs for children, the emphasis is on a creative and enjoyable, rather than formal, approach. It is important to select songs that will be attractive to children, placed in a comfortable key, with easy-to-remember melodies and choruses. Folk songs are among the most suitable, particularly songs of other lands which give children a sense of experiencing foreign cultures and even singing in foreign languages. Rather than a line-by-line learning of words and melody, as songs have traditionally been taught, it is

wise to teach the song by singing it through several times. Gradually it will become familiar, and, when repeated, it will be performed with increasing confidence and success.

Children themselves may be encouraged to suggest or ask for songs they know or have heard. Sometimes it is a good idea to have a song-listening session by playing records of folk songs. All children should be encouraged to take part; even if a child cannot sing on pitch to begin with, he or she should not be left out. By the same token, no child should be forced to sing. Hopefully, (although the child may lack confidence to begin with), being part of the group and the gentle encouragement of the leader will lead the child to join in before too long.

With young children, song arrangements should be extremely simple, without part singing or the attempt to introduce harmony in singing. By the age of seven or eight, however, children should be ready to explore the following ways of singing.

Rounds. Here, children are divided into groups, usually three or four, according to the construction of the song. One group begins to sing. When it has reached the end of the first phrase or line, the second group starts the song from the beginning. Then the next group comes in in turn. Usually, the entire song is sung through three times, with each group stopping in turn the final time through.

Harmony. This is a form of part singing, in which one set of voices sing the set melody while another group of children sings a melody that blends harmonically with the first group. To do an expert job of song leadership using formal arrangements with harmony, the music leader should be able to read music and teach the different parts clearly. Sometimes, however, particularly if he or she has sung a good deal and has a good ''musical ear,'' the leader can teach harmonies without a formal music background.

Part Song. Other songs may be sung contrapuntally—different sets of words or melodies are sung against each other simultaneously by groups of children. Or there may be arrangements in which children sing only portions of the song, as in a ''question and answer'' type of folk song, in which one group may sing a verse asking a question, and another group may respond in alternate verses.

In singing, it is important to cultivate sensitivity to the sound of the words and music. Children should have a sense of being part of something lovely and creative, and should listen to the others as they sing, rather than just shouting or drowning each other out. For this reason, it is important to select songs with a wide variety of moods. In addition to songs which are spirited, happy, and lively, or forceful and strongly rhythmic, some songs should be sad, slow, and moving. Often it helps to use the ''crescendo-diminuendo'' approach, in which children begin by singing very softly, build up gradually to a strong volume, and gradually back to a low volume again, almost whispering by the end of the song.

Singing with Other Groups. In addition to singing with children, this activity can be extremely useful with teenagers, young and middle-aged adults, family groups, and senior citizens. Singing is often the ''magic'' catalyst that gets everyone swinging along in rhythm on a hiking trail, or that livens up a boring bus trip. It is a spirited "waker-upper" as a break in a club meeting or business meeting of a PTA or civic association. In social clubs, on picnics and outings, at church parties and barbecues, singing appeals to all!

How much leadership is actually required for singing in social recreation? This depends on the circumstances. If the group is a small, friendly one, with the members knowing each other well, it is likely that not too much actual leadership will be required. If one or two individuals happen to have guitars for informal accompaniment, the singing will flourish spontaneously—almost with a life of its own. On the other hand, if the group is large, if the intention is for them to learn a number of new songs, or if they are new to each other and have not sung together before, a song leader is necessary.

Guidelines for Song Leadership

Some guides for group singing might include:

1. Get the singing under way quickly, by introducing a familiar song or two. This creates confidence and a spirit of participation. Gradually, new or unfamiliar songs may be taught, although at the beginning and end of the session, the songs chosen should all be well known.
2. There should be variety in the songs that are chosen—including some fun songs, action songs, or other novelty numbers—but with the main emphasis on doing songs that are just plain good singing. This should also include variety in the mood, tempo, and musical quality of the songs.
3. The leader may, if he or she can, use the traditional hand gestures to show the meter (Figure 9–1). If not, the leader may simply move his

FIGURE 9–1

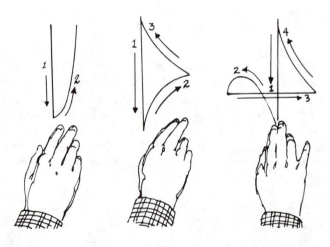

or her hand in a small arc to indicate the rhythm. With a large group, gestures should be rather large and dramatic, to be visible and unmistakable. In a small group, no gestures at all may be necessary, except to indicate the beginning tempo, or when a note is held or cut off.

4. Song leadership should be enthusiastic, although not artificially so. It is important to begin a song in the correct pitch and to keep the tempo at a comfortable level. An accompanist is helpful; with a large group, this should be someone playing an instrument like a piano or accordion. In a smaller group, a guitarist or banjoist is excellent.

Some other guides for effective song leadership are:

Announce the song you are about to present clearly.

If you are using an accompanist, make sure that he or she is placed close to you, and can see you as you lead the singing.

In presenting a new song, it is a good idea to tell the group something interesting about it or its background, and then to sing it through while they are listening.

Have the participants learn it one line at a time, becoming familiar with the words and melody, and then review the entire song. If necessary, use song sheets, slides with words on them, or similar devices.

When they are fairly sure of the song, have them do it. Make sure the accompanist gives a good introduction, and the singers know when to come in.

Attack and release each line or stanza of the song clearly. Be definite, not fuzzy, in your leadership.

If singing with children, pitch songs at an appropriate key—usually higher than for most adults. Encourage them to sing softly and with feeling, not simply to shout out the words.

Do not neglect any of the singers; encourage those who are not singing to join in.

In acknowledging requests, do not hesitate to choose those which *you* feel will be most suitable for the group.

If you use conducting motions, make large gestures, with your hands and arms well away from the body; keep the movements graceful, and capture the spirit of each song with them.

In ending a song session, choose a familiar song that everyone enjoys which will provide an effective, relaxed end to the singing.[3]

While it is helpful to have a good voice and a knowledge of music structure, it is just as important to have a warm personality and sound judgment about the songs to be presented. The author has observed some song leaders who had very little technical knowledge of music, and in fact had rather poor voices, but who nonetheless had the gift of getting groups to sing with deep feeling and great pleasure. They hardly used their own voices, but they drew out the best that was around them.

Examples of Songs
For Community Singing

The More We Get Together

A lively song of good fellowship, fitted to an old German folk tune.

English verse:

English Anonymous   German Folk Tune

The more we get to-geth-er, to-geth-er, to-geth-er,

The more we get to-geth-er, the hap-pier we'll be.

For your friends are my friends and my friends are your friends,

The more we get to-geth-er, the hap-pier we'll be.

German verse:

Ach, du lieber Augustin, Augustin,
  Augustin,
Ach, du lieber Augustin, Alles ist hin.
Stock ist weg, Hut ist weg, August selbst
  liegt im Dreck,
Ach, du lieber Augustin, Alles ist hin.

Actions to be performed while singing: During first two lines of song, do rhythmic action in 3/4 time. *Clap* own hands once, then *pat* knees twice. Beginning on the first "more," do this action seven times, ending with a *clap* on the "be" at the end of the second line. Then extend arms along neighbors' arms and sway in rhythm to the *left* and *right* two full times during the next line. On the last line, do *clap-pat-pat* action again, starting with the word "more," three times and end with a *clap* on the word "be."

Kookaburra

The kookaburra is an Australian bird, very much like a woodpecker, which has a raucous cry that sounds very much like laughter—thus this popular round.

The group divides into four sections, since there are four lines in the song. Each section in turn comes in after the first line has been sung. The entire song is done three times through, as in all rounds.

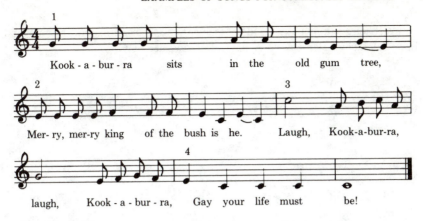

Kook - a - bur - ra   sits   in the   old gum   tree,

Mer- ry, mer-ry king   of the bush is he.   Laugh,   Kook-a-bur-ra,

laugh,   Kook - a - bur - ra,   Gay your life must   be!

Where is Thumbkin?

A simple action song with finger play for younger children.

Words	*Action*
Where is thumbkin? Where is thumbkin?	(hands are hidden behind singer's back)
Here I am.	(right fist makes appearance, thumb pointing up)
Here I am.	(left fist appears, in same way)
How are you today, sir? Very well, I thank you.	(right thumb ''nods'' four times) (left thumb does the same)
Run away. Run away.	(right hand disappears behind back) (left hand does the same)

Sweetly Sings the Donkey

This rousing three-part round may also be used as an action song, to enliven a drowsy group.

After the words have been learned, practice this action: place thumbs at the ears and flap hands forward in rhythm like a donkey's ears. Then do the song as a round, with each section in turn standing up and doing the hand-flapping routine on the last line: "Hee-haw! Hee-haw! Hee-haw, hee-haw, hee-haw!"

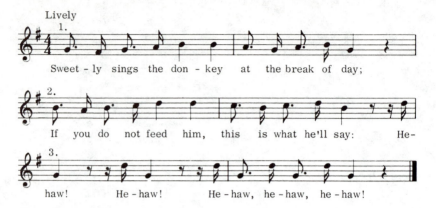

White Coral Bells

A traditional old song with a lovely melody is this two-part round.

Little Tom Tinker

A livelier action song—sure to create laughter in groups of any age. Incidentally, the word "clinker" means a red-hot coal.

As the song is sung three times, the following action is done: (a) the first time, everyone quickly raises his hands twice, on the words "Ma! Ma!"; (b) the second time, everyone rises and sits quickly while singing "Ma! Ma!"; (c) the third time, both actions are done simultaneously, during "Ma! Ma!" When the group is familiar with words and action, they may also do the song as a round in four parts.

Lit - tle Tom Tink - er got   burned by   a   clink - er   and

he   be - gan   to   cry.   Ma!

Ma!   What   a   poor   fel - low   am   I!

Old MacDonald

In this lively song about a well-populated barnyard, each time the verse is sung, the name and sound of a new animal or bird is added to what has gone before.

The next time it is sung through, add "ducks" and sing:

Oh, old Mac-Don-ald had a farm,   ee - i - ee - i   -   o.
And on this farm he had some chicks,   ee - i - ee - i   -   o.

With a   chick-chick here,   and   a   chick-chick there,

Here a chick, there a chick,   ev' - ry where a chick - chick,

Old Mac-Don-ald   had a   farm,   ee - i - ee - i   -   o.

And on this farm he had some ducks, ee-i-ee-i-o.
With a quack-quack here and a quack-quack there,
Here a quack, there a quack, everywhere a quack-quack,
With a chick-chick here, and a chick-chick there,
Here a chick, there a chick, everywhere a chick-chick,
Old MacDonald had a farm, ee-i-ee-i-o.

Other animals:
Cow—moo moo
Donkey—hee-haw
Pig—oink-oink
Cat—meow-meow
Turkey—gobble-gobble

Eentsy, Weentsy Spider

Another children's action song that may also be enjoyed by teenagers or adults.

The action fits the words like this:

Words	*Action*
The eentsy weentsy spider Went up the water spout.	Touch forefinger of one hand to thumb of other, then rotate back and forth, "climbing" up.
Down came the rain and washed the spider out.	Shake both hands rhythmically in front, up and down, to suggest "rain."
Out came the sun and Dried up all the rain.	Raise arms slowly in front, in large circle, to suggest "sun."
And the eentsy weentsy spider Went up the spout again.	Repeat first action.

The song and action may be done three times: (a) singing words and doing action as above; (b) humming melody and doing action; and (c) humming melody mentally (but not making a sound) and doing action.

The eent - sy, weent - sy spi - der Went up the wa - ter spout. Down came the rain And washed the spi-der out. Out came the sun And dried up all the rain. And the eent - sy, weent - sy spi - der Went up the spout a - gain!

The Tree in the Wood

Another favorite ''add-on'' song—a real test of memory!

3. And on this limb, there was a branch,
   The finest branch you ever did see,
   The branch was on the limb,
   The limb was on the tree,
   The tree was in the wood, etc.
4. And on this branch, there was a nest, etc.
5. And in this nest, there was an egg, etc.
6. And in this egg, there was a bird, etc.
7. And on this bird, there was a wing, etc.
8. And on this wing, there was a feather, etc.

NOTE: Repeat bracketed measure as often as needed, as verses are added.

In selecting songs for recreational programs, it is a good idea to include newer or currently popular songs, including novelty songs that participants may be ready to teach each other. At the same time, familiar old stand-bys should not be ignored; although the leader may sometimes feel jaded about them, they are often new and quite enjoyable for younger participants.

DRAMA IN RECREATION

Dramatic activities are another major form of community recreation today. It has been estimated that there are over 3,000 amateur theater groups in the United States today, with well over 100,000 nonprofessional stage performances presented each year. Community drama programs may include a wide range of activities, such as charades and dramatic games, choral speaking or dramatic readings, pantomime workshops, mobile theaters and show wagons, talent or variety shows, play festivals, storytelling, or puppetry.

Perhaps the most unique quality of drama in recreation is that it is an important means of communication and entertainment. As no other artistic medium does, it expresses humans' hopes and fears, life experiences, triumphs, defeats, and comedic episodes. It may be serious or trivial, based on reality, or fanciful. It reflects, interprets, and enriches life.

As a recreational activity, drama has the advantage of offering participants many different forms of involvement. In addition to acting, they may do any of the following: dancing, singing, stage lighting, carpentry, ushering, costume design and producing, staging, makeup, publicity, music, and ticket sales. Like other performing arts, it places a heavy premium on whole-hearted cooperation by all participants, and, by having clear-cut production goals to achieve, usually manages to sustain a high level of interest over a period of time.

Examples of Community Theater

Many examples of community theater have been widely publicized. Washington, D.C., for example, has had an extremely successful, nonprofit Children's Theater, carried on with the sponsorship of the District's Recreation Department. The city of Downey, California, has had as many as 2,000 children a year take part in a similar children's theater program, with many workshops and performances each year. The Oak Park, Illinois, Stevenson Players, are a popular teenage drama group that has been performing steadily since the 1940s. The Cultural Arts Divisions of cities like Los Angeles have often included adult professional theater groups that perform throughout the city's neighborhoods.

Therapeutic Uses of Drama.   Many hospitals, nursing homes and other rehabilitation programs also make use of drama programs. In some cases, it is simply presented as a form of enjoyable recreation, with the techniques and subjects adapted to the abilities and interests of the patients or clients being served. In others, psychodrama or sociodrama techniques may be used, particularly in the case of drug or alcohol abuse group programs.

Theater programs have also become popular in recreation centers serving the elderly. For example, in a study of seventy-eight residential care settings, twenty-three respondents indicated that they had dramatics programs for the elderly. In a similar study of senior centers, twenty-five of fifty-eight respondents indicated that they had dramatics as an important part of their program.

Similarly, a number of prisons and other correctional facilities have organized theater groups. In some cases, they have developed repertoires based on works written by convicts themselves, drawn from their life experiences:

> One such group is "The Family," which began with eight inmates at the Bedford, New York, Correctional Facility who became involved in group therapy experiences such as theater games, exercises, role-playing and psychodrama, in which inmates acted out traumatic scenes from their own life. The prison theater workshops gave rise to a dozen new plays presented in homes for unwed mothers, drug rehabilitation centers, and even leading professional theaters in the East. Ultimately, "The Family" became a touring professional company of 150 actors and stage technicians in the outside community.[4]

Approaches to Community Drama

These examples make it clear that theater activities may take many forms within community recreation or therapeutic settings. The municipal recreation and park department, voluntary agency, or other leisure-service organization that wishes to develop a sound drama program should seek to develop programs serving various age groups, at different levels of performing skill.

Guidelines for Leading Informal Dramatics

At a beginning level, many kinds of dramatic activities may be enjoyed on playgrounds or in community centers. These include the following: (a) pantomime and improvisation; (b) dramatic games, charades, stunts, and skits; (c) puppet shows or shadow plays; and (d) performances which are put on for children, often with the use of mobile theaters or show wagons.

Pantomime and Improvisation

These are particularly useful in leading up to more advanced dramatic activities and provide great enjoyment in themselves. They help children become aware of their own expressive potential and make them more sensitive to sensory perception. Several categories of pantomimes follow:

1. "Acting out" activities, which other children may guess at. Such humorous ideas may be presented as:
   a lady trying on a new hat
   a man stifling a sneeze in a movie theater
   a boy taking castor oil
   stepping into an ice-cold bath or pool
   having your arms full of packages while a dog is snapping at your ankles
   coming up to bat in the big game with two out in the ninth

2. Pantomimes involving the senses:
   touch: picking up a soft kitten; sewing and sticking yourself with a needle; pulling taffy and getting your fingers stuck
   smell: smelling a delicious hot pie on a window sill and finding your way to it; trying to decide which perfume to buy as a gift; smelling a skunk
   hearing: listening to an alarm clock waking you up early in the morning; hearing a call for help while exploring in the woods; hearing an auto crash

taste: taking castor oil; finishing the chocolate icing in a bowl

3. Pantomimes expressing emotion, based on different settings or happenings:
   fear: going past a graveyard late at night
   anger: someone has taken your model airplane and carelessly broken it
   pity: a baby robin falls from a nest and dies
   surprise: you spy a house on fire, and rush to bring help

Pantomime may be taught as an art form, with a high degree of discipline and specialized training to increase suppleness, body control, and flexibility. Each portion of the body can be disciplined, with the use of hands, elbows, shoulders, feet, knees, head, and facial expressions analyzed for the fullest and most precise expressiveness. Effective pantomime is more than simply copying movement accurately. It must involve gathering the *essence* of a movement and showing it with a real sense of what the person performing it is like.

Charades

Many games are based on pantomimic action; a number of these may be found in game collections. The most useful ones are basically *charades,* which involve acting out a famous name, play, movie or book title, saying, or proverb, so that others may guess it. Charades are usually done without speaking, although in some cases sounds may be permitted. Several types of charades follow:

Individual Charades

One person acts out a name, title, or saying, while others try to guess what he has in mind. He usually begins by showing the category of the charade (if it is a title of a book, he pretends to read a book; if it is a television show, he describes with his hands the shape of the television screen; if it is a saying, he holds up two fingers of both hands, indicating "quotes"). He then proceeds to act out word by word, or syllable by syllable, the title or saying to be guessed. Thus, he holds up one finger and the others say, "First word." He holds up two fingers, and they say, "Second syllable." As he continues to act, the others guess the words or syllables, and he nods affirmatively when they are correct. When one player guesses it correctly, that player will be the next to act out a charade.

Team Charades

Each group of about six or eight players selects a title or phrase. They prepare a group charade, either giving the whole title at once, or showing it word by word in several short scenes. Then they act it out for the others to guess. Each team in turn acts its charade out for the other.

Team "Pass" Charades

A variation of the preceding is for each team to select a title or phrase, write it on a slip of paper, and pass it to the team on its right to act out. Or the leader may prepare a number of titles, and each team acts out the title it is given.

Relay Charades

The group divides into several teams, which must be spaced at a distance from each other. The leader has a list of several titles. Each team sends a player up; she is given the first title and must run back to her team and act it out as rapidly as possible. When her team guesses it satisfactorily, a second player runs up; she is given the second title, which she must act out quickly. This is continued until the first team to complete the entire list is the winner.

Groups that play a great deal of charades learn to use specific gestures to speed up the guessing process. For instance, holding up the thumb and forefinger close together indicates "small word." The other players quickly call out "the," "it," "and," and similar words, until the "actor" indicates by nodding which is correct. If the other players are calling out a word which sounds like the one being acted, the "actor" indicates this by pointing at his ear. He may indicate that the word being sought is a longer form of a word they are guessing (by stretching his hands apart) or that it is a shorter form (by making a chopping gesture). Thus charades may become a fairly skilled activity, or they may be approached on a very simple basis and still provide much enjoyment.

Other Dramatic Games

Other dramatic games involve use of pantomimic movements or verbal role playing. Here are several of the most appealing.

I'm Thinking of a Noun

One player says, "I'm thinking of a one-syllable noun that rhymes with _____," and then he gives a rhyming word. For example, he might be secretly thinking of the word "jail," and as a clue he gives the rhyming word "mail." One at a time, the other players try to guess the correct word. However, they must act out their guesses using pantomime, and without saying a word. Each time a word is acted out (typical guesses might be "tail," "hail," "pail," or "rail") the leader must guess it, and then say whether or not it is the secret word. The player who *does* guess and act out the secret word becomes the new leader, and the game begins again.

Bird, Beast, or Fish

The players form several equal teams, who form small clusters around the room. Each team sends an "actor" to the leader, who is in the center. She gives the actors the name of some living creature to act out. They go back to their groups to act the word out with pantomime, without using any sound. If it is a bird, they return with arms waving as if flying. If it is a beast, they crawl or run on all fours. If it is a fish, or sea creature, they return with a swimming movement. As the actors pantomime the creature, the group members try to guess it; the actors may nod their heads to show if they are "hot" or "cold," but may not make a sound. The first group to guess the creature exactly gets one point. Then each group sends a new actor up, and the leader gives them a new creature to act out. The game continues until everyone has had a chance to act, and the team with the highest score is the winner.

Going to California

Players sit in a circle, and one player begins by saying, "I'm going to California, and I'm taking a _____ with me." Instead of saying the name of the object, he pantomimes it. Then the next player must repeat the sentence, pantomime the first action, and then say "and a _____," and show another object. So it goes around the circle, with each player in turn pantomiming the objects that have gone before, and then adding one of his own. The last player to be able to act out all of the previous objects in the correct order is the winner.

Continued Story

Players sit in a circle, and one player begins to tell a story. After a few moments, she stops abruptly, usually at a moment of suspense. The next player in the circle must pick up the thread of the action immediately and continue the story. Usually, tales of humor, adventure, or ghost stories are the most successful as the continued story travels from person to person around the circle. This game is particularly successful for campfires and similar occasions.

Skits and Stunts

Dramatic activities of this sort are extremely popular, particularly with teen-age or adult participants. They take two forms: (a) those made up in advance and acted out through memorization or using a script; and (b) those which are created by the group, possibly based on a common idea or suggestion given by the leader.

Examples of the former type include group gags, monologues, short poems, "blackouts," and other humorous skits, which may frequently be found in collections. It is important to scrutinize them carefully before using skits or stunts with groups. This is so for two reasons. First, many tend to be extremely old-fashioned and "corny," rather than topical and modern in their humor. Second, many of the older skits are offensive or in bad taste, since they use dialect that ridicules those of racial or religious minorities.

Improvised skits or stunts are often more genuinely amusing since they express the real ideas and interests of the group members, and give those who have a flair for humor or improvised acting a real opportunity to express themselves. While one talented member of the group may write such skits, it is often better if all the players join in preparing the script, letting their ideas stimulate other ideas, just as professional gag writers do.

There are also a number of devices that group leaders may use in informal dramatics as a basis for making up skits.

The leader may give each group several "props" (toys, knives, pens, ties, books, feathers) in a paper bag; each group must build a skit based on its set of props.

The leader may assign a one-sentence plot outline to each group; the players then develop their own skits, based on the outline. It is interesting to see the many variations that may be evolved from as simple a line as, "You are rushing to get somewhere, and there is an unexpected interruption."

Puppet Shows and Shadow Plays

One of the most popular forms of playground or community dramatic activity is the puppet show. Children and teenagers may enjoy making their own puppets of various types: sock puppets, which may be designed so fingers actually work the mouth and give expression to the face; puppets with papier-mâché or clay-model heads, with the fingers of the performer tucked into felt or cardboard hands and arms; paper-bag puppets, with the face designed with paint or crayon; tin-can puppets; and vegetable puppets, in which a large potato, apple, turnip, or carrot may serve as the head. Designing and making puppets for a playground performance provides an enjoyable arts and crafts activity (Figures 9–2, 9–3, and 9–4).

Many simple hand puppet stages may be built or improvised. These include a small cardboard carton with a stage opening cut out, which is placed on a table or desk behind which the players crouch; a "doorway stage," a broomstick stretched across a doorway or between chairs with "curtains" hung from it; or a more formally constructed stage involving a mattress or bicycle carton standing on end, or even a real stage constructed from two-by-fours and plywood panels (Figures 9–5, 9–6, and 9–7).

Children may use these to put on plays that they have made up themselves, or to present plays based on famous stories drawn from children's literature, just as in children's theater programs. They may be presented with a minimum of props or may involve real miniature stage sets and lighting.

FIGURE 9–2   FIGURE 9–3   FIGURE 9–4

FIGURE 9–5   FIGURE 9–6   FIGURE 9–7

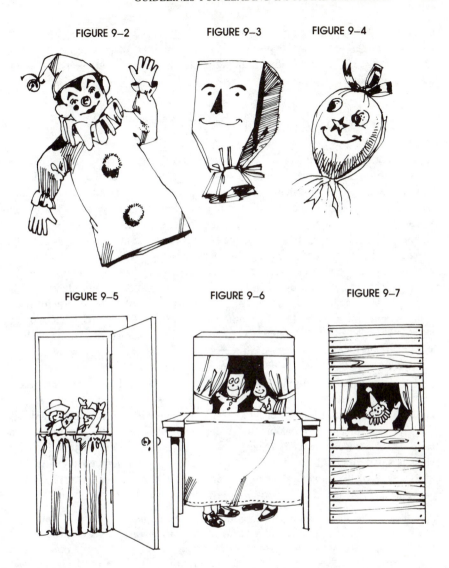

Shadow plays are usually done by having a large sheet hung between two posts, or in a doorway, with a strong light shining from behind. The players may then, by using puppets or appearing themselves, put on a performance (from behind the scene) in which the figures appear sharply outlined as silhouettes on the sheet. They may speak themselves as the action goes on, or they may perform to a prerecorded, taped sound track of voices and sound effects.

Mobile Drama Programs

More and more, many community recreation departments are using "stage wagons" or "stagemobiles," cleverly designed so that they can be transported by trucks that then open up to form compact stage sets. They can be quickly set up to permit traveling acting troupes to give performances on playgrounds throughout a city or in centers throughout a large county area. Such mobile units can be used to give young drama participants an opportunity to act or be part of performances in many settings. As such, they are an important part of the up-to-date cultural arts program in many communities.

DANCE IN COMMUNITY RECREATION

Many forms of dance may be sponsored by community recreation agencies, ranging from ballet or modern dance, to rock-and-roll events or aerobic dancing as a form of fitness exercise. Of these, the two major categories are: (a) creative or concert forms of dance: ballet, modern jazz, ethnic, and other performing kinds of dance; and (b) social forms of dance, including ballroom, folk, square, rock-and-roll, and round dancing. In addition to sponsoring instructional classes, performing groups, regularly meeting dance clubs, and recitals or concerts, many recreation departments also promote clinics, workshops, and leadership training in dance instruction. In some cases, they schedule large-scale band concerts which include popular dancing.

In approaching dance, one concern is that it has often been thought of as a primarily feminine activity. In many communities, men and boys have been hesitant to take part in it—particularly in its more creative aspects. However, with the decline of rigid sex stereotyping in other forms of recreation, such as sports, a growing number of males today are enjoying creative dance participation.

To illustrate, a high school dance teacher, Diane Pruett, has successfully involved many male students in modern dance classes in Miami Coral Park High School in Dade County, Florida. Increasingly, members of intramural and inter-scholastic sports teams have taken modern dance and have joined the performing dance group. Many have commented on the value of dance in contributing to their movement skills, posture, flexibility, and body alignment. However, Pruett considers an important outcome of the creative dance experience to be its effect on social relationships between male and female students. She writes:

> . . . I find it very pleasant to see the genuine friendships that develop in my modern dance classes. High school students often find it hard to develop friendships with members of the opposite sex in which there are no emotional attachments. Within a dance class, however, the students must learn to communicate verbally, physically, and aesthetically with each other. Barriers in communication break down. One of the biggest gains for the students in the class is that they begin to find themselves and learn to appreciate others.[5]

In numerous other ways, then, varied forms of dance may have important values for a wide range of participants, including all the major kinds of benefits ascribed to recreation generally: physical, social, emotional, and intellectual.

Types of Activities Offered

Different recreation agencies tend to emphasize contrasting forms of dance activity. For example, the Montgomery County, Maryland, Department of Recreation has for a number of years offered an extremely varied program of dance classes in the following areas: *ballroom dance* for teenagers and adults; *modern dance* for children, teenagers, and adults; *round dancing* (American set-pattern couple dances) for adults; *"slimnastics"* for adults; *ballet* for children, teenagers, and adults; *body rhythmics* for adults; *square dancing* for adults; and *tap* and *ballet* combined for children and teenagers. Included also are special square dance workshops, young peoples' ballet workshops, and a ballet theater production program.

In contrast, a city like San Antonio, Texas, has become known for its classes and performing groups in Mexican and Spanish dancing, reflecting the ethnic heritage of many of its residents. Classes are taught by dance authorities, who regularly choreograph such classical music as "Capriccio Espanol" and "The Three-Cornered Hat" for performance with the San Antonio Symphony Orchestra. Those taught in the program also take part in a summer spectacular, "Fiesta Noche Del Rio," a popular tourist attraction. The San Antonio Recreation Division also sponsors their perform-ances—as a free service—for conventions, service organizations, hospitals, the armed forces, the Red Cross, and similar groups.

Many voluntary agencies offer dance instruction and social activities as part of their program. In many YWCAs, for example, it is customary to have courses for adults in ballroom dancing and folk and square dancing, as well as weekly social dances for members and their guests. And, of course, dance is also offered by commercial organizations and private membership clubs.

Dance in Social Recreation

Social, square, and folk dancing are widely used as an important part of social recreation for teenage and adult groups in the community. Apart from rock-and-roll or "disco" dancing which normally does not require leadership, except for the role of the "disc jockey" who plays records or tapes, they may be approached on two levels:

Regularly Meeting Classes and Clubs.   There are today thousands of classes and clubs devoted to square, folk, and round dancing throughout the United States and Canada. Often these are devoted to fairly high-level skills, and involve couples or individuals who attend regularly, take part in special workshops, festivals, or weekends, and are serious enthusiasts of these dance hobbies.

Occasional Recreational Dance Programs.   A much greater number of individuals of all ages throughout the country take part occasionally in square and folk dancing as part of general social recreation activities. Thus, a church, Parent-Teacher Association, 4-H club, YM- or YWCA, hotel, teen club, or similar organization may plan a special social or party which introduces simple square and folk dance activities. Usually, when presented in such settings—if the instruction is brief but effective—participation is relaxed and enthusiastic.

There would be little point to providing descriptions of the more advanced square or folk dances in this book, although a number of sources are included in the bibliography. Instead, guides are offered for the successful leadership of these forms of dance in social recreation situations. In addition, several illustrative dances are given, which may be used for teaching assignments in recreation leadership courses.

Guides for Recreational Dance Leadership

Selection.   Dances should be chosen to suit the musical and rhythmic tastes of the participants, their physical status, and social needs and interests. Thus, in a senior citizens' center, emphasis should be placed on older, more traditional forms of ballroom or round dancing, on relaxed mixers and rather simple, slow square dances. Among teenagers, it is important to provide spirited dances with catchy melodies. Dances chosen should build on previously learned skills and should always include some new materials to keep interest at a high level.

Programming.   In any given dance session, dances presented should have variety, and should involve a gradual progression of skills. They should be blocked in groups: two or three folk dances or mixers, two or three square dances, and, if social dancing is part of the program, a period of time for general dancing. It is usually a good idea (if the group has not done this kind of dancing before and resistance may be anticipated) to begin with social dance icebreakers or circle dances without partners.

Instruction.   This should be clear, enthusiastic, and as brief as possible, so that people do not become bored with repetitious, drill-like teaching. The following steps are involved:

1. The appropriate formation should be taken and the dance introduced.
2. The dance should be demonstrated by having the group walk through the action. In a folk dance, this is usually done in "teachable units," sections of the dance that form recognizable blocks of action, fitted to sections of the music. Usually, in a square dance, the specific "figure" of the dance is explained and walked through all at once. If the activity is a social dance icebreaker or mixer, it may only be necessary to explain it briefly, and then begin.
3. If the dance is at all complicated, the separate parts should then be assembled and reviewed. If it is simple, this is not necessary.
4. The group then does the dance. If they have learned it correctly and the bulk are doing it satisfactorily (in any group, a few individuals may always have some difficulty), it should continue. If there is much confusion, it may be necessary to stop it, reteach the part that is causing difficulty, and then start over.

The following section includes a number of simple folk dances, traditional dance mixers, and square and line dances that are useful for informal recreational situations.

Examples of Folk and Square Dances

Shoo Fly
American Play Party Mixer

This lively, partner-changing dance is a good lead-up to square dancing.

Formation

A circle of partners with hands joined, all facing the center. Each girl is on her partner's right.

Words to be sung

Verse

Shoo fly, don't bother me,
Shoo fly, don't bother me,
Shoo fly, don't bother me
'Cause I belong to somebody.

Chorus

I do, I do,
I ain't goin' to tell you who,
I belong to somebody,
Yes, indeed, I do.

Phonograph record: RCA Victor, LE-3000 (words are sung on record).

FIGURE 9–8

Action

Keeping hands joined, all take four walking steps forward to the center, and four steps backward to place. Repeat entire action.

All swing partners. Children may use a two-hand skipping swing, or an elbow swing. Adults use a "buzz swing" (Figure 9–8). At end of verse, each boy faces the center and passes his partner across in front of him to his left side. Hands are joined in the circle again.

NOTE: The girl now on the boy's right is his new partner. The dance is repeated from the beginning, as many times as desired.

Oh, Susannah
American Play Party Mixer

This circle dance introduces the grand-right-and-left and promenade, and so might be done as one of the first numbers of a recreational dance program.

Formation

A circle of partners with hands joined, all facing the center. Each girl is on her partner's right.

FIGURE 9–9

Words to be Sung

Verse

Oh, I come from Alabama with
My banjo on my knee,
And I'm going to Louisiana
My true love for to see.

It rained all night, the day I left,
The weather it was dry,
The sun so hot I froze to death,
Susannah, don't you cry.

Action

All the girls walk four steps to the center, clapping hands on the fourth step, and four steps back to place. All the boys do the same.

Facing partners, all do a grand-right-and-left. Give right hands to partners, pass, left hands to next person, pass, and continue for remainder of verse (Figure 9–9).

FIGURE 9–10

Chorus

Oh, Susannah,
Don't you cry for me,
For I'm going to Louisiana
With my banjo on my knee.

Each person meets a new partner and swings this person with sixteen "buzz" steps.

Oh, Susannah
Don't you cry for me,
For I'm going to Louisiana
With my banjo on my knee.

In promenade position (Figure 9–10) new partners promenade sixteen steps counterclockwise around circle. At end of chorus, all face center, with girls on partner's right, ready to begin dance again.

Phonograph records: RCA Victor 45-6178 (without words on record); Educational.

Recordings of America S.G. 2 (with words on record).

Savila Se Bela Loza
Yugoslav Folk Dance

This is a lively, simple circle folk dance, an example of the popular Yugoslav "kolo."

Formation

Dancers join hands in a single circle, facing the center. No partners are needed.

Action

Part 1   With hands joined and beginning with right foot, run eighteen steps to the right (counterclockwise). Then step again on right foot, hop lightly on it, and swing left foot across in front.

Turning to left, run eighteen steps to the left (clockwise), beginning with left foot. Then step again on left foot, hop lightly on it, and swing right foot across in front.

Part 2   "Basic kolo step." Facing the center, with hands still joined, step on right foot, traveling to right side, cross the left foot in back, step on right foot again, and hop on it, swinging the left foot across in front.

The same action is done to the left: step on left to side, cross right in back, step left, and hop on it, swinging the right foot across in front.

The entire action is done three full times with small steps close to the floor. Then the dance is repeated from the beginning.

Phonograph record: Folkraft 1496X45-B (recorded in Yugoslavia by Dennis Boxell).

Seven Steps
German Folk Dance Mixer

A lively European folk dance which uses the schottische, a fundamental folk dance step.

Formation

A double circle of couples facing to the right (counterclockwise) in open position (Figure 9–11).

FIGURE 9–11

Action

Part 1   Starting with the outside foot (boy's left and girl's right), take seven running steps forward. Pause on the eighth count, lifting inside foot (boy's right and girl's left).

Starting with the inside foot, take seven running steps backward. Pause on the eighth count, lifting outside foot.

Part 2   Releasing partner's hand, and with both hands on own waist, each person does a schottische step away from his partner, to the side. Boy goes to left, stepping left, right, left, and hop, while girl does reverse footwork. Each person does a schottische step back to partner. Boy goes to right, stepping right, left, right, and hop, while girl does reverse footwork.

In shoulder-waist position (Figure 9–12) each couple does four step-hops, turning once clockwise. Boy begins with left foot and girl with right foot.

Part 3   The action of part 2 is repeated. The boy, however, instead of returning to his partner with a schottische, moves *ahead* to the

FIGURE 9–12

next girl, while his partner moves *back* to the next boy. In shoulder-waist position, they turn with this *new* partner, with four step-hops.

NOTE: The dance is repeated as many times as desired, each time with a new partner.

Phonograph record: Folk Dancer MH-1048.

Alley Cat
American Novelty Dance

This simple novelty dance, done without partners, is enjoyed by all age groups.

Part 4

Formation

Individuals scattered around floor (they may be in several rows), all facing in one direction. Leader stands in front of them, to show action.

Action

After the musical introduction, do following actions.

Part 1 Place right foot out to right side, toe touching floor, and bring it back to place. Repeat.
Do same action with left foot, to left side and back, twice.

Part 2 Place right foot back, toe touching floor, and bring it back to place. Repeat.
Do same action with left foot, placing it back and to place, twice.

Part 3 Bring right knee up across in front of body, and then return right foot to place on floor. Repeat.
Do same action with left knee, up and in front of body, and back, twice.

Part 4 Bring right knee up across in front of body and down, once. Do same action with left knee. Then clap hands and jump once in place, turning *one-quarter* to the right (clockwise).

The action is repeated several times. Each time, all the dancers rotate one-quarter position to the right, and do the dance facing in a new direction.

Phonograph record: Atco 45-6226.

Hokey Pokey
American Novelty Dance

This is a lively version of an old English singing game, Looby Loo, in which all the dancers do different hand and foot actions in turn.

Formation

All face center in a single circle, without partners.

Words

You put your right foot in,
You put your right foot out,
You put your right foot in,
And you shake it all about.
You do the Hokey Pokey
And you turn yourself around,
That's what it's all about.

NOTE: This action is repeated, each time with a different action: "right foot," "left foot," "right arm," "left arm," "right elbow," "left elbow," "head," etc. At end, as words on record repeat "You do the Hokey Pokey,

Action

All dancers touch right toe to floor in front, and then to floor in back. They put right toe forward again and then shake it in the air. Each dancer turns slowly to right with four strutting steps, to face center again. Then all clap own hands four times, slowly.

You do the Hokey Pokey," etc. all take four steps forward to the center and back, three times, then clap hands in place four times.

Phonograph record: Capitol Records, Starline 6026.

Doublebska Polka
Czech Folk Dance Mixer

This couple dance mixer using the polka step has become a favorite of many American folk dancers.

Formation

Couples scattered around the dance floor, in closed dance position.

Action

Part 1   All couples do sixteen polka steps, traveling counterclockwise around the hall and turning clockwise as couples.

Part 2   Forming small circles with six to ten couples in a circle, couples march counterclockwise. Each boy has his right arm around his partner's waist, and his left hand on the left shoulder of the boy in front of him. They take sixteen steps forward (Figure 9–13).

Part 3   Boys release partners and face the center. In the polka rhythm, they clap their own hands twice and then clap hands once with their neighbors. This clapping action is done sixteen times (Figure 9–14).

Meanwhile, the girls polka individually, without turning, sixteen steps clockwise around the outside of the circle.

NOTE: At the end of Part 3, boys turn to the outside to find a new partner. They form couples again and start the dance from the beginning. It is repeated as many times as desired.

Phonograph record: Folk Dancer MH-3016.

FIGURE 9–13   FIGURE 9–14

Virginia Reel
American Country Dance

This is probably the best known and liked of all the traditional recreational dances.

Formation

A line of boys, facing a line of girls. There should be between four and eight couples to a set, with six being the best number. The couple nearest the "caller" or source of music is the first, or "head," couple. If dancers turn to face the music, each girl should be on her partner's right.

Action

Part 1   Taking hands in lines (girls holding hands in their line, and boys in theirs), all take four walking steps forward toward opposite line, and four steps backward. Repeat this.

All walk forward, join right hands with partner's right hand, and walk clockwise around partner, returning to place with eight steps.

Repeat this action with left hands joined, turning counterclockwise.

Repeat this action with both hands joined, turning clockwise.

All walk forward and "do-si-do," passing around partner back-to-back (beginning with right sides passing) and returning to place.

Part 2   The first couple joins both hands and slides eight steps down the set (between the lines) and eight steps back up to their starting position.

The "reel" (Figure 9–15). The first couple does a right elbow-swing once, turning clockwise. The first boy then turns the next girl in the girls' line with a left elbow, turning counterclockwise. At the same time, the first girl does the same with the next boy in the boys' line. This action is repeated several times, with the first couple working their way down the set, first turning each other with a right elbow, and then the *next* person on the side with a left elbow.

"Cast off!" When they reach the "foot" of the set, the first couple joins both hands, and slides up to the "head" of the set. They face forward (toward the music) and "cast off." The first boy marches to the left and down to the foot of the set (with the other boys following him) while the first girl does the same to the right (Figure 9–16). When they reach the foot, the first couple joins both hands and makes an arch. The others go under the arch and back up to place, keeping the same order, but leaving the first couple at the foot.

NOTE: The dance is repeated as many times as there are couples, each time with a new first couple.

Phonograph records: RCA Victor 45-6180 (without calls); RCA Victor LE-3002 (with calls).

FIGURE 9–15   FIGURE 9–16

Duck for the Oyster
American Square Dance

This is one of the easiest of square dances, and may be done even by young children, although it will also be enjoyed by adults who are not square dance "addicts."

Formation

Four couples to a set, with each couple standing on one side of a square formation, backs parallel to one side of the room, facing in. Each girl is on her partner's right side. Make as many sets as you have room for!

Action   Following the caller's commands, all "honor partners," and then "corners." This means bowing or curtseying to one's own partner, and then to one's corner (girl on the boy's left, and vice versa).

All join hands in a circle and walk or skip to the left, and back to the right to starting position.

All face partners and do a grand-right-and-left (boys going counterclockwise and girls clockwise) halfway around the square. Meet partners, take promenade position, and promenade counterclockwise back to original home position (see *Oh, Susannah* for these actions).

The first couple (couple standing with their backs to the caller, or music), joins inside hands and walks out to the right, to face the second couple. They join hands with them, and circle to the left

several steps. The first couple does the "duck for the oyster" action, ducking halfway under the joined hands of the second couple, and then back. The second couple does the same thing, ducking under the joined hands of the first couple, and back. Then the first couple ducks through, and lets go of the second couple's hands. They go on to the third couple (facing their home position) and do the entire "duck for the oyster" action with them. They go on to the fourth couple (couple on the left of their home position) and do the same action with them. Then they return to place.

In turn, the second, third, and fourth couples each go out to the right, and do the same action with each of the other couples. As a "break," they may also swing partners and promenade, or do the grand-right-and-left.

Phonograph Record: RCA Victor Educational Records, "Let's Square Dance Series," LE-3000 (45 rpm or 33⅓ rpm). Record has calls for the action on it, and illustrated booklet of directions.

Social Dance Mixers and Icebreakers

Although folk and square dances are extremely useful activities for children's playground programs or for teenage and adult social recreation, the most commonly found form of recreational dance is couple social dancing. While fads may come and go, with new dances constantly being invented, this age-old social activity continues to have great appeal for all ages. In most situations, people will take part freely and confidently. However, in some situations, such as teenage school dances or adult "singles" parties, they may tend to be rather slow about inviting partners to dance. The social dance mixers and icebreakers presented in Chapter 10 will help to cut down shyness and reserve at such events, as well as provide lively fun at *all* parties and dances.

AEROBIC DANCE IN RECREATION SETTINGS

Although aerobic dance might have been presented in Chapter 6, as a popular form of fitness activity, it is also recognized as a type of recreational dance and is therefore included in this chapter.

Chiles and Moore describe aerobic dance as a fitness concept originated by Jacki Sorenson, made up of vigorous routines set to music:

> Routines consist of exercises, simple disco movements, ballet, and locomotor and non-locomotor skills (swinging, pushing, running, jumping, and hopping). The objective is to increase cardiovascular fitness, flexibility, and muscle tone . . . . Disco, rock and roll, and pop music—music that makes the students move—offer the best beats for aerobic routines.[6]

Typically, an aerobic dance session might consist of about 40 minutes of activity, with a ten-minute warmup, a 20- or 25-minute routine period, and a ten-minute cooldown. Unlike modern dance or ballet classes, where the pace is somewhat slower as the instructor demonstrates movements, has the class members practice them, and corrects individuals carefully, aerobic dancing moves rapidly, with the instructor demonstrating different movement sequences and having the class get into them very quickly. Usually, there are fairly long, sustained periods of activity without pause, with the instructor showing the action in front of participants as they dance, and calling out directions.

While the pace of aerobic dancing may vary from group to group, with middle-aged or elderly participants moving at a more relaxed pace than younger dancers, it generally consists of a highly vigorous workout, with excellent health benefits. There are many standardized routines, including numerous sequences on records or cassette tapes, and instructors may also feel free to compose their own routines and select their own music. As an example, a routine composed by Moore, set to the tune "Sandy," from the movie *Grease,* includes the following movements:

> 7 arm circles with both arms out
> 10 jumping jacks
> 8 straight leg kick steps (kick leg up straight in front, then step)
> jog 8 forward
> jog 8 backward
> 4 hustle steps to right (using a right, close, left sequence)
> 4 hustle steps to left
> Walk forward 4 and clap
> Walk 4 back and clap
> 1 head roll to the right (8 counts)

1 head roll to the left (8 counts)
Jump one step forward, one back, one right and one left
8 jumping jacks
8 step kicks and clap under knee
8 hops forward on right leg
8 hops backward on left leg
8 toe touches
8 jogs forward
8 jogs backward[7]

During the final part of the session, participants may lie down, stretch out, and relax, while the instructor leads the group in relaxation activities. Chiles and Moore conclude that aerobic dance often appeals to people with whom other fitness activities are less successful. For this reason, it has become extremely popular both in school physical education programs and in many leisure-service settings.

Summing up, this chapter has presented an overview of three major forms of performing arts activities that are popular in community recreation programs. Leadership methods are outlined within such areas as song leadership or dance instruction, and a number of useful, simple activities are presented, through which student leaders can begin to develop skills of working with groups in a social recreation setting.

NOTES

[1]Barry D. Mangum, "A Giant Step Forward for the Arts in Leisure," *Parks and Recreation* (July 1982): 30–31.

[2]John R. Kelly, *Leisure* (Englewood Cliffs, N.J.: Prentice-Hall, 1982), p. 361.

[3]*Leadership Manual* (Euclid, Ohio: Recreation and Park Dept., 1974).

[4]Richard Kraus, *Therapeutic Recreation Service: Principles and Practices* (Philadelphia: Saunders College Publishing, 1983), p. 348.

[5]Diane M. Pruett, "Male High School Athletes in Dance Classes," *Journal of Physical Education, Recreation and Dance* (May 1981): 45.

[6]Barbara Ann Chiles and Suzanne Moore, "Aerobic Dance in Public Schools," *Journal of Physical Education, Recreation and Dance* (February 1981): 51.

[7]Chiles and Moore: 52.

STUDENT PROJECTS

1. Select one major type of activity found in this chapter (music, drama, or dance) and analyze the various ways in which it may be presented in a community or voluntary-agency recreation program—i.e., the activity formats and types of population groups that might be involved. Develop an overall plan for its presentation.
2. As an alternative to Project 1, select a setting which serves special populations, such as a nursing home or psychiatric hospital, and develop a manual which includes guidelines for leading music, drama, or dance in this setting.
3. In class, have students lead a participation workshop in music, drama, or dance activities, to be followed by class review and evaluation.

SUGGESTED READINGS

John Batcheller and Sally Monsour, *Music in Recreation and Leisure* (Dubuque, Iowa: Wm. C. Brown, 1972).

Betty Casey, *International Folk Dancing, U.S.A.* (Garden City, N.Y.: Doubleday, 1981).

Frances C. Durland, *Creative Dramatics for Children* (Kent, Ohio: Kent State University Press, 1975).

Gladys Andrews Fleming, *Creative Rhythmic Movement: Boys' and Girls' Dancing* (Englewood Cliffs, N.J.: Prentice-Hall, 1976).

Emily Gillies, *Creative Dramatics for All Children* (Washington, D.C.: Association for Childhood Education, 1973).

Jane Harris, Ann Pittman, and Marlys Waller, *Dance a While* (Minneapolis: Burgess, 1968).

Sue Jennings, *Remedial Drama: A Handbook for Teachers and Therapists* (New York: Theater Arts Books, 1974).

James Leisy, *The Good Times Songbook* (Nashville: Abingdon Press, 1974).

Betty Lowndes, *Movement and Creative Drama for Children* (Boston: Plays, Inc., 1971).

Esther Nelson, *Musical Games for Children of All Ages* (New York: Sterling, 1976).

Audrey Wethered, *Music and Drama in Therapy* (Boston: Plays, Inc., 1973).

Social Recreation: Games, Mixers, Party-Planning, and Special Events

Social recreation consists of programs that bring people together for relaxed sociability in group settings. Usually, it includes activities such as games, songs, skits, or dances which place little emphasis on competition or a high level of skill, and instead promote friendly, cooperative participation.

Such organizations as religious or social clubs, teenage councils, church fellowship groups, or Golden Age Clubs sponsor social recreation. The events themselves may consist of festivals, parties, carnivals, covered-dish suppers, or similar programs that promote a positive, accepting group climate. In social recreation, participants are encouraged to do their own planning and provide their own leadership whenever possible.

This chapter presents a number of activities that are commonly found in social recreation, such as group games, social mixers and icebreakers, novelty stunts and contests, mental and word games, and similar activities. It concludes with party-planning guidelines, sample holiday parties, and a discussion of trip-planning and other special events.

SOCIAL RECREATION ACTIVITIES: GAMES AND MIXERS

Group games are an important part of social recreation. The games and mixers that appear in this chapter are distinctly different from those presented in Chapter 6. They are much less active and athletic, and represent the urge to play in its simplest form. People take part in them for sheer pleasure and enjoyment, rather than to gain prestige or other rewards through victory, as in many sports.

Useful for all ages, these group games range from the very simple to the highly complex, and from moderately lively to passive or quiet activities. They can therefore be carried on even by persons with limited physical abilities. They have a great potential for achieving desirable personal outcomes but this does not happen automatically. Whatever the game structure, the leader's goal at all times should be to ensure that all are involved as successfully as possible, and that all are gaining satisfaction from the activity. Throughout, values of acceptance, friendship, and good humor should be stressed.

The games that follow fall into several categories: (a) group games or contests, generally active or semi-active; (b) social mixers, icebreakers, and get-acquainted games; (c) novelty stunts and contests, primarily for children; (d) mental games, quizzes, puzzles, and word games; (e) so-called magic stunts and tricks; and (f) table games and contests. In general, these games are familiar, tried-and-true activities. A few are of recent origin, come from unusual sources, or represent interesting and new variations of older activities.

They are suited for use in several different kinds of recreational situations: (a) playgrounds, community centers, summer camps, or other settings where groups of children and youth can be active in vigorous games, or where quieter indoor games are useful for rainy days; (b) any group situation, such as a couples club, senior center, or other social event, where games offer the opportunity for friendly mixing; and (c) special programs or parties, such as carnivals, game nights, or banquets, where mixers and stunts lend spice to the occasion.

GUIDELINES FOR LEADING GAMES

What are the steps of successful game leadership? To begin with, it is most important to pick the right activity. Gauge the ability and interests of the group; take their age, number, mental ability, physical status, and previous recreational experiences into account. Ideally, your choice (or choices, if you are planning a *session* of games) should be based on activities that you have enjoyed personally, or that you have seen work well with similar groups.

1. Prepare yourself. Become completely familiar with the game, so there is no question in your mind about its rules, purpose, or strategy. If special equipment or materials are required, get them ready.
2. In presenting the game to the group, do so in as lively and enthusiastic a manner as possible. First, have them take the appropriate formation or divide into whatever teams, lines, or other arrangement may be necessary. Then introduce the activity, arousing their interest with a brief explanatory phrase or two.
3. Explain the game. This should be done as quickly as possible, but the basic point must be understood. Too often a leader gets all tangled up in explaining rules, roles of different players, or strategy, without making it clear that the purpose is to catch someone, to gain the highest point total, to guess the correct answer, or to complete the action. The essential purpose of the game *must* be made clear.

4. Briefly demonstrate the game, either yourself or with participants carrying out the action as you tell them what to do. As soon as it is generally understood, *get started*. There should not be a long-winded delay before the game is actually played.

5. If the contestants are carrying on the game successfully, do not interfere; in fact, it is appropriate in most games for the leader to play along with the others. Only if there is confusion or disagreement, or if certain individuals are having a great deal of difficulty, should the leader step in to iron out the difficulty and help the action resume. If some players are unsuccessful in a certain role—such as the "chaser" in a tag game—the leader may quickly step in to change or rotate roles.

6. Cut the game off while interest in it is still fairly high, rather than have it drag on and grind to a dull ending.

In selecting games for a whole session, it is important to provide variety. Some games should be familiar, others introduced for the first time. Similarly, there should be a healthy balance between vigorous and quiet games, and some mental or social games as well as physical ones. Every effort should be made to give each participant some degree of success, rather than permit some players to be "steady losers" and (as may happen with children) become the butt of jokes or ridicule. Now, on to the games themselves!

Group Games and Contests

These are games which tend to be moderately active, designed for groups of as few as eight or ten to as many as fifty or sixty participants. They are generally most suitable for children and youth in centers, playgrounds, clubs, parties, or similar situations, although in many cases they are also suitable for adults in informal recreation situations.

Indian Chief
Semiactive; 10–30 players

Players sit in a circle. One player in the circle is chosen as "It," and is asked to leave the room. The group then selects a secret leader, or Indian Chief. The Chief begins to lead the group in performing some action, such as hand-clapping or lightly stamping a foot. "It" returns to the room, walks around inside the circle, and tries to guess who the Chief is. The Chief continues to lead the group in various actions, waving hands, standing up and sitting down, etc. He must change the action every fifteen or twenty seconds, and the other players copy him quickly, being careful not to keep their eyes fixed on him.

"It" is given three chances to guess who the Indian Chief is. If he is successful, that player becomes "It" and the game is played again. If not, it is usually best to pick a new "It" and a new Chief.

Hot Potato
Semiactive; 8–25 players

This is a very easy and familiar game that is always popular with children. They stand or sit in a circle and, while music plays, pass a ball or beanbag from person to person around the circle. The music is suddenly stopped after fifteen or twenty seconds, and the child holding the "hot potato" is eliminated. A whistle may also be used as a signal. The game continues until only one player remains—the winner.

Musical Chairs
Active; 8–30 players

A number of chairs—one less than the number of players—are placed side by side in a line, facing in alternate directions. On signal, the players walk counterclockwise (to the left) around the line of chairs, to the accompaniment of a piano or music from a record player. When the music stops, each child tries to find a seat. The boy or girl who cannot get a seat drops out of the game and the action is repeated, with a new chair taken away, so there is one chair less than the number of players. The game goes on until there are only two children left. They go round the last chair, and the child who sits in it when the music stops wins the game.

Square Relay
Active; 16–40 players

Players sit in four equal teams, on sides of a square, facing inward. A chair is placed in the center of the square. Each player on the left is given a rubber playground ball or beanbag. At a signal, each team passes the ball along the line to the right, to the right-hand player. When he receives it, he runs forward, *around* the chair in the center and back to the chair on the left side of his line. Meanwhile, all players shift one seat to the right. The action is repeated, with each player having a turn at running. The first team to complete the action is the winner.

Magic Carpets
Semiactive; 8–30 players

A number of newspapers or large sheets of cardboard (as many as there are players) are scattered around the room on the floor. Music starts, and players march around the room single file, to the right. When the music stops, each player must find a sheet of paper to stand on. The player who cannot find a "magic carpet" is eliminated, since the leader has removed one sheet. The action is repeated, until only one player—the winner—remains.

Simon Says
Active; 6–50 players

Probably the most famous of "elimination" games! One player, the leader, is Simon. He faces the other players, and commands them to do certain actions, such as: "Clap hands!" "Turn around!" "Touch your toes!" As Simon gives each command, he does the action himself, and the other players must immediately imitate the action—but only if the command was preceded by the words, "Simon says!" If Simon does not say "Simon says," the players should ignore the command and do nothing. Any player who makes a mistake, by not moving when he should or vice versa, is eliminated. To make the game trickier, Simon may try to trick the players by giving a rapid string of commands with "Simon says," and then suddenly giving a command without the phrase. The last player to survive is the winner.

Dog and Bone
Quiet; 6–20 players

Here's a different kind of game. Players sit on chairs arranged in a semicircle. One player, the "dog," sits blindfolded on a chair about fifteen feet in front of them, facing them. Directly in front of the "dog" on the floor is a book; this is the "bone." The leader points to one player, who tries to creep or crawl silently forward, and take the "bone" back to his or her place without being heard by the "dog." If the "dog" thinks he hears him, he points directly at him. If he is pointing in a reasonably correct direction, the player must give up the "bone" and go back to his place. Another player then tries to steal the "bone." If one succeeds, he takes the place of the "dog," and the game begins again.

The Ocean Is Calm
Semiactive; 8–40 players

Players sit in chairs scattered around the room. Each child thinks of the name of some creature that lives in the sea, without saying it aloud. One player is picked to be the fisherman. He rises and says, "The ocean is calm.'' He then walks around the room, calling out the names of various sea creatures: ''Sharks!'' ''Squid!'' ''Whales!'' ''Sea turtles!'' ''Oysters!'' When a player hears the name of his creature, he gets up and walks behind the fisherman, calling out the names of other sea creatures. When most of the players have been called out of their seats, the fisherman shouts: ''The ocean is stormy.'' All the players—those still seated as well as those standing—must find new chairs. The last player to find a seat becomes the new fisherman.

Fox, Gun, Hunter
Semiactive; 8–40 players

Players divide into two teams. Each team goes into a huddle and decides to be one of three things: a fox, gun, or hunter. These choices rank as follows: (a) fox outranks hunter; (b) hunter outranks gun; (c) gun outranks fox. After selecting their roles, the two teams stand in lines facing each other and, on signal, advance three steps. They then show what they have chosen. If a team has chosen to be the fox, players put hands to their ears and bark. If they are a gun, they take aim and fire, shouting ''Bang!'' If hunter, they cross arms and shout ''Hey.'' The team that outranks the other scores a point. If they have both chosen the same, there is no score. The game is repeated, with teams huddling each time to decide what they want to be, until one team has won five points.

Social Mixers and Icebreakers

These are mixers and get-acquainted games, and are generally more useful for teenage or adult groups in party situations than for other age levels. Despite the range of participants suggested, it is possible to play them with much larger groups, provided that the leader's directions can be heard.

Hidden Names
Semiactive; 10–50 players

Each player is given the name of a famous person on a slip pinned to her back. She also has pencil and paper. The object is to circulate, reading and writing down as many names of other players as possible. But the object is also to keep others from reading the name on your back. Players therefore back up against the wall, dodge around speedily, and lie on the floor to avoid having their names read. It can be quite acrobatic. After about five minutes, a signal is given, and the lists are totaled to find the winner.

Who Am I?
Quiet; 10–50 players

As in ''Hidden Names,'' the names of famous men and women are printed on slips of paper and pinned to the back of each player entering the room. Each player tries to find out his own famous identity by circulating around the room, letting others read the name on his back, and then asking them questions about the famous name that can be answered by a ''Yes'' or ''No.'' Gradually, he establishes whether he is a human or animal real or fictional, individual or group, alive or dead, male or female. When he has guessed his own identity, he may continue to play by answering the questions of other players. There is no real winner in games like this. The real purpose is to encourage friendly mixing and conversation.

Yes or No
Quiet; 10–50 players

Players are given ten or fifteen dried beans each, and are told to circulate around and ask each other questions on any subject. Any player who answers with a ''Yes'' or ''No'' must pay the questioner with a bean as forfeit. Sounds or gestures like ''Uh-huh'' or ''Nope,'' or shaking one's head to indicate ''Yes'' or ''No'' are also penalized. The game continues for several minutes, as players move around rapidly trying to win beans from each other. At the end, they count their trophies, and the player with the most beans wins.

Odd or Even
Quiet; 10–50 players

This mixer begins like "Yes or No," with each player being given a handful of beans. A player takes any number of beans from her stockpile, holds them in her right fist, and asks any other player, "Odd or even?" The opponent guesses. If she is right, she gets those beans from the questioner. If she is wrong, she must turn over that number of beans to the questioner. After several minutes of play, the contestant with the most beans is declared the winner.

Name Game
Quiet; 15–50 players

Each player is given a sheet of paper and a pencil. He then prints his full name down the center of the sheet, letter by letter, from top to bottom. Nicknames are permitted, if they are shorter than the surname. Each player then goes round the room, asking the names of the other players. Each time he hears a name that includes any of the letters in his own name, he prints that name (it can be either the first or last name) across his sheet in such a way that his name and the other name are joined by the common letter. The winner is the first player to match every name in his name with the name of another player. Each name may be used only once.

Name Bingo
Quiet; 15–50 players

Each player is handed a sheet of paper that is marked off in five rows of five boxes each for a total of twenty-five squares, as in a Bingo card. If there are fewer than twenty-five players, it may be best to have sheets with three rows of three boxes each, for nine squares. The mixer is played like *bingo*, except that names substitute for numbers. Players move around the room, asking others their names, and printing each one (first and last) in a square, until all the squares are filled. Then the game leader calls out the names of players, one by one, from a list she has made up. When a player sees that a name on her sheet has been called, she draws a line through it. The first player to cross out an entire line of boxes (horizontally, vertically, or diagonally) wins, and calls out, "Name Bingo!"

Lucky Fifteenth
Quiet; 20–50 players

At a party or games session, the leader announces that one of the players has a "secret treasure"—a shiny new quarter—which he will give to the fifteenth person who shakes hands with him. Nobody knows who has the treasure; the players circulate around and begin shaking hands with each other and chatting briefly, until suddenly the "treasure holder" announces the winner.

Pairing Mixers

There are many interesting stunts which help get players to take partners. Some of these may be done with young children in order to have them pair off for games. Others may be useful with teenagers and adults in choosing partners for dancing, or in helping people circulate at a social event. Several examples follow.

Animal Pairs
Quiet; 10–50 players

The leader prepares pictures of animal pairs, by cutting pictures of animals out of magazines and then cutting each picture in half. Each child is given half a picture and then, on signal, all scurry about to find their partners by matching halves to form a whole animal.

Animal Calls
Quiet; 10–50 players

This is like the preceding game, but players are given a slip of paper with the name of an animal on it. Two of each animal are given out; they must be animals with a familar call, like wolves (howl), lions (roar), or pigs (grunt). At a signal, children circulate, making their animal noises and looking for their partners.

Animal Teams
Quiet; 20–70 players

A humorous variation of "Animal Calls" is one in which, in a somewhat larger group, several people each are given a slip with the name of the same animal. Thus, there might be eight roosters, eight horses, eight donkeys, etc. At a signal, they close their eyes and circulate, calling out their animal noises and joining hands with others of the same species when they find them. The mixer concludes when all the members of the same groups have found each other, thus forming teams which may be then used in other games. Although this may appear a rather childish activity, it is surprisingly popular with teenagers and adults.

Singing Teams
Quiet; 20–70 players

This is like "Animal Teams," except that each player is given the name of a familiar song. Eight players might be given a slip for "Oh, Susannah," eight for "Home on the Range," eight for "You Are My Sunshine," and so on. At a signal, they circulate, each person singing his song loudly. When they find others singing the same song, they link arms with them and continue to march around and sing until all the singing teams are formed. The leader might then ask each group to sing its song for the others, in an informal concert.

It should be noted that this and other games like "Animal Teams" are described as "quiet" only because they are not physically active. In terms of noise, they are certainly *not* quiet!

Matching Cards
Quiet; 20–70 players

There are many variations of mixers like "Animal Pairs," in which players are each given a card or slip, and asked to find the person whose slip matches theirs. Here are a few of the possibilities:

Split Valentines

For St. Valentine's Day, large red hearts are painted or drawn on cards. Each card is then cut in half a different way, some with a straight vertical cut, others a wavy cut, etc. Half of the group gets one half of the cut cards, and the other players the other half. They circulate to find the player whose card matches theirs.

Christmas Tree Mixer

Like the preceding mixer, but with green Christmas trees as the cut card.

Famous Couples

Particularly for dance icebreakers to match partners of the opposite sex, paired slips are made up with the names of famous couples— "Antony" and "Cleopatra," "Romeo" and "Juliet," or more recent couples. Boys receive the male names and girls the female names. At a signal, each person circulates to find his or her partner for the next dance. With a very large group, there might be several paired slips for each famous couple, to help players locate their partners more easily.

Go-Together Words

Paired slips may also be made up using words which commonly go together, such as "Bacon" and "Eggs," or opposites, like "Night" and "Day." It is easy to make up long lists of such paired words, for matching slips.

Dance Icebreakers

There are many other simple stunts or icebreakers which can be used to help participants take partners at a dance or party. Some good examples follow.

Multiplication Dance
Semiactive; 20–100 players

The dance floor is cleared, and one couple is designated to begin dancing when the music starts. After a moment or two, the music stops, and the first couple separates. Each of them invites a new partner to dance from the sidelines, so two couples are out on the floor. This is repeated several times, with the number of dancers doubling each time until all the participants are dancing.

Backward Choice
Semiactive; 20–100 players

Boys and girls, or men and women, form two separate lines at opposite sides of the room, facing away from each other. As the music begins, they begin walking slowly backward toward each other. When they make contact, by bumping into a person of the opposite sex, they become partners with this person for the next game or dance.

Color and Clothing
Semiactive; 20–100 players

As the leader looks around the room, she notes what people are wearing. When the music stops, she makes sure that everyone is on the sidelines. Then she announces, "All boys (or men) in brown slacks, please invite a new partner to dance." A few moments later, she asks those couples to remain on the floor and says, "All girls (or women) in pink dresses, please invite a fellow to dance." So it goes, naming a new article of clothing, or possibly glasses, jewelry, beards, moustaches, or braids, until all the dancers are out on the floor.

Conversation Mixer
Semiactive; 20–100 players

This is a variation of the old Paul Jones mixer, in which girls form a circle on the inside (hands joined, facing out) while boys join hands in a circle around them (facing in). At a signal, music plays and they all start to walk to their right, girls going clockwise and boys counterclockwise. When the music stops, everyone is facing a new partner. The leader assigns a topic of conversation—preferably a timely or humorous one—and everyone must talk for a minute or two on this topic. The music plays and they dance together for a few moments. The entire "Conversation Mixer" is usually repeated several times, each time with new partners and new topics of conversation.

Broom Mixer
Semiactive; 20–100 players

As the dance begins, everyone is dancing with a partner, except one person who dances with a broom. After a few moments, that person presses the end of the broom to the floor, puts his foot against it, and snaps the other end down sharply, making a loud noise. At this signal, all the dancers quickly change partners, while the person who had the broom makes sure to find a new partner. When everyone else is paired off again, a new person is left without a partner. This person picks up the broom and dances with it, and the mixer is repeated several times.

Elimination Dances

These are simple contests which lend excitement to the party, and which gradually eliminate each of the couples in turn until only one couple remains. As in many elimination contests, a simple, inexpensive prize may be given to the winning couple, although this is not essential.

Broom Dance Elimination
Active; 20–100 players

As all the couples begin dancing, one of them is given a broom. They must try to give it to another couple as quickly as possible, and the dancing continues with the broom passing from couple to couple. Suddenly the music stops, and the couple holding the broom is eliminated. This is repeated again and again, usually with the music and action growing faster and faster, until only one couple remains—the winner. The leader should stress that each dancer must remain with his or her partner rather than chase other couples around the floor with the broom, and that it is necessary to accept the broom when it is offered to you. Also, if there is a very large crowd of dancers, it is a good idea to use two or three brooms to begin with, or it will take much too long to eliminate all the dancers.

Balloon Buster
Active; 20–100 players

Each couple is given an inflated balloon and a piece of string. The balloon is tied to the foot of one of the partners, so it trails behind by about a foot. As the couples dance, they try to maneuver close enough to other couples so that they can stamp on their balloons and break them. At the same time, they try to avoid other couples trying to break *their* balloon. The couples may not separate or stop dancing, and the contest continues until only one couple—the winner—remains with an unburst balloon.

Orange Dance
Active; 20–100 players

Each couple taking part in the contest is given an orange. As the music begins, they must place their orange between their foreheads and hold it there by pressing their heads forward. They may not touch it with their hands, once it is in place. They continue to dance with their partners, and whenever a couple drops its orange, it is eliminated. To add excitement to the dance, the music is at first played slowly, but gradually speeds up until it is very lively. Varied dance rhythms—Latin, rock-and-roll, polka, or waltz—may also be played and dancers required to dance to these, which makes keeping the orange in place all the harder.

Last Couple Stoop
Active; 20–100 players

After doing social dancing for a time, this elimination dance is a welcome novelty. Boys form a large circle around the outside of the room facing to the right (clockwise). Just inside that circle, girls form a circle facing left (counterclockwise). As the music plays, each person walks forward in single file, away from his or her partner. Suddenly, the music stops, and each person must quickly rush toward his or her partner, take both hands, and quickly squat. The last couple to complete the action is eliminated. Then the circles are re-formed and the action is repeated. The contest continues until only the winning couple remains.

Statues
Semi-active; 20–100 players

A very simple elimination dance, in which every couple dances around the floor and, when the music stops suddenly, must "freeze" and remain motionless. Any couple moving, even slightly, is eliminated, and the action is repeated until only one couple remains—the winner.

Silly Statues
Active; 20–100 players

As a variation of the preceding contest, when the music stops, the leader calls out, "Silly statues!" and each couple must freeze in the most extreme and unusual position it can think of. Quickly, one or two judges selected by the leader survey the floor and agree on the couple that has taken the most unusual pose. They select this couple as the winner.

Novelty Stunts and Contests

These are unusual, humorous stunts and contests which are chiefly suitable for children at parties or game sessions, although they may also be done by teenagers and adults. They are usually quite easy to teach, and may involve different groupings of players—individuals, teams, or *en masse*.

Shoe Hunt
Semiactive; 8–20 players

Each child takes off both shoes, and puts them in a large cardboard box in the center of the room. As the children form a large circle around the box, the leader mixes the shoes up thoroughly. At a signal, all the children run forward, find their own shoes, and put them on. The first player to come to the leader with his or her shoes on and fastened (tied or buckled), wins the game. For younger children, the requirement of tying laces may be waived.

Peanut Hunt
Semiactive; 8–25 players

The leader hides unshelled peanuts in every possible nook or corner of the room, behind curtains, under furniture, etc. At a signal, each child sets out in search of the hidden peanuts, collecting them in a dish or pan. Players may hunt as individuals, or divided up into small teams. After eight or ten minutes, the search is ended, and the player or team with the most peanuts is the winner. This game may also be played outdoors, by scattering peanuts over a playground or other play area.

How Many Beans?
Quiet; unlimited

Before the event, the leader fills a large glass bottle or other transparent container with beans, marbles, or large pebbles. Only the leader knows exactly how many are in the bottle. Children have a chance to look carefully at the container; they then write their estimates of the number of beans or other objects on a sheet of paper. When every player has turned his or her estimate in (this may be done at any time during the party or game session), the leader announces the correct number. The child with the closest guess is the winner and is awarded an appropriate prize—such as a handful of beans.

Baby Picture Contest
Quiet; 5–15 players

Each child is asked to bring a picture of himself or herself as a baby to the party or game session. The pictures are numbered and put up on display. When the game is played, children try to guess the subject of each picture, writing down the names of the other players and putting the number of the correct picture next to each name. After a few minutes the leader collects the lists, and the player who has succeeded in identifying the most baby photographs is the winner.

Tangled Teams
Active; 12–20 players

The group divides into two teams. One player is selected to be "It" for each team. He goes to the other team (they are holding hands in a circle) and, at a signal, begins to "tangle" them. This is done by winding them up, raising arms over heads, having them duck under arms and legs, and so forth, to make the most complicated tangle possible—still holding hands. After about two minutes, they should be thoroughly snarled. Each "It" then goes back to his own group and, at a signal, begins to untangle his teammates, who are still holding hands firmly. The first "It" to restore his group to the original circle wins.

Reuben and Rachel
Active; 10–20 players

Two players, a boy and a girl, are chosen to be Reuben and Rachel. They stand in the center of a circle formed by the other players, whose hands are joined. To begin, Reuben is blindfolded. He calls out, "Rachel," and she must answer immediately, "Here, Reuben." Reuben tries to catch and tag Rachel. If he succeeds, they reverse roles, Rachel being blindfolded and trying to catch Reuben. The two players should keep calling and answering each other rapidly, to make it possible for the blindfolded player to locate the other.

Rattler
Active; 10–20 players

This is just like "Reuben and Rachel," except that the two players do not call out to each other. Instead the player being pursued shakes a tin can with pebbles in it, and the blindfolded player chases the rattling noise.

Novelty Games

These are games using simple items that are usually available around a home, such as beans, potatoes, bottle tops, and tin cans. They may be played as separate contests at a party, or as part of a "carnival" or game session in which players are on teams and pile up scores, competing against each other.

Potato-Spearing Contest
Semiactive; 4 or more players

Each player is given a large uncooked potato and a fork. At a signal, players throw their potatoes into the air and try to spear them with a fork as they come down, getting one point for each successful spearing. This game is not for very young children, and even older ones should stand a few feet apart to make sure they do not spear one another instead of the potato.

Pie-Eating Contest
Semiactive; 4 or more players

Children kneel on the floor in a circle, with hands behind their backs. A paper plate with a section of a pie is placed on the floor in front of each contestant. On signal, the boys and girls lean forward and eat the pie as quickly as they can. The first child to finish the pie and pick up the empty paper plate with his teeth is the winner. Newspapers should be spread carefully over the floor, since the game is a messy one—especially if cherry or blueberry pies are used.

Community Sneeze
Quiet; unlimited

An unusual novelty stunt, in which all the players stand or sit facing the leader. He divides them into three separate groups, indicating the sections with his hand. He then has the group on the left practice saying, and then shouting, the word "Hishee." The middle group practices the word "Hashee," and the other group does the word "Hoshee." Then, on signal, all three groups shout their word at once. The result sounds very much like a giant sneeze. The leader smiles and says, "Bless you!"

Candle Shootout
Quiet; 4 or more players

A lighted candle is put on a plate or tray about six or eight feet away from a line of players. Boys and girls on the shooting line take turns in trying to shoot out the flame with a water pistol. When a player succeeds, he wins one point, and the candle is relighted for the next player. The game may also be played by setting up several lit candles in a row, with a point given for each candle shot out with only a single pistol-load of water. This contest must be played outdoors, or in a place that will not be damaged by the water. Also, because of the open flame, adults should supervise it carefully.

Hammer Contest
Active; 4 or more players

A very popular contest at carnivals or play days! The game leader drives nails into a long piece of softwood lumber, just far enough to secure them. Each contestant takes a turn trying to drive his nail all the way into the wood. The player who can do this with the fewest hammer blows is the winner. Or the leader can give a set number of blows to children according to age level (five to seven-year-olds have fifteen chances, eight to ten-year-olds ten chances), with any child driving the nail within his limit considered a winner.

Speed Shaving
Quiet; 4 or more players

Players divide into teams of two. Using a shaving foam dispenser, one player covers the lower part of his partner's face with foamy cream. Then, with a wooden tongue depressor or plastic spoon, he begins to shave his partner's face clean. The action is then repeated with the other partner doing the shaving. The first team to complete the entire action is the winner.

Apple-Ducking Contest
Semiactive; 6–15 players

Children gather around a large tub of water, in which several apples are floating. They compete to get one of the floating apples out of the water without using their hands. If all the children duck at the same time, the winner is the first to get an apple. If they take turns, they should be timed with a watch with a second hand, to see who gets the winning time. If stems are left on the apples, players may simply be able to lift them out with their teeth. If stems are removed, they usually have to duck their heads right into the water and bite the apples to get them out. Keep plenty of paper towels and a mop on hand to dry up after this one.

Stepping-Stone Race
Active; 8–20 players

Boys and girls line up behind a starting line about fifteen feet away from a turning line. Each player has two shirt cardboards or other pieces of cardboard; these are the "stepping stones." At a signal, each player must travel to the turning line and back, stepping *only* on the cardboard. This is done by stepping forward on one piece of cardboard, then moving the rear one forward to step on it, and so on. The contest may be played as a competition between several players, or as a relay race among several teams.

Cracker Whistle Contest
Semiactive; 8–20 players

Players divide into two or more relay teams and line up behind a starting line. About fifteen feet in front of each team is a chair. At the signal, the first person on each team runs to his or her chair, sits down, is given two salted soda crackers, and eats the crackers. He or she must then whistle audibly (hard to do with a mouth full of half-chewed crackers), run back to his or her line and touch the next player. The first team to complete the action is the winner.

Hat and Coat Relay
Active; 8–20 players

Players divide into two or more equal teams. Each team is given a hat and coat. At a signal, each first player runs forward to a turning line and puts on the hat and coat, completely buttoning the latter. He or she then runs back to his line, takes the hat and coat off, and hands them to the next player. This action is repeated until one team wins by having all its players complete it.

Fanning Football
Active; 10–30 players

Somewhat like "Balloon Fanning." Goal lines are marked near opposite ends of a room, and two teams of children stand in positions spaced around between the goal markers. Each boy or girl has a shirt cardboard (the fan). A ping-pong ball (the football) is thrown into the center of the room. Using their cardboards as fans, players try to move the ball from teammate to teammate toward the opposite goal. The ball may only be fanned, not hit directly, and when it goes through the goal markers (two chairs, a yard apart) the scoring team gets six points. Should a player hit the ball by mistake, his or her team is penalized one point. A touchdown scored by a hit does not count. After several minutes of play, the team with the higher score wins. To prevent children crowding around the "football," each child may move only three feet from his starting position.

Novelty Olympics

There are also many other novelty contests which can be played within a comparatively small space where action must be kept to a minimum. The following scaled-down Olympic contests do not measure real athletic skill, of course, but children—or other age groups—will enjoy them.

Discus Throw

Players are given paper plates and line up at one end of the room. A small circle is marked off at the other end. The leader shows how to throw a discus, throwing the plate with a sideways motion. Each player is then given three tries to throw his or her plate into the circle. The contestant with the best score—or the one who comes closest—is the winner.

Reverse Bull's-Eye

Players stand on a line, holding a mirror, with their backs to a large hoop that has been hung from a ceiling fixture, beam, or door frame. Using the mirror to take aim, they take turns in throwing a ping-pong ball or beanbag back over their shoulders toward the hoop. Each player has five tries, and for every throw that goes through the hoop, he gets a point. The player or team with the most points wins the event.

Broad Jump

The players line up, and each one smiles as broadly as he or she can. The leader measures the width of each smile with a ruler or tape measure. The boy or girl with the broadest grin wins the event.

Mile Walk

Players line up at one end of the room. At a signal, they race across the room and back by placing the heel of one foot against the toe of the other at every step. The first player to get to the turning line and back wins.

High Jump

Each contestant takes a turn at taking a deep breath and then whistling a long, high note. The whistle is timed, and the contestant who holds a note for the longest time is the high jump champion.

High Dive

Each player is given ten corks. A glass half full of water is placed on the floor in front of him. With his arm outstretched at shoulder height, he tries to drop the corks one at a time into the glass. The boy or girl who manages to get the most corks into the water becomes the winner of the high dive contest.

Other Tests of Accuracy

In addition to the preceding stunts, many other simple games may be improvised using home equipment, such as the following: (1) throwing beans, one at a time, into a small aluminum plate floating in a large tub of water; (2) bouncing ping-pong balls or tennis balls so they land in a plastic pail; (3) tossing beanbags at a board with numbered holes (each hole is given a specific value, and the total score adds up the values for the holes the beanbags go through); (4) tossing quoits at an upright board with nails driven in at an angle (each nail has a value, and a score is made when a quoit hangs on a nail); (5) throwing darts (preferably suction-tipped) at a target; (6) "Landing on the Carrier" (throwing paper airplanes so they come as close as possible to a "carrier" chalked on the floor); (7) "Ring the Bell" (throwing a rubber ball at a bell hung at eye level).

Mental and Word Games and Puzzles

These include group games based on word knowledge, as well as puzzles, tricks, and other contests featuring mental agility, and paper-and-pencil games involving drawing. For the most part they are suited to teen-agers and adults, although children are able to play many of them. None of them, obviously, is physically demanding, and they are best played in groups of four to twenty.

Coffeepot

A player leaves the room while the others pick a secret verb. The player returns and tries to find out what the secret verb is, by asking questions that may be answered only by "Yes," "No," or "Sometimes." When he asks questions, he must substitute the word "coffeepot" for the verb. For example: "Do you coffeepot out of doors?" "Can you coffeepot at any age?" or "Is it hard to coffeepot?" When he has a good idea of the word, he may take a guess at it. If he is right, the last person to answer a question becomes "It," and the game begins again. If not, he is allowed two more tries. If the third guess is wrong, he is told the word, and may then select the next player to be "It."

Animal, Vegetable, or Mineral

In this game, one person goes out of the room while the others think of some real or fictional person, object, place, or thing. When "It" returns, he is given the clue that the group has thought of something that is either animal, vegetable, or mineral (or possibly a combination of these). A person, an animal, or anything made of animal substance would be classified as animal, for example. An automobile might be classified as all three, in that it might include animal (leather seat covers), vegetable (rubber floor mat), and mineral (steel body).

"It" asks as many questions as he needs to identify the thing they have in mind. His first questions should establish major categories and make clear whether or not it is a real or fictional person or thing, a single object or a class of objects, in the past or present, etc. Since this game may drag on if the choice is a very difficult one, it may be wise to set a time limit.

Twenty Questions

This is very much like the preceding game, except that one player is chosen to think of a person or object that is also familiar to the other players. The entire group tries to guess it, asking questions one at a time which must be answered by only "Yes," "No," or "Sometimes." They are allowed twenty questions to do this, and should begin by establishing broad categories (human, alive or dead, male or female). When this has been done, they can try to guess the actual answer. If the subject is named within the twenty-question limit, the person who guessed it begins a new game by thinking of another subject.

Buzz

Here's a lively and somewhat nerve-wracking game, based on quick thinking. The group sits in a circle. The first player calls out the number *one*, the next *two*, and so on. The only catch is that when *seven* is reached (or multiples of seven, or numbers containing seven, like 14, 17, 21, or 27), the player involved must quickly stand and say *Buzz*. If he makes a mistake, he is given the first letter of *Buzz* (B), and the game is started from the beginning. When a person is given all four letters (B-u-z-z), he is eliminated. A skillful group may go up to the hundreds, but this is rare.

A variation of this is "Fizz," a word which is used whenever *five* or a multiple of *five* appears. The game may also be played as "Fizz-Buzz," which combines the two games.

Observation

About fifteen or twenty small household objects are placed on a table. They may include such items as a spoon, knife, pencil, sneaker, pitcher, fan, ash tray, or pipe. Players all stand around the table for two or three minutes and try to memorize the objects. Then they are covered with a sheet, and the players try to write down as many as they can remember. After five minutes time is called, and the lists are turned over to the leader. The contestant who has correctly remembered the greatest number of objects is the winner.

Sense of Touch

This is very much like "Observation," except that the objects are placed in a large paper bag or sack. In turn, each of the players puts his hand into the sack and is permitted to explore its contents for a minute or two. All players are given five minutes to write down the objects hidden inside. Then the lists are compared, and the player with the best sense of touch—and keenest memory—is the winner, having identified the greatest number of correct objects.

Sense of Smell

Here, the sense tested is smell. The leader places a number of substances, each with a distinctive odor, in small paper cups on the table. They might include chopped onion, mustard, wine, sliced apple, and charred wood. Players are blindfolded and brought into the room one at a time. Each player is permitted to sniff each substance for a moment or two and then must try to identify it. A score of correct answers is kept for each contestant. When the game is over, the player—or team—with the highest score wins.

Advertising Slogans

Have one or two people help in compiling a list of well-known advertising phrases or slogans, taking them from television commercials or magazines. The group is divided into two teams. The leader calls out a slogan, and the first player to call back the name of the correct product wins a point for his team. Or the game may be played with the first player of one team given the chance to answer (if he cannot, his opponent may), and then the first

player of the opposing team given a turn, and so on down the line.

Picture Charades

Players divide into teams of at least five or six each. Each team is given a pencil and a pad of paper. It selects an "artist." The artist from each team goes up to the leader (who has prepared a list of titles, famous names, or proverbs). The leader shows them all the first title or other phrase. They hurry back to their groups, and, without saying a word (although they may shake their heads or nod, to indicate "hot" or "cold"), they draw a picture to get the idea across. The group members keep guessing until they have the solution. The first team to get it has its "artist" run up, and the leader gives his or her team one point. The game is continued several times, until each player has been an "artist."

Progressive Pictures

Each player is given a sheet of paper and a pencil. She begins by drawing a head (any age, either sex) at the top of the paper. She then folds the sheet so that the head is hidden, but a bit of the neck still shows. At a signal, all the players pass their folded sheets to the next player on the right. They then draw the upper part of the body down to the waist, including the arms. This is folded and passed to the right. The total drawing is completed in two more stages (to the knees and then to the feet). The drawings are then unfolded and displayed. The varied drawing styles, sizes, clothing, and mixed genders are bound to make the "Progressive Pictures" hilarious, and appreciated by all!

Word Games

Many popular mental games are based on spelling, word discovery, or deciphering skills. Here are several.

Scrambled Holiday Words

At any holiday party, the leader may prepare a set of cards on which he has printed, in large letters, a particular word or phrase commonly attached to that holiday. One by one, he holds up the cards, and the players, in teams,

try to identify the words or phrases. The catch? The letters are scrambled, like this:

Halloween Words

bogsnil (goblins)	chitw (witch)
skopos (spooks)	raertikotrtc (trick
nukpmip (pumpkin)	or treat)

Christmas Words

gamern (manger)
fitsg (gifts)
galens (angels)
Linsegnitht (Silent Night)
Luassacant (Santa Claus)

Depending on the group, these may be scrambled so they are more or less easy to decipher. Also, phrases with two or more words may have the words kept separate, so they are easier. Thus, Santa Claus could be: Tasan Sluac.

Super Brain

A somewhat similar word game is one in which the group divides into small teams, each with a pencil and paper. The leader gives them a two-word combination, each with five letters, like "super brain.' Each team must then make up a list of as many four- or five-letter words from the letters in "super brain" as it can within ten minutes. The team with the greatest number of correct words at the end wins.

Examples: brine   spear   pear   pain
            spare   raise   barn   rain

Hidden Proverbs

One player leaves the room while the others agree on a well-known proverb or popular saying. The player comes back and tries to guess the proverb by asking the other players in turn a series of questions. In their responses, they must each use a word of the proverb. The answer to the first question must contain in it the first word of the proverb. The answer to the next must contain the second word of the proverb, and so on. Although the players try to conceal these words as cleverly as possible, the player who went out is given three chances to guess the proverb—and he usually can do it! Then, the player who gave the last clue becomes "It" and the game starts again.

Silly Milly

The leader begins by telling the other players, "I'm Silly Milly. I'm odd and queer, but not peculiar." The others try to guess why these words were used to describe Silly Milly, and what other things she would like, or not like. The leader gives some additional clues: "I like floors, but not ceilings." "I like apples, but not oranges." The secret is that Silly Milly likes any word that contains a double letter, and dislikes all other words. As the others keep guessing, some of them begin to guess the secret and identify Milly's likes and dislikes. However, they do not give it away, and the others keep trying to figure out the puzzle. Finally, it is explained to all. There is no winner or loser in this game—just the fun of trying to figure out a real brain-teaser.

Magic Stunts and Tricks

There are many so-called magic puzzles and tricks which both children and adults enjoy, not the elaborate tricks that real performers put on, but simple little novelties requiring only a moment's preparation. These include: (a) humorous stunts which may involve a play on words; (b) so-called mind-reading activities, based on prearrangement; (c) simple manipulation of cards, coins, or other props; and (d) paper-and-pencil puzzles, mathematical tricks, and stunts. Several of these follow.

The Amazing Nut

One person boasts to the others that he will show them something they have never seen before, and will never see again. When they indicate loud disbelief, he cracks a peanut, shows them the nut—which they've never seen before—and eats it. They'll never see it again.

Poke Your Foot

The same person holds up a key ring and states that he can poke his foot—shoe and all—through it. Not likely? When others confess they don't see how it can be done, he promptly puts his forefinger through the key ring and pokes his foot—to a chorus of groans.

Slim Jim

The leader announces to the others that he is so slim that he can actually slide himself under a closed door. When the others challenge him, he says, "All right, I'll do it! I'll slide myself under the door." He has the others go into the next room. Then he prints the word "myself" in big letters on a sheet of paper, and slides it under the closed door. When they see it, there are loud hoots—but the other players must admit he did what he said he would!

Hypnotized Knee

The leader announces that he can hypnotize anyone's knee so it cannot be lifted. When one of the other players doubts this, he shows them how it is done. He has that player stand against a wall, with his right side touching the wall (shoulder, arm, hip, knee, foot—all must be as close as possible). Then the leader kneels and pronounces a "magic" incantation over the left knee. He rises and says, "It's hypnotized! You cannot lift it." When the player tries to lift it, he finds he cannot without losing his balance and falling over. Try it!

In Cahoots

In this "magic" stunt, one person goes out of the group. The players then select some object in the room. "It" comes back in. The leader of the group points to one object after another. When he comes to the right one, "It" promptly says, "That's it." The secret? The leader and "It" have previously agreed that the correct object would be the first one named after any piece of furniture with legs. Thus, if the correct object was to be a *lamp,* the leader would point to: a rug, a picture, a window, a *chair*—and then the *lamp.*

Okay, All Right, Ready

In a similar stunt, three persons are chosen to stand facing the group. One of them is designated as the secret one who must be identified, while "It" is out of the room. The leader calls "It" to come in, and goes out of the room himself—so that no one can accuse him of giving the plot away. Yet, when "It" comes in, he promptly points at the right person. How? The secret is in the word the leader used to call him in. It was either, "okay," "all right," or "ready." Reading from left to right, the first letters of these spell "oar," a convenient memory clue. If the word was "okay," the secret person was the first on the left; if "all right," the middle person; if "ready," the one on the right.

Pick the Card

This is another "magic" stunt. The leader deals out nine cards, in three rows of three each, as "It" goes out. The group selects one card, which "It" must then identify when he returns. The leader points to each card in turn, without saying a word. When he points to the correct one, "It" says, "That's it!" The secret is that when the leader points to the very first card, he touches it on one of nine spots, which indicates which card (upper left, upper middle, upper right, etc.) is the correct one (Figure 10–1).

FIGURE 10–1

Head Through a Card

Not "magic"—and quite different from "poking" your foot through a ring—is this one. You offer to put your head through a small calling card. When the scoffing is over, and you've assured the others that you are really going to do it, you take a scissors and cut the card from alternate sides as shown (Figure 10–2). When you've gently unfolded it, it will open up to a sizable paper circlet that you can put your head through.

FIGURE 10–2

Turn the Glasses Over

Here's a puzzler involving three drinking glasses, which are placed on the table in a row. The first is right side up, the second upside down, and the third right side up. The task is to turn all three glasses so they are upside down, in *three moves*. Each move consists of turning two glasses over at one time but you can't turn the same two glasses over more than once. How does it work? First, turn over the second and third glasses. Then turn over the first and third glasses. Finally, turn over the second and third glasses again— and you'll have them all upside down!

FIGURE 10–3

There are hundreds of mathematical puzzles involving diagrams, number manipulations, and simple calculations. Here are a few:

Which Bills

A man bought an overcoat for $103. He paid for it with eight bills—but they were *not* five twenty-dollar bills and three one-dollar bills, which would be the easy answer. In fact, there were *no* one-dollar bills used at all. What were they? The answer: a fifty-dollar bill, two twenty-dollar bills, a five-dollar bill, and four two-dollar bills.

Amazing Nines

Ask the group to take any three-digit number; if they will reverse it, and then subtract the lesser from the greater number, you will tell them what the middle digit will be—nine. Try it! For example, 678, when reversed, becomes 876. Subtract one from the other and the answer is 198.

The Mysterious Number

When you add 100 to a certain number, the total is actually more than if you multiply the number by 100. What is this mysterious number? The answer—one.

Your Age, Madam!

The magician asks for a volunteer from the audience. A woman comes forward. He tells her that he can guess her age by using a secret magic formula. He gives her a piece of paper and a pencil and asks her to do the following calculation:

Her age: 30
Multiply by 3: 90
Add 6: 96
Divide by 3: 32

He then asks her for the last number. She tells him, and mentally he subtracts 2, and tells her the correct age: 30. It doesn't matter what the original number is; if you carry out the calculation and subtract 2, the answer will be right!

TABLE AND EQUIPMENT GAMES

There are many useful table games involving homemade or specially built pieces of equipment. These are especially suited for small groups of participants, two or three at a time, in a game room, a lounge, or even in a hospital ward where patients may not move from their beds or wheelchairs. One very popular form of fun in such settings is playing cards, and it is extremely useful for a recreation leader to know a variety of simple card games, such as solitaire and its variations, casino, the various forms of rummy, concentration, war, slapjack, old maid, hearts, fan tan, and others which are not basically gambling games. There are several good collections of card games.

Board games are another good kind of intriguing pastime for small groups or twosomes. Such games as chess, checkers, Monopoly, Chinese checkers, Parcheesi, backgammon, Scrabble, and some of the more recently invented games, such as Clue or Detective, hold appeal for young and old.

Essentially, these are mental games, involving a knowledge of strategy and alertness. Other kinds of equipment games, such as Nok Hockey (a miniature form of hockey played within a boxlike frame), Skittles (a game using a spinning top which knocks down pins within a box frame), Puff Billiards (a circular-table game in which players squeeze rubber bulbs to shoot a cork ball into opponents' goal pockets), and Labyrinth (a Swedish game in which a steel ball must be passed along a numbered route without falling into holes along the way) are becoming increasingly popular. These involve a high degree of dexterity, and, in most cases, excitement and a great amount of rollicking laughter.

ORGANIZING THE GAME ROOM OR LOUNGE

A game room or lounge is an area set aside for activities such as party games, table games, paper and pencil games, board games, and the like. In an armed forces center, or recreation center serving young adults, it may also involve informal dancing, music, refreshments, or other social activities. When it caters to children and youth, it should be based on a variety of different games: (a) games such as Nok Hockey, involving noisy competition; (b) quiet two-player games such as checkers, cards, chess, or dominoes; (c) games requiring a larger area, like table tennis, billiards, or table shuffle-board; and (d) games involving targets and longer distances, like horseshoes or duckpins. In organizing the room and its program, the following guides are helpful:

1. Tables and chairs should be grouped together according to type, separating quiet games from the noisy or more vigorous ones.
2. If possible, particularly when children with a wide age spread are using the game room, equipment for each major age grouping should be placed in a separate section of the room, so that children have a feeling of ''our'' section and do not squabble about the use of equipment.
3. Make the room attractive by displaying posters, tournament charts, pictures of game room activities and sports events, and even mimeographed or hand-printed newspapers placed on the bulletin board.
4. Organize the program so that each group has some individual attention and guidance during the session; this can best be done if organized games for each age group are not taking place at the same time.
5. Special events, such as demonstrations or tournaments, should be used to increase interest in game participation on each age level. Tournaments of short duration, lasting for a single session or possibly one week, are often more useful and manageable than longer tournaments. For greatest interest, these should be of many types, such as checkers or chess tournaments, Nok Hockey, table tennis, top spinning, billiards—or almost any sort of game that can be played within a fairly short span of time and result in a definite winner.

PLANNING PARTIES AND OTHER SPECIAL EVENTS

Social games, mixers, stunts, and other novelty activities are useful in planning parties and other special events. Many organized recreation programs conduct community-wide celebrations, festivals, play-days, exhibitions, demonstrations, trips, and outings. Summer playground programs may include such events as art fairs, bicycle rodeos, fishing contests, hobby shows, cookouts, aquatic meetings, stunt nights, and similar special programs.

Of all of these, parties are perhaps the most useful. Every age level enjoys parties—either to celebrate holidays, birthdays, special themes, or simply to have fun in an informal way. Parties may be extremely casual, or may involve complex planning and elaborate provision for decorations, refreshments, and program activities that fit a specific subject or theme.

In general, the process of planning any special event includes the following tasks:

Program.   Careful planning of the program is essential to every special event. The program includes the games, music, dancing, entertainment, presentations, talks, films, or other activities that people will take part in. Planning a program involves handling any necessary arrangements, such as locating a film projector or record player, hiring an orchestra, selecting prizes, or securing other needed materials or leaders.

Facilities.   Arrangements must be made to secure the space, equipment, and other major items needed for an event, including rooms, halls, picnic grounds, buses, parking areas, coat rooms, and permits to carry on activities.

Publicity and Invitations.   A key element in the success of any event is making sure that people know about it and will attend. Thus, all publicity—whether it be announcements, posters, fliers, or mailed invitations—is critical. Sometimes the function of creating publicity is directly attached to the job of selling tickets. Promotional materials can be sent out with tickets, or those who sell tickets can be responsible for spreading the word as well.

Decorations.   Decorations add to the spirit and enhance the chances for success of most parties and therefore should be chosen in a creative and imaginative way. Decorations are not always involved in special events, however; certain events may have no decorations at all.

Refreshments.   Refreshments also add to the enjoyment of participants at special events. Like decorations, they may be used to express the theme of a party and to promote its special quality. Refreshments may in some situations be sold; selling them is a major money-raising activity for many organizations.

Financial Management.   At most special events, other than the simplest, home-based parties, financial management is an important responsibility. Planning for the payment of the costs of printing fliers and tickets, renting a hall, buying food and drink, and hiring a band or entertainers with income from ticket sales, refreshment sales, raffles, auctions, game booths, gift item sales, or other sources is a critical management function.

Crowd Control and Safety.   For large carnivals, picnics, or shows, it is necessary to make careful arrangements concerning the assignment of areas or booths and the maintenance of access and exit routes. Police or paid guards should be on hand to protect the safety of participants and the operation of the event itself. Arrangements also should be made to promote safety and to provide medical care or first aid if necessary.

Clean-up.   Cleaning up must be carefully planned for in most medium- or large-sized events. Dismantling booths, removing garbage and debris, and restoring a hall or outdoor area to its original state are not glamorous responsibilities, but they must be organized and carried out effectively.

Follow-up.   When the curtain has come down, the show is not really over. Any special event should be carefully evaluated, in order to determine strengths and weaknesses and the degree of success attained. Recommendations must be made for improving possible future events of the same type. Reports must be written and filed or submitted. Thank-you letters should be sent to those who assisted or contributed to the program, and postevent publicity in the form of news releases should be sent out.[1]

Particularly for larger or more ambitious programs, it is advisable to form a steering or planning committee, and to assign each important responsibility to *one* committee member. If it is a really huge event, each committee member might also be assisted by a smaller subcommittee—to sell tickets, for example, or to prepare refreshments. If the event is relatively small and simple, each committee member might have two or three responsibilities. However, each responsibility should be clearly assigned to one person, so that everyone knows who is in charge of it.

Examples of Theme Parties

In carrying out specific theme parties, which might be done in a recreation center, Golden Age Club, or other setting, program activities should be carefully chosen to fit the subject. Three popular party themes for the mid-winter season are: Patriotic Party (held in February, at the time of Washington's and Lincoln's Birthdays), Valentine's Day Party (February 14), and St. Patrick's Day Party (March 17). Examples of suitable games and mixers for each of these parties follow.

Patriotic Party

The theme of patriotism should be illustrated by decorations, flags, red-white-and-blue bunting, and cherry tree and log cabin decorations. Patriotic music would be played, and games would include:

Cherry Tree Relay

Players line up in equal teams. With cardboard hatchets, each first player runs up to a "cherry tree" (which may be improvised by placing cranberries or other small canned fruit on a cut sapling). He takes a "cherry" and, holding it on his hatchet, runs back to his team. The action is continued until one team, the winner, is finished.

Log Cabin Building

Guests divide into small teams. Each team is given a milk bottle and a box of wooden matches. Players take turns in placing the matches, one at a time, on the bottles, trying to build a "log cabin" that is as high as possible. After ten minutes, a whistle is blown, and the team that has the highest structure wins.

Scrambled Presidents

The leader holds up placards on which the names of presidents have been painted with the letters "scrambled." Thus—NNLIOCL (Lincoln) or EGIDOLOC (Coolidge). The guests are divided into teams, and must either guess the correct name as in a spelling bee, with the first player of each team taking a turn, or with the first player who guesses the name ringing a bell and then identifying it. Each correct answer is a point scored for the player's team.

"Honest Abe" Quiz

In this contest, the guests divide into teams. The leader asks a series of questions, each of which must be answered by a word containing the syllable that *sounds like* "Abe" (Although it need not be spelled this way). Examples:

"What Abe sends a message?"	Cable
"What Abe do you find at the race track?"	Stable
"What Abe is the littlest of all?"	Baby
"What Abe do you find on a tin can?"	Label
"What Abe is a lady's name?"	Mabel

Valentine's Day Party

Here's a party with the popular theme of romance. Decorations and refreshments include pink streamers, hearts, proverbs about love, red jello or ice cream in heart-shaped molds, and pink lemonade. Favorite songs like "Let Me Call You Sweetheart" or other old-time love songs would be played or sung. Games and mixers include:

Matching Partners Mixer

To take partners for social dancing or other activities each guest is given a red heart with a name on it. The names represent "famous couples." The boy with "Julius Caesar" must find the girl with "Cleopatra," the boy with "Napoleon" must find "Josephine," etc.

Heart Hunt

Before guests arrive, hide numbered hearts throughout room or hall where party is to be held—under chairs, behind curtains, in flower pots. There should be at least five hearts for each number, and as many numbers as there will be guests. At a signal, they are asked to hunt for hearts, the object being to see which player can first collect five hearts bearing the same number. To do this, they will also have to circulate around and "swap" hearts with each other. The first player to have five hearts with the same number is the winner. This may also be done in couples.

Famous Proposals

Guests divide into couples. Each person is given the name of a famous historical figure on a slip of paper. One couple then performs: the boy must propose to the girl in the style of *his* character and she must reply in the style of hers. Thus, he might propose as "Genghis Khan" or "King Henry the Eighth," and she might reply as "Joan of Arc" or "Florence Nightingale." After the dialogue has gone on for a few minutes, the others try to guess who they are.

St. Patrick's Day Party

Here, of course, invitation, decorations, and food all reflect typical Irish customs; the shamrock is widely displayed and the color green appears wherever possible. Irish songs like "McNamara's Band" or "Did Your Mother Come From Ireland?' may be sung. Irish jigs may be played—and if anyone can teach the step, others may enjoy trying it. Games and mixers include:

Shillelagh Duel

Three boys stand in a circle. Brown paper bags are put on their heads, and they are given shillelaghs (rolled up newspapers, in this case). They are then blindfolded and, at a signal, try to knock the brown paper bags off each other's heads. To help them locate each other, each one must keep calling out his own name: "Pat," "Mike," and "Kevin." This slapstick stunt provides informal fun and no one will be hurt.

Irish Potato Race

Just like a regular potato race, but with popular Irish tunes playing in the background, and with players scooping up potatoes using green cardboard shamrocks instead of large spoons. This is played as a relay.

Drawing the Pig

Otherwise known as "Blind Pig." Each player is given a large sheet of drawing paper and green crayon. The lights are turned out (or several players at a time are blindfolded), and while unable to see, must draw a pig smoking a little clay pipe and trying to scramble over a stile. When everyone has had a chance, the drawings are exhibited, and the one that gets the most applause wins.

"Pat" Who?

Like the "Honest Abe" quiz, this is a contest in which the correct word containing the name "Pat" must be given in reply to each phrase:

"Pat in the army"	Patriotic
"Pat in the nobility"	Patrician

"Pat sewing a tear in his coat"	Patching
"Pat on the police force"	Patrolman

Other ideas may readily be found in the dictionary.

Other easily adaptable party themes are for holidays like Independence Day, Hallowe'en, or Thanksgiving. Still other themes include a Rodeo or Western Party, a Gay Nineties Party, Hawaiian Luau, Father-and-Son or Mother-and-Daughter Party, Circus Party, Easter Egg Hunt Party, Space Age Party, and numerous similar ideas. Such events provide an opportunity to use many of the games, mixers, songs, dances, and dramatic activities found throughout this book, and to involve group members in program planning and providing their own leadership.

LEADERSHIP GUIDELINES

In terms of leadership guidelines for planning and carrying out parties, the following list was developed by program specialists in Dayton, Ohio:

Build Up.   Build up anticipation and curiosity about the coming event— through word of mouth, impromptu skits given prior to the actual event, unusual posters, bulletins, clever invitations, and other forms of publicity.

Atmosphere.   Set the stage for the party through costuming and decorations, and give the first arrivals something specific to do, which puts them at ease and gets them into the "party spirit." Part of the costuming or decorating job may be left undone, so they may work on it when they arrive.

Program.   See that the most people have the best time possible, and everyone goes home a little better person for having participated in the party. Specific hints include:

1. Remember the size of the group, the age, and the space you have to work in when selecting activities.
2. Balance your program so that it will appeal to a wider group than just those people who have enough nerve to request activities they like especially.
3. Balance the leadership so that no one person is too outstanding—help new leaders emerge at each session.
4. Plan simple activities early in the evening and more demanding stunts after the group has warmed up.
5. Strive to have smooth transitions from one activity to the next, so that time is not wasted in taking different formations, teams, partners, etc.
6. Gradually "taper off" the party, ending with a mellow and pleasant feeling after its climax.

Refreshments.   Keep refreshments simple but make sure they fit into the party theme. Instead of having people "line up" to be served, try a method of serving that will be unusual; also try variations in chair arrangements, such as little "conversation circles" that will bring people together in friendly groups.

Finally, the Dayton party planning guides offer the following suggestions for the direct leadership of activities in social recreation:

1. In teaching, demonstrate more and talk less. Stand where everyone can see you. Be a part of and not apart from the group.
2. Your attitude will be contagious, so make it enthusiastic and friendly.
3. Maintain control of the group by: (a) having a hand signal or musical signal to get quiet and attention (particularly with younger groups); (b) using members of a committee to quiet people in different parts of the room; (c) speaking in a slow, controlled voice, and varying the range and tempo of your voice for emphasis; (d) being continually alert to how participants are getting along; mentally "standing in their shoes."[2]

OUTINGS, TRIPS, AND PICNICS

A final form of special event which is useful in adding variety to recreation programs include various forms of outings and trips. These may include simple picnics at nearby wooded areas, lakes or beaches; brief excursions to amusement parks, community buildings, or sites of historic, environmental, or other special interest; or much more ambitious, distant, and extended trips. Many corporate/employee programs today sponsor chartered flights for their employees to distant points in this hemisphere, or even to Europe and the Orient. Travel has become an increasingly important part of the total modern recreation picture, and in one form or another, is a useful and adaptable program feature.

Tips for Leaders

Successful adventure trips don't just "happen"; they require thoughtful planning for before, during, and after:

Before the Trip
1. Let the group help plan and make arrangements as far as possible.
2. Decide on place, date, time, meeting place.
3. Contact place to make reservations, if necessary.
4. Secure volunteer transportation.
5. Secure an adequate number of volunteer adult leaders and teen aides, if appropriate. Explain their responsibilities.
6. Publicize—by word of mouth, posters, press, invitation.
7. Secure parental permission slips for children and youth.
8. Register participants.

9. Discuss the trip: where going, what to look for, how it is related to us.
10. Discuss what to wear, trip manners, what to bring (picnic lunch, entrance fee, pocket money).

During the Trip

1. Keep group together. Having a leader at front and back of group helps.
2. Be alert to safety practices, especially crossing streets and going to and from cars.
3. Good manners will make your group welcome and pave the way for other groups. Thank those who serve your group.

After the Trip

1. Send a "thank you" letter to the management of the place visited. Let a participant write the letter.
2. Thank volunteer leaders and aides.
3. Reinforce the experience through group discussion (or talking with individuals) about the trip and its special points of interest.
4. Follow up with some related activity in program, as a pet show or animal drawings after a zoo visit.
5. Plan another trip to the same place or to a related place for experience in depth, if interest warrants.

Picnics.   Picnics are a time-honored and always enjoyable form of outing for families or organized recreation groups. The City Division of Recreation in Louisville, Kentucky, offers a number of "picnic planning pointers":

1. In choosing a location, be sure to have some shade available, a level, open space for games and other activities, good drinking water, a shelter in case of rain, toilet facilities, tables, and a cooking fireplace.
2. Appoint committees or persons for specific duties: such as transportation, equipment, program events, food, etc.
3. Arrange games, contests, and stunts in which everyone can participate on a team or group basis.
4. Be sure to take along a first aid kit.
5. Inexpensive and humorous prizes add to the fun and enjoyment.
6. Direction signs are always helpful, especially near the picnic spot.
7. Be sure to clean up after the picnic; put out cooking fires; dispose of all waste paper, scraps, etc., and leave the picnic area ready for the next user.
8. Novel invitations always add a touch and may be prepared in the form of maps on brown wrapping paper, picnic basket folders, nature materials pasted on card folders, clever rhymes, etc.
9. Provide something to do for the "early birds." Guessing contests (items in a jar . . . identification of nature objects, etc.), puzzles, horseshoes, and beanbag or board games.[3]

To help stimulate and encourage picnics, the City Recreation Division in Louisville offers community groups a planning and picnic equipment lending service without charge. They also provide personnel to conduct picnic programs at a nominal charge, the cost dependent upon the size of the group, the length of the picnic, and the time required. The equipment that they make available to organized and responsible groups includes such sports and game items as: badminton; beanbags; burlap sacks; croquet; dart boards; horseshoes; softballs, bats, bases, and gloves; tug-of-war rope; and volleyballs and volleyball nets.

This chapter has described several different types of special events, celebrations, parties, and outing programs that may be sponsored by organized recreation groups. In addition, programs and guides for successful leadership are included.

In concluding, it should be pointed out that the task of organizing special events and leading the kinds of activities presented in this chapter provides an ideal way to develop leadership skills and responsibilities among group members. At every stage, from the initial planning of an event to its final evaluation, all participants should be encouraged to provide input and to share planning and leadership responsibilities. Thus, special events provide not only fun and a sense of group accomplishment, but important social growth and learning experiences.

NOTES

[1]Adapted from Richard Kraus, *Social Recreation: A Group Dynamics Approach* (St. Louis: C. V. Mosby, 1979): pp. 116–17.

[2]*Party-Planning Manual* (Dayton, Ohio, Recreation Bureau, n.d.)

[3]*Picnic Booklet* (Louisville, Kentucky, Department of Parks and Recreation, n.d.)

STUDENT PROJECTS

1. Have different small teams of students plan and carry out social recreation events for the class, such as holiday or theme parties, carnivals, or even trips and outings. Such projects may require considerable preparation, and therefore should be scheduled well in advance of the actual presentation.
2. As an alternative to Project 1, student groups may plan and carry out one or more social recreation events for an outside organization or institution, possibly in connection with a fund-raising effort on their part.
3. Individual class members may lead different social games and mixers, stunts, or other activities with class participation, followed by a critique of their leadership approach.

SUGGESTED READINGS

Catherine Allen, *Fun for Parties and Programs* (Englewood Cliffs, N.J.: Prentice-Hall, 1956).

Israel C. Heaton and Clark T. Thorstenson, *Planning for Social Recreation* (Boston: Houghton Mifflin, 1978).

Richard Kraus, *Social Recreation, A Group Dynamics Approach* (St. Louis: C. V. Mosby, 1979).

PART **3**

Specialized Functions
and Career
Development

Young recreation leaders learn basic musical skills in Reading, Pennsylvania; retired Honeywell Corporation employees enjoy a special event. Methods of leading swimming for the handicapped are taught in Omaha. Career development in commercial recreation may begin by being part of the show at a popular theme park--in this case, Busch Gardens' The Old Country. Staff members work with community groups in the Philadelphia Police Athletic League sports award program, while a Volunteer Youth Coaches training program is presented by the Naval Air Station, Point Mugu, California.

CHAPTER 11

Leadership of Human-Service Activities

A unique development in many leisure-service agencies today is that programs frequently include activities and services which are not recreational in the strict sense of the word.

Instead, these may be programs that contribute to the physical or mental health of participants, to their vocational or educational development, or to other vital areas of daily living. Such program elements might well be described as *human-service activities*. In public, voluntary, corporate/employee, military, and other types of leisure-service programs, recreation personnel are frequently called upon to direct or administer the provision of such services.

RATIONALE FOR ASSUMING HUMAN-SERVICE FUNCTIONS

Although some recreation and park professionals have resisted such program functions, a strong case can be made to justify their inclusion in leisure-service agencies.

First, it is generally recognized that recreation in itself provides far more than simply ''fun'' or ''pleasure.'' It helps meet many critical personal needs of participants related to health and emotional and social development. In the broad sense, recreation helps participants meet their total life needs and achieve their fullest potential as holistic human beings. Beyond this, it has also been shown that recreation is provided as a form of community-based service to meet other important societal needs—for group participation and community action, to reduce anti-social uses of leisure, to provide celebration and ritual, or to contribute to environmental values.

However, there are a number of other convincing reasons that justify recreation agencies' assuming nonrecreational responsibilities. In many community centers or similar agencies, recreation serves as a "threshold" activity that helps to attract potential participants into a facility. Typically, teenage youth may enter a neighborhood center to play sports or "hang out" in a lounge, but then become involved with the staff of the center and begin to reveal their other problems or concerns. Often, recreation staff members are the only adults who are in a position to know and relate to young people on a daily basis, who are not perceived as threatening or coercive figures, and to whom they can relate in a friendly, trusting way. Recreation personnel come to know entire families over a period of time, and are able to involve children and their parents in meaningful programs that enrich their lives and help to build positive bonds and relationships.

In many cases, it may not be possible for an overall recreation program to function effectively unless social problems in the center or the surrounding neighborhood are dealt with. If a youth center is dominated by fighting gangs, or by problems of drug dealing or other forms of delinquent activity, it cannot operate in a positive, successful way. Therefore, it becomes necessary for the center staff to deal with the underlying problems that affect participation and programming, using their own and other available community resources, through referral and consultation.

Similarly, in a senior center serving elderly men and women, it is often likely to be the recreation director or leader who is in the best position to know the participants well, to gain their confidence, and to plan program activities that meet a wide range of their life needs. These may relate to nutritional programs, counseling, legal and transportation assistance, medical or dental clinics, and similar services. Often, such services may be scheduled as part of the overall range of agency activities, and may be publicized and coordinated with other activities to provide a well-integrated range of involvements for elderly participants.

In a growing number of communities, the public recreation and park department may be designated by civic officials as the appropriate branch of community government to deal with the needs of special populations, such as youth, the aging, or the handicapped, simply because it has already established regular, meaningful contact with such groups through ongoing programs.

In other cases, the fact that many recreation and park departments operate substantial tracts of land, water-based facilities, or other community structures, may provide the basis for assigning them responsibility for running other community facilities or services. For example, in some cases, recreation and park functions have been linked to the management of streets and highways; shade trees; libraries, museums, and other civic institutions; or marinas, stadiums, and even community airports!

In institutional settings, such as psychiatric hospitals or physical rehabilitation centers, recreation personnel frequently carry out programs that are intended to achieve specific treatment goals for patients or clients. Often, these involve the application of varied forms of therapy or educational experiences that are not in themselves recreational—but that may readily be carried out by therapeutic recreation specialists.

Summing up, there is a convincing rationale for having recreation professionals assume responsibility for other nonrecreational human-service functions. Beyond this, the fact that leisure-service organizations are meeting important community needs helps to gain public respect and support, at a time when such backing is vitally needed.

ADMINISTRATIVE ARRANGEMENTS
FOR HUMAN-SERVICE FUNCTIONS

There are several types of administrative arrangements under which recreation professionals may carry on human-service functions, or may be closely integrated with such services.

First, recreation may be part of a total multiservice agency structure, in which two or more different departments or agencies are situated in a single community center, working cooperatively with each other. For example, recreation personnel may operate a leisure-service program in a large community center, in which the public schools also provide a day-care program, or an adult evening center education program. Within the same facility, the municipality's youth board may provide counseling or drug and alcohol abuse programs, or a health-service group sponsor clinics or diagnostic services.

Second, in some situations the overall program may be administered by recreation personnel. However, they may employ other skilled specialists to work with clients within their areas of professional expertise. For example, in a large senior center, medical services might be provided by public health nurses, under the administrative direction of the center's manager. In the San Francisco Recreation Center for the Handicapped, qualified social workers are employed by the agency (see page 232), to handle functions related to intake, family counseling, or referral. In some cases, it may be possible to give members of the recreation staff in-service training so they are qualified to carry out a number of the less technical functions.

Third, in some cases recreation may not be identified as a separate, independent area of responsibility, but rather as an area of service administratively attached to other related functions. For example, in many corporate/employee programs one or more staff members may be assigned responsibility for coordinating various personnel-related functions. Typically, these might include personnel benefits; stress counseling; the administration of weight-loss, alcohol, or drug-abuse programs; career development; preretirement workshops, and similar services.

Having examined the rationale for recreation agencies or departments conducting human-service programs, we now examine examples of such programs in several types of settings.

HUMAN-SERVICE PROGRAMMING IN PUBLIC AGENCIES

In Huntington Beach, California, the overall Community Services Department is separated administratively into a Beach Division and a Recreation and Human Services Division. The Beach Division includes both marine safety, involving an extensive beach supervision and lifeguarding program, and the maintenance of two miles of beach and parking and piers.

The Recreation and Human Services Division includes the operation of several parks, community centers, nature centers, adventure playgrounds, and similar facilities—along with a diverse range of sports, hobbies, special events, "contract" classes (conducted by paid outside specialists), and other recreation programs. The

Human Services program is particularly active with respect to the handicapped and aging populations in Huntington Beach, and is best illustrated in these areas. For example, the Seniors' Recreation Center, which serves as the hub of activities for thousands of senior citizens, provides numerous courses offered through community colleges or adult education programs in the area, as well as the following services offered free of charge to seniors:

Job Employment Bank	Glaucoma Testing
Discount Booklets	Podiatrist
Blood Pressure Checking	Elderly Care
Flu Clinic	Registration for Voting
Legal Assistance	Energy Crisis Assistance
Income Tax Assistance	Utility Tax Exemption and Certificate
Tax Rebate Assistance	

Other special programs for seniors offered through the Recreation and Human Services Division, or with its cooperation, include an outreach program for the homebound, a meals-to-the-home service, transportation assistance to needed locations, friendly visitations, information and referral services, and a special Christmas program for several hundred needy or isolated seniors.

Another example may be found in the city of Nepean, Ontario, Canada. Contrary to the prevalent view that social services tend to be needed primarily in low-income, congested metropolitan areas, the City of Nepean represents a relatively affluent suburban community, with outstanding public recreation and park facilities and a highly developed and well-supported program.

Nonetheless, this Canadian community also offers a number of unique, experimental programs designed to meet the special recreation and social needs of special populations in the city. For example, it offers several different weekday afternoon series designed particularly for women, titled Wide World and Women's World, consisting of speakers, luncheons, discussions, seminars, film showings, and other events, on such themes as: "Coping with Grief and Loss"; "The History of the Feminist Print Media"; "Legal Issues in Today's Society"; "Disarmament and the Nuclear Issues"; "The Cancer Society: Working for You and with Youth"; "De-Mystifying the World of Investing"; "International Women's Week Workshop," and other cultural events and workshops.

The Nepean Parks and Recreation Department also offers:

1. An After-Work Employee Fitness Program and a Lunch-Hour Employee Fitness Program;
2. A Friends for Fun Program designed for mildly retarded adolescents and young adults;
3. An Inter-Action Program designed specifically to integrate "special participants" (those with emotional, mental, physical, or learning disabilities) into regular recreation programs;
4. A Recreational Swim Program for the orthopedically disabled;
5. Outlook, a project providing social/recreational after-care programs for discharged psychiatric patients in the area, with group and one-to-one

activities pairing community volunteers with clients, on a ''buddy-system'' basis.

Such programs are not found only in public recreation and park departments. Instead, as the following section shows, they are offered in numerous other types of agencies.

HUMAN-SERVICE ACTIVITIES IN VOLUNTARY AGENCIES

Many voluntary agencies, particularly in the youth-serving field, provide social programs and services that extend far beyond recreation as such. Indeed, most such organizations regard themselves as multiservice agencies, with recreation seen not as an end in itself, but rather as a means of achieving other important goals.

These may include such purposes as spiritual development, providing guidance in key areas of personal development, contributing to vocational or career development, or helping to promote desirable causes related to the community, the nation, or even the world environment. For example, in addition to sponsoring numerous courses or workshops designed to help girls and women function more effectively in modern society, the YWCA has initiated many action programs designed to overcome specific problem areas:

> Almost 200 YWCAs have initiated programs for battered women, and the National YWCA has initiated national conferences and workshops on domestic violence. Hundreds of YWCAs provide career-planning and employment programs; others focus on juvenile justice needs to reduce delinquency among ''high-risk'' young women, or developmental day-care programs and therapeutic services for the disabled.[1]

Numerous Girls' Club programs include individual, group, and family counseling dealing with such problems as truancy, running away, incorrigibility, or other symptoms of family dysfunction. Similarly, the Boys' Clubs of America sponsor numerous national and local projects dealing with health and physical fitness goals, problems of juvenile delinquency, and youth employment.

In some cases, organizations like the CYO or YM–YWHA may deal not so much with specific social needs or community problems, as with the overall need to help people enrich and strengthen their personal values, and become more able to deal with life constructively, both as family members and within the broader community. For example, the Philadelphia YM–YWHA has sponsored a successful Institute of Awareness for a number of years, which is designed to offer both men and women courses and workshops dealing with their basic life orientations and important areas of personal growth and understanding. In a recent year, such offerings included these subjects:

> Born to Win: Personal Awareness Through the Use of Transactional Analysis
> Success Strategies: Make Your Career/Life Goals Happen
> Sales Dynamics: Power Approaches to Successful Selling
> Weight Control through Behavior Modification
> How You Can Break the Worry Habit Before it Breaks You
> Living with Death, Dying, and Loss: Learning to Make Each Day Count

Still other workshops and mini-labs deal with time management, assertiveness training, self-hypnosis, channeling anger effectively, surviving stress, communication for couples, personal investments, money management, art and life, setting personal priorities, and practical law.

EMPLOYEE RECREATION PROGRAMS

As described in Chapter 4, many major companies and industrial organizations provide or assist in recreation services for their employees. While these may include games and sports, social programs, hobby classes, or travel activities, they also tend to give heavy emphasis to physical fitness activities, as well as other personal needs of employees.

In a recent study of 221 Fortune-500 companies, Taylor and Weiner of the University of Kentucky found that employee services and fringe benefits included many programs related to education, social welfare, and related needs:

> Of the 221 respondents, 98 percent (N = 216) offered some kind of employee service or fringe benefit program for their employees. The most popular programs were tuition refund programs (98 percent, N = 216), preretirement education (52 percent, N = 115), adult education (46 percent, N = 102), and discount cards (43 percent, N = 93). Other employee services included various recreation clubs, family stores, season theater passes, annual health examinations, counseling, YMCA memberships, cafeterias, credit unions, trips and tours, etc. Fifty-seven percent (N = 125) of respondents had organized recreation programs for their employees.[2]

In many cases, recreation has been linked administratively with other personnel services and programs. For example, the Atlantic-Richfield Company (ARCO) has initiated an extensive employee health and fitness program, for reasons that are very practical and realistic. Sparks writes:

> Wellness in the work force is important to any company because healthy employees are more productive and lose less on-the-job time to minor ailments. Also, healthy workers tend to be happier and promote goodwill in the workplace.
>
> Perhaps the stronger motivation for corporate health education is less visible. It is the high cost of health care, underwritten by corporations in the form of insurance premiums which most companies subsidize for employees in group plans.[3]

In 1982, Americans spent $300 billion (almost 9 percent of the Gross National Product) on health care with indications that this may rise to 20 percent of the GNP by the year 2000. For this reason, preventive medicine has become the key focus for corporate interest in the health field, with physical fitness an important component. ARCO's wellness campaign has many elements, including clinics, promotions, and special activities in the areas of stress management, smoking cessation, nutrition, hypertension control, heart attack prevention, cancer detection, and physical fitness. An extensive range of sports and other physical activities, including racquetball, aerobics, running, weight-training, softball, volleyball, basketball, badminton, golf, hockey, paddle tennis, karate, and personalized exercise programs contribute to the overall fitness effort.

MILITARY RECREATION PROGRAMS

Most recreation programs that are sponsored by the Morale, Welfare, and Recreation (MWR) divisions of the major armed forces branches include such traditional activities as games and sports, social recreation, arts and crafts, and hobbies.

During the past several years, increased emphasis has been given to fitness programs, and to youth and family-oriented activities designed to meet the needs of dependents of military personnel living on or close to military bases. Many programs are specifically for children and youth, including teen councils and centers, youth sports leagues, and other recreational activities.

In some cases, MWR provides assistance to working parents with younger children. The Charleston, South Carolina, Air Force Base, for example, sponsors a Child Care Center for preschool children, in addition to an After-School Care program for elementary-age children, and varied family-geared events. Its Recreation Supply Office lends camper trailers, backpacks, tents, sleeping bags, stoves, cooking kits, and other gear to military personnel and their dependents, to use in the more than 16,000 campsites available in South Carolina.

Other armed forces units sponsor programs intended to strengthen family unity and counteract some of the inevitable stresses found in military life. At the Naval Air Station in Lemoore, California, for example, Marriage Encounter weekends, workshops on family violence, and family stress counseling are all provided by varied base offices—usually in cooperation with the Morale, Welfare, and Recreation division. Increasing numbers of such activities are being developed at many military bases in the United States and abroad, and military personnel have been seeking new and more effective ways of contributing to positive and healthful family life in the military.

THERAPEUTIC RECREATION SERVICE

By its very nature, therapeutic recreation service is designed to provide significant human service benefits to its participants, whether programs are being carried on within treatment setting, or simply being provided for persons with a significant degree of disability who live in the community.

What is not generally recognized is the extent to which recreation may provide a core or key element of an overall program which also addresses many other important needs of the disabled. The San Francisco Recreation Center for the Handicapped, for example, is noted for its outstanding leisure-service programs for children, youth, and adults with varying forms of disability. Established in 1952, it has become recognized nationally and internationally as a model in developing community-based recreation, education, socialization, and habilitation programs for the severely disabled through lectures, workshops, conferences, seminars, films, and publications.[4]

The Recreation Center's services include: (1) a wide range of year-round adapted recreation activities; (2) preschool and day-care readiness-for-school programs; (3) infant stimulation and early childhood development activities; (4) resocialization and community integration of long-institutionalized mentally retarded and mentally ill adults; (5) instruction in independent living skills; (6) adult education instruction; (7) outreach programs for homebound, severely handicapped, and elderly clients; (8) on-the-job training and employment of handicapped; (9) transportation services for all; (10) case work, social services, information, and referral to other agencies; and (11) meals served at all programs.

The Adult Day Care Division, for example, seeks to provide each adult participant the opportunity to achieve his or her maximum social, physical, intellectual, and emotional functioning potential. Each client has individualized goals and objectives, through which recreation leaders develop group program plans. The overall objectives of the Adult Day Care Division include: basic skill development; self-help skills; recreation skills; travel skills; social skills; physical fitness development; and communication skills.

Camping as Program Focus.

As an example of the wide range of its programs, the Recreation Center for the Handicapped sponsors camping programs of three basic types: *day camping* at a site adjacent to the Center; *wilderness* and *winter trip camping* in the High Sierras; and *resident camping* in a regular YMCA camp facility.

All Center participants are regularly enrolled in some type of camping program, and the majority attend all three types of camps. In a recent year, 1300 participants, ages 14 months to 93 years, took part in camping. Most were multi-handicapped, including mentally retarded individuals of all ages; some in wheelchairs, on crutches, or bedfast, and many with severe speech impairments, visual handicaps, and hearing losses. Many are unable to feed themselves, and require assistance with toileting.

While the San Francisco Center for the Handicapped represents an outstanding example of such programs, many other therapeutic recreation agencies offer similar activities. In many cases, recreation personnel take direct responsibility for directing Activities of Daily Living (ADL) programs, which help severely impaired individuals learn to care for themselves in such areas as maintaining an apartment, cooking, cleaning, and other self-care responsibilities. In other cases, they learn to travel independently, an essential for clients who seek to work and live in the community. Leisure counseling programs help them begin to make the fullest and most satisfying use of their own leisure, while other discussion groups and counseling services help them deal positively with issues related to courtship, marriage, and sexual involvement.

In still other programs, recreation personnel may either direct or coordinate program activities such as *Sensory Training, Remotivation, Behavior Modification,* or *Reality Orientation*—all recently developed techniques designed to help individuals participate more fully in group life, and to bring them more fully in touch with their physical and social environment.

Typically, recreation personnel focus on program responsibilities related to the life interests, personal needs, and social involvements of participants. As a simple example, arranging religious activities or political campaign appearances or discussion groups in nursing homes is usually the function of recreation leaders.

IMPLICATIONS FOR LEADERSHIP

This chapter has described a considerable number of human-service functions which either are assumed directly by recreation specialists in different types of agencies, or which they coordinate or help to plan. Obviously, it is essential that they do so with an awareness of the special expertise required to carry on such services, and that they either develop the needed understandings and skills themselves, or make sure that the individuals who conduct such programs are qualified to do so.

In campus recreation programs, for example, recreation personnel must be familiar with the overall goals of higher education and current thinking with respect to the developmental needs and psychosocial processes of college students, as well as the philosophical orientation of their own institutions.

In corporate/employee recreation programs, those in charge frequently must develop a basic understanding of personnel management practices, as well as skills related to counseling, the administration of benefits programs, and similar functions.

In some cases, it may be necessary for recreation personnel to develop and sharpen their skills if they are to be able to provide other specialized forms of activities or services. In some psychiatric hospitals, for example, therapeutic recreation specialists are given the opportunity to practice leadership in group therapy programs under the supervision of qualified psychologists or other mental health professionals. In nursing homes or geriatric care units, they may be able to take special training sessions in other types of adjunctive therapy, or in group awareness techniques.

When recreation professionals are not able to lead programs directly because of the special expertise or qualifications that may be required, they should be able to work closely with specialists in these fields and to coordinate their programs with them. Ideally, recreation should be fully integrated with all such services—as in the case of health and fitness programming—and should be regarded as a vital area of agency service with clearly identifiable goals and outcomes that contribute to overall organizational or community needs and values.

NOTES

[1]See *Annual Report of National YWCA*, New York, N.Y., 1982.

[2]Frances W. Taylor and Andrew I. Weiner, "The Status of Recreation and Fitness in Fortune 500 Companies," Research Presentation, NRPA Congress, Minneapolis, 1981.

[3]John Sparks, "ARCO's Ambitious Program to Promote Employee Fitness," *Parks and Recreation* (December 1983): 46.

[4]*Annual Report and Fact Sheet* (San Francisco: Recreation Center for the Handicapped, 1983).

STUDENT PROJECTS

1. Hold a class debate on the proposition that it is appropriate for recreation and park agencies to assume human-service functions as an important ongoing responsibility.

2. Form visitation teams to go out to different community agencies and examine their programs and functions within the human-service area.
3. Develop guidelines for leadership within the human-service field, including specific approaches related to helping, referral, advocacy, and similar roles, and also dealing with cooperative agency relationships with other human-service organizations.

SUGGESTED READINGS

Richard Kraus, Gay Carpenter, and Barbara Bates, *Recreation Leadership and Supervision* (Philadelphia: W. B. Saunders, 1981), Chapters 8, 9.

E. William Niepoth, *Leisure Leadership* (Englewood Cliffs, N.J.: Prentice-Hall, 1983), Chapters 1, 4, 8, 9.

H. Douglas Sessoms, *Leisure Services* (Englewood Cliffs, N.J.: Prentice-Hall, 1984), Chapter 7.

CHAPTER 12

Problem-Solving:
Principles and Methods

Having examined several of the major areas of recreation program activity leadership, we now move to a final important aspect of leadership concern—the task of resolving problem situations, where the appropriate solution or course of action is not readily apparent.

This chapter gives the reader an opportunity to apply many of the guidelines and concepts described in earlier chapters, in the problem-solving process. Additionally, the reader is encouraged to apply his or her own judgment, experience, and powers of critical analysis in examining the case studies that conclude the chapter.

DISTINCTION BETWEEN PROBLEM-SOLVING AND DECISION-MAKING

First, it is important to make a distinction between problem-solving and decision-making. While similar, the two are not the same.

All of us make many decisions as a matter of daily routine. We must decide what magazine to buy, where to eat, what clothes to wear, who to call, or what movie to see. Most such questions are relatively inconsequential; if a poor or unwise decision is made, the results are not usually too serious. However, we also tend to face more serious questions in our lives—how to expand our incomes, how to cut down on drinking or overeating, how to relate to a rebellious child or domineering parent, or similar concerns. Such issues may indeed represent critical problems in our lives, which demand serious effort if they are to be satisfactorily resolved.

Similarly, recreation leaders or supervisors make many routine decisions. These may relate to choices of program activities, scheduling an event, determining what fee to charge for a class registration, or which official to hire to "work" a game. Such questions usually are handled in one of two ways. First, they may fall directly under existing policies or procedural rules which make the decision automatic. Or, they may represent a matter of personal judgment, in which the leader makes a decision quickly with relative confidence that it will be a sound one.

Causes of Difficulty

Whenever policies or procedures are applicable that will permit a routine decision to be made, this is an ideal solution. However, from time to time more serious difficulties may emerge, which demand a more thoughtful, cautious, or systematic approach to arriving at a solution. This is likely to be the case when any of the following conditions are present:

1. *Complexity of Problem.* This includes situations in which there are a number of variables or conditions that might justify more than one possible solution, and in which there is no clear-cut argument that any one decision would be correct.
2. *Extent and Duration of Problem.* In some cases, a problem may be widespread and may have existed over a period of time, with past efforts to resolve it having repeatedly proved unsuccessful.
3. *Political/Personal Complications.* It is frequently difficult to apply rational solutions or policies when a problem situation is made worse by political pressures or influence, or by personal complications that involve strong emotions, favoritism, or other complications.
4. *Falling Between the Cracks.* Another cause of difficulty may occur when a problem "falls between the cracks," in the sense that it does not fit cleanly or neatly under any given policy or procedural guideline.

Roots, Not Symptoms

The problem-solving process may be approached on two levels. First, there are the obvious manifestations of the problem, the "symptoms" that cause concern and demand action. On the other hand, there are "roots," which represent the underlying causes behind a difficulty.

To illustrate, an employee may be erratic in his or her work record, frequently coming late or missing assignments. These are symptoms. The causes may be found in the employee's own character and life situation, or possibly in the job situation if there is a lack of structure and supervision or a generally poor state of morale on the part of staff members.

It is essential to identify the underlying causes of problem situations and to deal constructively with them, rather than concentrating solely on preventing or solving symptoms. To accept pat solutions dealing only with the surface manifestation of a problem is like putting a bandaid on a serious internal injury. It will provide neither real relief nor a cure.

Instead, a systematic approach that analyzes the overall problem and its causes and that identifies appropriate solutions is called for. While problems may be approached in various ways, a commonly found model of problem-solving includes six stages: (1) recognition and definition of the problem; (2) assigning responsibility for its solution; (3) investigating and diagnosing the problem; (4) identifying possible solutions, and selecting the most appropriate one; (5) action implementing the preferred solution; and (6) monitoring and evaluating the solution.

SIX-STAGE PROBLEM-SOLVING MODEL

Each of the six stages has several steps which may need to be taken, depending on the complexity of the problem and the leadership style of those involved.

1. *Recognition.* While there may be general awareness that a problem exists, there may also be unwillingness to recognize and deal with it. The first step in problem-solving is to recognize the difficulty as a serious one, and to define it. This means that the nature of the problem must be understood, in terms of its being a breakdown in staff relations, an interpersonal conflict, or other type of disagreement. At the same time, a determination must be made to resolve it, because of the damage, confusion, or poor morale that it is causing.

2. *Assign Responsibility.* There are a number of possible choices here, including any of the following:

a. *Avoidance.* This consists of avoiding the problem, refusing to deal with it, and hoping that it will go away. Like most problems, it usually does not. As a modified approach, one may seek to ''smooth it over,'' minimizing its importance and not dealing with it.

b. *Buck-Passing.* An easy approach is to take the position that the problem is too difficult or too risky to deal with, and to push it elsewhere, either to the next level of management or possibly to the governing board or commission.

c. *Unilateral Decision.* The leader or supervisor may simply make an authoritarian decision, without consultation with others or seeking their support.

d. *Grudging Consultation.* Here, the individual in charge asks the opinions of others, but essentially makes his or her own decision, without sharing the decision-making power in a meaningful way.

e. *Task-Group Assignment.* A small group of employees may be assigned to investigate the problem and bring in a recommendation.

f. *Consensus Approach.* This represents a participative-management approach, in which a considerable number of those in the agency share in the process of analyzing the problem and deciding on a course of action.

According to current management theory, the collective judgment and analytical ability of groups generally are superior to those of individual members. Therefore those approaches that emphasize participative goal-setting and problem-solving are preferable to other approaches. In addition, personnel in an agency are generally more willing to accept and support a decision in which they have had a voice, than one which has been imposed on them without consultation.

3. *Investigate Problem.* It is impossible to make an informed decision without a full investigation of the scope of the problem, its history, possible underlying causes, and different points of view about it. Many problems involve sharp disagreements among participants, staff members, or community groups, and it is essential that all conflicting opinions and explanations be examined. This process may involve any of the following actions:

a. *Gathering Data.* The problem-solving group should examine all available documentation in the form of personnel or program records, correspondence, newspaper accounts, department reports, or similar sources.

b. *Interviews and Observation.* Involved parties should be interviewed in person or possibly be present for hearings or "town meetings," to explore the issues. In addition, those investigating the problem may need to visit the site where the difficulty is occurring or to observe programs in action.

c. *Staff Consultation.* Knowledgeable or involved staff members should be consulted for relevant information, and to learn their views as to possible solutions for the problem.

d. *Search for Precedents.* Precedents showing how similar problems have been handled should be sought, either within the agency itself, or in the literature or similar organizations.

4. *Identify Alternative Solutions.* When the problem has been carefully investigated, the next step is to identify possible alternative solutions, consider their strengths and weaknesses, and select those that are most feasible and likely to succeed. This may include the following methods:

a. *Group Discussion.* Through group discussion, several alternative plans may be identified and discussed, with emphasis on exploring their strengths and weaknesses fully. It should be noted that decisions may take two forms: (1) a single decisive action; or (2) a plan of action or program that will take a period of time to carry out. In each case, the ease of implementation, including possible obstacles and costs, must be considered—as well as the degree of probable success of the approach.

b. *Simulation Approaches.* Simulation is the process of setting up a hypothetical situation and either acting it out through role-playing, or using electronic data-processing methods to determine possible outcomes. Computer-based decision-making is frequently used in business, government, or military settings, where masses of statistical data are available, and there can be reasonable control of the key variables in the model.

c. *Select Alternative.* At the conclusion of this stage, the strengths and weaknesses of each possible solution must be weighed, and the most promising alternative chosen—bearing in mind that it must be accept-able to the key authority figures involved, and appropriate in terms of legal restrictions, Civil Service codes, the mandate of the agency, union contracts, or other binding agreements.

5. *Implement Solution.* Before the decided-on solution is put into effect, several steps should be taken:

a. *Inform Parties.* It is extremely important to inform all parties of the decision that has been reached—if possible at a meeting where there can be a full discussion of the reasons for the plan, and an attempt to moderate hostile feelings or opposition to it. Nothing is more annoying than to find out indirectly, or at second-hand, about a decision affecting you seriously. It is therefore critical that there be a dialogue among interested parties at this point, in order to build acceptance and support for the decision.

b. *Consider Human-Relations Effect.* Similarly, when decisions are made that directly affect the lives or careers of people—as in the case of employees who are being disciplined or demoted—it is important that this be done in as constructive a way as possible, without damaging their self-respect or dignity in the eyes of others.

c. *Providing Full Support.* Finally, in implementing the decision, it is essential that needed support be given to the action taken. Not infre-quently, when the comment, ''We tried that before and it didn't work,'' is heard, the true meaning is that a decision was made, but was not given full logistical or enforcement support. Understandably, it may have failed. It is therefore critical that needed administrative approval and back-up be given to putting the solution into effect.

6. *Monitoring and Evaluating Outcomes.* The last step in the problem-solving process is to observe and monitor the effects of the action that has been taken. In some cases, where a single decisive action has been taken (such as the decision to build a new center, or promote an employee), it cannot easily be rethought or reversed.

In other cases, such as in the possible effort to enrich programs and partici-pation in a given agency, if one approach is observed not to work over a period of time, the original plan may be changed, and new approaches implemented. Evaluation, as described here, may be either *informal,* in the sense of involving observation and periodic discussions, or *formal,* through the use of systematic instruments and data-gathering procedures.

USEFUL PROBLEM-SOLVING TECHNIQUES

The preceding pages outline specific steps to be followed in the problem-solving process. In order to carry them out effectively, there are a number of tech-niques that can be used to identify possible creative solutions or to get parties to a dispute ready to mediate their differences and accept a group decision.

The following methods are helpful in this solving process. Typically, they do not represent strict methods of analysis or rigorous ways of assessing the value of potential solutions. Instead, they facilitate the group process, and help to bring groups to readiness for taking needed action. While they are described here very briefly, fuller details of each approach may be found in texts on leadership and group dynamics and problem-solving by Joseph J. Bannon,[1] David W. and Frank P. Johnson,[2] and H. Douglas Sessoms and Jack L. Stevenson.[3]

Values Clarification Exercises

These represent group exercises which help participants recognize their own value systems and ways of relating to others in group situations. For example, an exercise might be done in which group members respond to a series of statements built around McGregor's Theory X and Theory Y (see p. 263). During the course of this, they come to realize whether or not they hold traditional or forward-thinking views with respect to the motivations of employees, on-the-job needs of employees, and effective ways of promoting work output.

This approach is particularly useful if the problem being explored is one in which there are sharply contrasting values at stake, or in which there may be a degree of personal conflict linked to professional philosophy or leadership styles.

Role-Playing Approaches

Psychodramas and sociodramas represent two forms of role-playing, in which parties to a dispute or problem-solving effort act out the problem situation. In so doing, they may vividly experience the feelings and attitudes of other "actors," and may be helped to confront and understand their own attitudes and positions more fully.

Role-playing exercises may range from dramatic sessions which are carefully orchestrated and directed, with people playing very specific roles in carefully designed sequences of action, to much less structured sessions in which people verbalize their views freely.

Usually, all relevant individuals in a problem situation are identified and acted out; in addition, the audience may enter in with its own questions and reactions. In some cases, the technique of "role-reversal" may be used, with individuals acting out parts directly opposed to their own real-life identities. For example, an angry and frustrated parent may be asked to act out the part of his or her rebellious teenager, or vice-versa. By exposing emotions and heightening conflict in visible form, often it is possible to see and understand problems and the issues involved in new, helpful ways—rather than through rational analysis alone.

Computer-Based Simulation Models

As suggested earlier, the use of simulation models which involve testing the value of various strategies or problem solutions has become increasingly popular in government, political science, business, the military, and other major systems today. Computer games are being used to teach human relations skills, tactics of warfare, and a host of other types of personal or professional abilities.

A clever programmer should be able to make use of electronic data-processing to analyze data and project the probable results of different courses of action, or to train personnel to function effectively in different problem situations. While the human, social, and economic factors involved in recreation-related problems are often less predictable than the elements involved in business or military strategy, certainly this is a technique which may be used in a challenging and entertaining way to analyze recreation problems.

Brainstorming

This is a relatively familiar technique which is used to generate a high level of creative thinking and possible solutions within a given problem area.

Simply described, the group assembles to review the problem and to suggest, in rapid-fire order, a wide range of possible ideas and actions that might be taken. As they do this, two or more recorders use a blackboard or large paper pads to print the suggestions that are made, as quickly as they are voiced. The rules are simple: (1) feel free to suggest anything; (2) do not criticize or "put down" anyone else's suggestions; and (3) where appropriate, "piggy-back" or build on other persons' ideas. Within a climate of creative excitement and humor, a host of ideas are likely to emerge—many of them impractical or useless, but others with real potential.

The initial phase of idea-generation is usually followed by having a smaller group of participants go over the suggestions, placing them in appropriate categories and culling out those which are obviously irrelevant or inappropriate. As a second stage, the overall group may again go over the ideas, or may deal with them through a process of group discussion.

Other Small-Group Techniques

In addition to these approaches, Sessoms and Stevenson have identified a number of other techniques which can be used to explore issues and develop possible problem-solving solutions. These include: (1) *buzz groups,* a familiar method of involving small groups of perhaps two to six members in quick discussions (between five and ten minutes) of issues or problems that have been faced by a larger group or body; (2) *fishbowl technique,* a means of having group members become more aware of discussion techniques, by having one group carry out discussions or exercises, while others surround them in an observing and encouraging role; and (3) a *panel approach* called the *colloquy,* in which three units of participants (involving a panel of two to four outside resource persons, three to four representatives chosen from the audience, and the audience itself) examine a problem.[4]

Group Discussion

This is probably the most popular problem-solving technique, and often is used after other methods have contributed to the group's thinking or attitudinal change process. It may be carried on with small or large groups, and usually includes the following elements:

All those involved form a circle, to permit free discussion without any one person dominating or "lecturing" the group in a formal sense. One individual acts as the leader; his or her role is to keep the discussion on track, recognize speakers and encourage as many as possible to participate, and gradually move the group toward the identification of an appropriate solution. In addition, one group member should serve as a recorder, to keep a record of major points covered, and decisions reached.

Other group members are encouraged to take part, and to play appropriate roles in the discussion, such as opinion-seeking and giving, information seeking and giving, clarifying and elaborating, testing for preliminary group attitudes, suggesting ideas or plans for action, and summarizing the discussion.

It is important that a positive group climate be maintained, and that the discussion not deteriorate into personal attacks or recriminations. The ideas of all individuals should be respected, although it is appropriate to argue against them in a constructive way.

The tendency to rush into a decision, or to quickly accept the ideas of individuals who are highly verbal and confident, or who hold high-status roles (sometimes called "group-think") should be avoided. At the same time, the group should not take longer than necessary to move toward resolution. If the same ideas are being expressed again and again, or if the mood of the group becomes irresolute or aimless, it is probably time to begin to consider a decision.

"Straw votes" may be used as a way of testing the direction in which the group is leaning. Ultimately, if there is an apparent consensus, the decision may be reached without taking any formal vote. If there is still some disagreement, it may be necessary to take a formal vote, although ideally it is best if those in the minority can be persuaded in a friendly way to accept the ideas of the majority—rather than hold out in opposition.

When the decision has finally been reached, it is important to state it very precisely and clearly for all to hear and agree with, so there can be no possible misunderstanding of the solution that has been arrived at, and in order to get clear-cut statements of support.

ADHERENCE TO AGENCY PHILOSOPHY AND POLICY

A final important principle to be considered is that any decision that is reached must be in reasonable harmony with the agency or organization's fundamental philosophy and policy structure. If not, it will inevitably lead to repercussions, resistance, and second thoughts.

Unfortunately, not all leisure-service organizations possess clearly stated philosophies or policy manuals. Many public recreation and park agencies do have fairly precise statements of goals or purposes set forth in their charters, or in departmental manuals. Voluntary organizations often have broad goals statements and procedural manuals, but may tend to lack the middle-ground of detailed policy statements. Therapeutic agencies often have policies which are enunciated by department heads subject to the approval of trustees, or in some cases accreditation standards developed by national professional organizations or accrediting bodies.

In addition to formal statements of this type, it is important to recognize that many leisure-service organizations today adhere to a specific model of priorities and service-delivery approaches. Three major models of program emphasis that are particularly applicable to public and voluntary agencies (the quality-of-life, marketing, and human-service approaches) were described in Chapter 1. Although this type of emphasis may not be stated explicitly in department or agency manuals or guidelines, it obviously tends to influence the basis on which staff members must approach the problem-solving process.

PROBLEM-SOLVING PROCEDURES IN DEALING WITH CASE STUDIES

We now move to a consideration of case studies, each of which provides a fairly typical problem that might be faced by a recreation, park, or leisure-service agency. Each of these descriptions outlines some type of conflict situation, a difficult choice among priorities, or managerial strategies. In some cases the problems are of a fairly personal nature; in others they involve struggles between community groups or agencies.

It should be clearly emphasized that conflicts are *not* inherently bad. Sessoms and Stevenson point out that, although we usually regard conflict as undesirable, and although we often try to avoid or eliminate it, there are many positive possibilities in conflict. Indeed, it is a *given* in human interaction, and is inevitable when human beings deal with each other. They write:

> Conflict is natural and healthy. Properly handled, it aids in clarifying the issues, brings solutions into focus, and stimulates action. It is essential to creativity and production. Effective leaders actively use conflict as a dynamic to strengthen the group. . . . The crucial task, therefore, is to find ways of dealing creatively with conflict.[5]

Ideally, this can best be achieved when all involved persons are encouraged and helped to search for mutually acceptable solutions through a process of creative interchange of ideas, attitudes, needs, and suggested actions. The task is to apply such an approach in solution of the problems found in the following case studies.

As a class project, it is suggested that small groups be formed to deal with the case studies that follow. In each case, between three and five students may be assigned to deal with a problem situation. It is their responsibility to read and discuss the case, "flesh out" its skeletal outline with additional, plausible details, and then to determine how they want to approach it. Following a period of planning, each group then presents its case to the entire class. They may use role-playing, brainstorming, buzz groups, or other techniques for analyzing the problem, and should, if possible, involve class members in the problem. Ultimately, they arrive at a recommended solution; both the solution and the method used to arrive at it should be reviewed and evaluated by the class.

Using this general approach, each instructor and class are encouraged to develop their own ways of using the case studies that follow.

Case Study 1: Birds or Bikes?

The South Onondaga Special Park District has acquired a substantial tract of almost untouched land by purchase. Following the transfer of title, two outdoor enthusiasts' associations, the Onondaga Motorbikers' Club, and the Weymouth County Snowmobile Dealers and Riders Club, present a set of proposals for the development of the tract. Their view is that a number of trails should be cut into the land for use by their members, and they support an additional proposal for establishing a hang-gliding area and sportsman's center and rifle range in its center. Since these groups were extremely helpful politically in getting approval for the bond issue to buy the land, the Park District Board is prepared to view their requests favorably.

Suddenly, however, a deluge of protests from environmental groups, bird-watchers' clubs, and wilderness societies descends on the board. There are popular petitions, editorials, sermons, and threats to impeach the entire board, if a single tree in the new tract is cut down. But the motorbikers and snowmobilers are determined to cash in their chips, and will not back down. What's the solution?

Case Study 2: Unexpected Fees: A Budgetary Crisis

Janice Brown, Recreation and Park Director for the City of Fallsburgh, is faced by a sudden financial crisis. For years, her department has made use of gyms, indoor pools, and auditoriums owned by the Fallsburgh Board of Education for its indoor programming during the winter months—without charge. Similarly, the school system has used outdoor sports facilities and nature-study areas owned by the Recreation and Park Department—also without charge.

Suddenly, Janice is informed by the chairman of the school board that beginning in the spring semester, there will be substantial custodial charges and utility costs, amounting to thousands of dollars, for the use of school facilities for recreation. This will affect not only the Recreation and Park Department, but also various community groups that have scheduled activities in the schools' facilities, an arrangement normally coordinated by the Recreation and Park Department. While the new policy has not yet been implemented, the plan is to put it in action within two months. How should Janice deal with it?

Case Study 3: The Local Residents Complain

The Morgan Township Recreation Commission has owned a large public park for a number of years, known as Crowley Park. However, in recent years, it has not had sufficient funding to maintain it effectively, and it has become decayed and overgrown. Under a new agreement with a township-wide sports association which sponsors seasonal sports for youth and young adults, the Overton Sports League, it was agreed that the members of this association would become responsible for maintaining the park and would also have the right to schedule its uses.

Within a few months, the Overton Sports League cleaned up three ballfields and a track, improved fencing, and rehabilitated a shelter facility in Crowley Park. They initiated a fund-raising campaign to install night lighting for evening sports events, and public use of the park began to expand tremendously. The new policy appeared to be a success, until a committee of Morgan Township residents in the neighborhood of the park appeared at the Commission's monthly meeting to complain. They claimed that the Overton people were totally dominating the use of the park's facilities and were not granting permits to any other groups—even neighborhood youth, who had formerly used the park for informal sports competition. In addition, neighborhood residents were concerned about the traffic and parking problems, as well as noise that would probably occur at night, with the new lighting system.

How could this problem have been avoided through better planning at an earlier stage? What are the alternative approaches for dealing with it now?

Case Study 4: A Controversial Employee

Dan Finnerty, Supervisor for the Easttown District in the City of Las Venturas, has had considerable difficulty with an employee, Jane Townsend. She has been an inconsistent employee at best, often being absent or late, and frequently being unwilling to accept responsibility, although she can be a talented leader when she wants to be. Other employees have often complained about her ''goofing off,'' and have asked that she be transferred to some other location. However, Jane happens to be the close friend of an influential member of the Las Venturas City Council, who helped her get the job in the first place.

Matters reach a crisis when Jane Townsend fails to supervise a sports event properly, and two younger children are injured as a result. There is the threat of a potential lawsuit, and other employees indicate that they are no longer willing to work with her. However, at the same time, her friend on City Council is putting pressure on Dan Finnerty to have her promoted in rank and given responsibility for directing the center where she now works. How should Dan deal with this controversial employee?

Case Study 5: The Unwelcome Participants

Bob Porter has been program director of the Wabash Community Center, a nonprofit youth-serving agency on the South Side, for several years. Based on his personal commitment to the human-service approach to recreation management, he has introduced varied social-service program activities at the Wabash Center, and has cooperated closely with other governmental or voluntary agencies meeting social needs in the city.

He has now agreed to let two such organizations use facilities in the Wabash Center on a rental basis. A group of outpatients from an alcohol and drug abuse center will be using his gymnasium two afternoons a week, and a nearby mental health center will be holding a weekly party in his auditorium for ex-mental patients. While such uses are in agreement with the principle of mainstreaming special populations, and with Bob Porter's own philosophy of service, he recognized that there might be some problems stemming from this arrangement. These began when a parents' group strenuously objected to the idea of having "drug addicts, winos, and crazy people" using the center—and to the possible dangers to their children. Up in arms, they threatened to take the issue to the board of trustees of the Wabash Center, and there appeared to be no possible basis for compromise. Unfortunately, Bob had not cleared the policy with his board in advance. What does he do now?

Case Study 6: The Card Players

In another nonprofit voluntary agency, the Millville Senior Center, there seems to be a problem based on sex (or at least on the gender of the participants).

About two-thirds of the Center's membership is female, and one-third are male. All are over sixty, with the average age in the mid-70s. The typical pattern of involvement at the Center is for the women members to take part in a wide range of activities, including hobby classes, music, dancing, and discussion groups. The men, in contrast, generally play cards at one end of the lounge, and with few exceptions, do not take part in any other activities. When it comes time for the monthly party, or other special events, the women members usually do all the work, although the men show up for refreshments and a little conversation, before going back to their pinochle and gin rummy games.

Suddenly, several of the most active women in the Millville Senior Center decide that they are no longer willing to put up with the situation where the men segregate themselves most of the time, take part in few "mixed" activities, and are unwilling to be officers or carry any of the responsibility of the club. One woman says angrily, "It's like my marriage. I did all the work, and he came home at six-o-clock, had supper, watched T.V. and did nothing else." The reaction of the men is that the women are just being silly. What should the director of the Center do about it?

Case Study 7: Can We Improve Intergroup Relations?

The Oroville Police Athletic League is a nonprofit youth center in an older section of town, which has been primarily white for years. There is a fairly sizable black population now, and the blacks have been showing increasing hostility toward a number of Asian boys and girls whose families have just begun to move into the area. Similarly, there is one street with a number of Hispanic families, and their young people have begun to use the center. Racial taunts have become commonplace, and there have been a number of fights in the town's parks and schools.

Thus far, the Oroville Police Athletic League has not experienced any direct conflict, but the director is sure that it is going to happen. With this four-sided racial situation (black, white, Asian, and Hispanic), what can be done to improve intergroup relations?

Case Study 8: A Problem of Professional Acceptance

In a private mental health center, the McCray Clinic, several of the activity therapists are concerned about their professional acceptance by the medical and nursing staff, and by other professional staff members.

The activity therapists, who include three recreation specialists, as well as dance and art therapists, feel that they are regarded as diversional workers, used chiefly to fill empty time, rather than as meaningful members of the treatment team. They are rarely brought into team meetings to review patients' progress and develop treatment plans. Although lip-service is given to their value, the medical and nursing staff often feel free to break into their schedules without warning, taking patients away for medication or other purposes. The most serious problem occurred when several patients who had been scheduled to go on a community trip were suddenly taken out of the group by the director of nursing, for some apparently administrative reasons. The morale and feeling of professional worth of the activity therapists is at a very low level. They make an appointment to see the McCray Clinic's director. How can this problem be solved, not only with respect to the community trips that were disrupted, but in terms of the overall image and status of the activity therapy program?

Case Study 9: The Right to Mainstream

In a suburban branch of the Cerebral Palsy Association, one of the staff workers has developed a social program serving older adolescents and young adults with cerebral palsy. In addition to parties, discussion groups, and trips, the group has enjoyed square dancing from time to time. A local caller, making use of very simple dances called at a slow pace, has been quite successful in arousing and maintaining the interest of the group members.

One of the goals of the program has been to encourage group members to "mainstream" themselves whenever possible, by joining existing community recreational programs serving nondisabled populations. Because of their success in square dancing at the Cerebral Palsy Center, several young men and women decide to attend a square dance club meeting at a local YWCA. However, they find the dancing very complex and rapid, and have trouble doing it; other members of the Y club avoid dancing with them, and are discourteous to them.

When they talk to the caller of the Y group, he comments that probably they should recognize that the dancing, as done at the Y, is beyond their capabilities, and that they should not attend. Angrily, they charge that his group is unfair to disabled persons, and that they intend to file a charge of discrimination against the Y.

The caller suggests that they go back to discuss the matter with their program director at the Cerebral Palsy Center. What should this person say to them? What new approach to leadership may be called for?

Case Study 10: Nude Sunbathing at the Private Club

Roswell Heights, a private residential community, operates a sports and recreation center for its membership, with a swimming pool, tennis courts, health club, and clubhouse for classes and other social events. Operating under an Activity Council, the club employs a recreation director, who schedules and plans activities. The policy of Roswell Heights is that residents may bring guests in to use the facilities at a charge, and that outside groups may also reserve facilities on a rental basis.

This policy has caused few problems through the years. However, several couples who are residents of Roswell Heights now approach Jane Paolone, the recreation director, with an unusual request. It seems that they enjoy nude sunbathing and have often gone to nudist beaches or on tours where this activity is popular. They would like to be able to swim nude at the club's pool and invite a number of outside friends who are nudists, to join them—paying a fee, according to the established policy. When Jane suggests that other club members may resent this, they ask that some special hours be set aside for their use, at which time other members might choose whether or not they wish to join them. There is a high fence around the pool, which would assure reasonable privacy. Jane consults with members of the Activity Council regarding this request; it appears that no existing policy or club by-law covers the matter. How should she handle it?

Case Study 11: Behavior Modification—But How?

Jim and Martha Gottschild have sent their teenage son Fred to a private summer camp that operates a behavior modification program. Fred has been a difficult child for the Gottschilds to handle since he was a boy. He has a volatile temper, refuses to take orders, often fights with his peers, and has been a low achiever at school, although he scores high on intelligence tests. The summer camp is run by a nonprofit community mental health association, under the direction of Mark Parsons, an ex-marine.

On visiting day, when Jim and Martha talk with Fred, he complains of the methods that have been used to discipline him and some of the other boys and girls. When they disobey camp rules, they have been forced to stand outside in the cold rain for hours, wearing only their underwear. Carrying pails of rocks, they have been made to scramble up and down a steep hill until exhausted, and have been subjected to other humiliating forms of punishment.

When Jim and Martha Gottschild discuss these practices with Fred's counselor, he indicates that all of the camp's policies, including punishment and other behavior modification strategies, are established by Mark Parsons, the director. Parsons is a very forceful, dynamic, and opinionated person. None of the counselors feel able to challenge him. While they are concerned about the methods used in the camp, the Gottschilds have a feeling that their son Fred appears to be somewhat more reasonable and self-disciplined than he has often been in the past. What should they do?

Case Study 12: Making a Go of the Campground

Two sisters, Alice and Marge Hough, have inherited an old farm situated on a pretty New England lake. Being outdoor recreation enthusiasts and having camped for years, they decide to begin their own business on the farm property—a commercial campground. After developing twenty campsites, a road, beach area on the lake, a toilet, and other needed facilities, they advertise the campground. Starting with a few families, the venture becomes modestly successful, and they expand the campground, adding a pier and sailboats for water fun. Campers hike in the woods beyond the campground, and enjoy other nature activities in the area.

However, Alice and Marge begin to recognize that they have one major problem. Attendance is fairly good from late June through the first two weeks in August. On weekends such as the July Fourth or Labor Day weekend, there are far more requests for campsites than they can possibly fill. However, from early September to the beginning of June, the campground is totally unused, and as a result, their income from it is simply not enough to justify the operation. What could the Hough sisters do to make the campground more of a year-round operation, and boost the profit of the operation?

Case Study 13: Justifying Employee Recreation

The Tra-Ject Corporation, a high-tech research and development company in the aerospace field, has developed an outstanding employee activities program, with two full-time staff members and a large employee recreation association. With increased economic competition, the Tra-Ject officers feel they must cut back on nonessential company expenses. They are considering firing the full-time employee activity directors, and reducing the program to a completely voluntary operation, without any subsidy from the company.

The two directors meet with the officers of the employee recreation association, to see what they can do about this threat. What can they do to convince the company administrators of the worth of the program? What proof will satisfy them? What new program features might be developed that would contribute directly to the welfare and successful operation of the company?

Case Study 14: Expanding the Human-Service Function

Ron Cohn is a civilian recreation employee at a U.S. Army Air Force base in Germany. The recreation program has been quite successful, with good participation in organized sports, crafts, social events, trips, and other activities. However, the base itself has had a serious problem of drug abuse and alcoholism among many enlisted personnel. In addition, there is a high level of tension on the base, with many service men and women suffering from stress and burnout; marital difficulties are common among the families attached to the base.

Ron is asked by his commanding officer to come up with a plan for attacking these problems, as part of the total Morale, Welfare, and Recreation operation. He has never had experience in running such programs. Where should he begin?

Case Study 15: Not Enough Gym Space

In another armed forces recreation program, the problem is one of not having enough gym space to conduct varied types of needed activities during the week. The commanding officer believes that competitive sports do the most to raise the morale of those on the base, and help promote its favorable image. He therefore makes heavy use of the one major gym facility available on the base, for teams to practice—not only basketball, boxing, or other indoor sports, but baseball and football teams to do agility drills, conditioning programs, and similar activities. This emphasis is year-round, with teams constantly practicing for competition with other bases in the region, or higher levels of competition in interservice meets. As a result, there is almost no opportunity for low-pressure intramural sports, or for teenage leagues to play various sports in the late afternoon or early evening, or for fitness or dance activities in the gym.

Sue Parker, who is in charge of the recreation program on the base, has had difficulty in making a case for these other activities with the base commander. In part, she feels it may be because she is a woman. However, she also feels that it is a matter of conflicting philosophy. What can she do to persuade the base commander that a more balanced sports program is desirable, or to find other available space to run a comprehensive program?

Developing Other Case Studies

In addition to reviewing and analyzing the fifteen cases described here, classes may develop their own cases, based on their personal experiences or on problem situations they may encounter in observing community leisure-service agencies or interviewing professional personnel. These cases may also provide the basis for class problem-solving exercises using the techniques described in this chapter.

NOTES

[1]Joseph J. Bannon, *Problem Solving in Recreation and Parks* (Englewood Cliffs, N.J.: Prentice-Hall, 1981).

[2]David W. Johnson and Frank P. Johnson, *Joining Together: Group Theory and Group Skills* (Englewood Cliffs, N.J.: Prentice-Hall, 1982).

[3]H. Douglas Sessoms and Jack L. Stevenson, *Leadership and Group Dynamics in Recreation Services* (Boston: Allyn and Bacon, 1981).

[4]Sessoms and Stevenson, Chapter 5.

[5]Sessoms and Stevenson, p. 174.

STUDENT PROJECTS

1. Form small groups to experiment with techniques designed to assist in the problem-solving process, such as role-playing, brainstorming, buzz-group methods, or values-clarification exercises (for additional information on these, see Suggested Readings below).
2. Form small groups; have each group select one of the cases presented in this chapter, and apply an appropriate small-group problem-solving technique in analyzing it and arriving at an appropriate solution. This may be done as a class exercise, with the small groups demonstrating the process, or involving other class members in it.
3. As a follow-up to Project 2, individual class members may present their own cases, based on their past experiences and observations, for groups to use in problem-solving exercises.

SUGGESTED READINGS

Joseph J. Bannon, *Problem Solving in Recreation and Parks* (Englewood Cliffs, N.J.: Prentice-Hall, 1981).

Richard Kraus, Gay Carpenter, and Barbara Bates, *Recreation Leadership and Supervision* (Philadelphia: W. B. Saunders, 1981), Chapter 14.

Christopher R. Edginton and Charles A. Griffith, *The Recreation and Leisure Delivery System* (Philadelphia: W. B. Saunders, 1983), Chapter 10.

H. Douglas Sessoms and Jack L. Stevenson, *Leadership and Group Dynamics in Recreation Services* (Boston: Allyn and Bacon, 1981), Chapters 5, 6, 7.

CHAPTER 13

Professional Development in Recreation Leadership

There is a time-worn cliché that says, "Leaders are not born; they are made." It would be foolish to suggest that many individuals did not seem to possess apparently innate personality traits that helped them gain success as leaders. However, it is also obvious that many important leadership qualities and skills may be nurtured and developed in a purposeful, deliberate way.

In examining the role of leadership in leisure-service agencies, it is therefore helpful to examine several key stages of staff development which are intended to improve the quality of professional practice, and which contribute to the career patterns of recreation leaders.

STAGES OF STAFF DEVELOPMENT

The stages of staff development include the following: (1) personnel recruiting; (2) hiring procedures; (3) orientation and probationary period; (4) in-service education; (5) supervision; (6) evaluation; and (7) promotion, transfer, termination, or other appropriate personnel actions. This chapter examines these processes, and concludes with a number of recommendations to students in higher education curricula in this field, or those who are considering recreation as a career.

In reading this chapter, students should understand that the professional development practices it presents are those that should be encountered within any effectively administered leisure-service agency. At each stage, they may recognize staff development techniques observed in agencies where they have done field work, or carried out part-time or seasonal leadership assignments. This is not to say that all leisure-service organizations carry out all elements of the staff development process in a fully professional way. However, most well-managed organizations must be concerned with carrying out each of these steps as effectively as possible.

Taking the application a step further, readers should also recognize that, as they move into professional roles where they will be supervising and directing personnel, the techniques presented here may become an important part of their responsibility. The very first step in the process, of course, involves recruiting and selecting personnel.

Recruitment

It is essential to attract and employ the most highly qualified individuals available on the labor market, if recreation and park programs are to be successful. A variety of techniques are used in this process. Hiring agencies may make up special fliers or brochures, giving full details of openings or career possibilities within a department. They may also by law be required to advertise openings in county or city newspapers. Positions may be advertised in listings in professional publications or employment services, or in "job marts" at professional conferences. Realistically, many positions are filled through word of mouth, or by hiring individuals who have previously worked for the department on a volunteer, part-time, or seasonal basis.

Many organizations, particularly commercial recreation businesses, establish internship programs for college majors in recreation and parks. Through such programs, they are able to identify highly qualified young people, and to select them for continuing full-time employment, following their graduation.

As part of the recruitment process, written job descriptions should be prepared, giving essential information about the responsibilities, salary, Civil Service grade (if governmental), personnel benefits, and hiring qualifications, as well as application procedures. Job descriptions should be concise and attractive, completely accurate, and approved by appropriate personnel officials in the agency or department. They should include deadlines for filing applications, examination dates, and other needed information. See Figure 13–1 for an example of job notices.

Hiring Procedure

With a substantial number of recreation and park majors graduating from professional preparation programs today, as well as others who have studied in allied fields, it is usually not difficult to attract job candidates. The real challenge to administrators is to attract, identify, and hire the very best candidates. This can only be done through effective recruitment, and the careful screening of applicants through interviews, reviews of past experience, references and education, examinations, and other procedures designed to measure real leadership potential.

Depending on the level of the position to be filled, the selection and screening process may be relatively brief, or may be complex and drawn out. If it is in a public agency, it may require examinations, with qualified candidates being placed on a list of eligible applicants. Careful attention should be paid to checking references and the interview process should involve, if possible, a team or committee of supervisors or

FIGURE 13–1 Examples of Employment Opportunities in U.S. Navy Recreation, Stateside and Overseas

Naval Support Office, La Maddalena, Italy is recruiting for a Recreation Specialist, UA–188–09 to handle the general recreation program. SF–171's should go to Consolidated Civilian Personnel Office, U.S. Naval Support Office, La Maddalena, FPO New York 09533.

Naval Support Activity, Naples, Italy is recruiting for a Recreation Specialist, GS–188–09 to serve as point of contact and liaison between all Mediterranean Area Afloat Units. Insures that Afloat Command are informed of available recreational and athletic programs, facilities, and competition. Prepares appropriated and NAF funded budgets for Fleet Support for Supervisor's review. SF–171's should go to U.S. Naval Support Activity, Box 29, CCPO, FPO New York 09521. October 1984.

Naval Air Station, Sigonella, Italy is recruiting for a Recreational Services Officer, UA/GS–0301–12 (pending classification and approval). SF–171's should go to Consolidated Civilian Personnel Office, Sigonella Branch, Naval Air Station, Sigonella, FPO New York 09523.

Norfolk Naval Shipyard, Portsmouth, VA is recruiting an Assistant Club Manager, UA–1101–7/9 for the Enlisted Mess. Position open until filled. No travel or relocation expenses. SF–171's should go to Coordinator, Recreational Services, Norfolk Naval Shipyard, Portsmouth, VA 23709.

Naval Weapons Station, Yorktown, VA is recruiting for a Golf Course Manager, GS–1101–07 to operate a 9-hole golf course with 18 tee grounds. SF–171's should go to Recreation Director, Naval Weapons Station, PO Box 88, Yorktown, VA 23691.

Commander, Naval Military Personnel Command, Washington, DC is recruiting for a Management Analyst, (Field Representative) UA–188–9/11 to serve as Fleet Recreation Coordinator, Traveling Field Rep. SF–171's should go to Commander, Naval Military Personnel Command, Recreational Services Department, Code N–113, Washington, DC 20370.

---

managerial personnel to ensure that the hiring decision is not based primarily on one individual's judgment.

An important element of the selection process involves the need to comply with equal opportunity regulations. In all types of organizations today, it is essential to avoid any form of discrimination based on race or ethnic origin, religion, sex, age, marital status, or similar factors. Questions in these areas may be asked only when there is a clear need to determine a legitimate occupational qualification.

Orientation and Probationary Period

The chief purpose of orientation is to familiarize new employees with the job setting and their own responsibilities as quickly and thoroughly as possible, in order to get them off on the right foot. Too often, individuals are thrown into a work situation without adequate preparation or briefing, and flounder unsuccessfully for a period of time, which is destructive both to the program and to their own morale. Effective orientation should be done as soon as the newly hired employee comes on the job. It may include any or all of the following procedures:

1. Preliminary meetings with all key personnel or department heads, both in their own department, and in other branches, divisions, or services related to recreation.

2. Tour of facilities, to become familiar with all important offices, parks, playgrounds, or centers in a district—or treatment or residential areas in an institution.

3. Detailed and thorough briefing on responsibilities and how these are to be performed, as well as personnel regulations. Normally, these, as well as basic information on personnel benefits, are included in a personnel manual which goes to all employees.

4. Putting the new employee under the direct supervision of a skilled staff member for a set period of weeks or months, to provide on-the-job training in the work situation before assigning him or her to more independent responsibilities. This is sometimes done by rotating the new employee to several different job settings, each for a brief period of time, in order to provide overall familiarity with the agency.

5. Finally, if enough individuals are being hired at one time, as in the case of an institution that is setting up a large new unit, or a summer program that is getting under way with many inexperienced young leaders, orientation may include special workshops. These usually extend over two or more days and include philosophy, policies, and principles of the agency's program, and also direct leadership techniques.

Use of Agency Manual. Most public recreation and park departments, as well as many voluntary or therapeutic agencies, have developed formal personnel codes or manuals of personnel practices.

These deal with such matters as: (a) employment (needed qualifications, examinations, and application procedures); (b) required participation in in-service training courses; (c) probationary periods of employment; (d) leaves of absence, for vacation, holiday, illness, maternity, or educational reasons; (e) retirement plans, joint-contribution pension plans, disability retirement plans, death benefits; (f) legal assistance for suits related to job occurrences; (g) overtime pay or compensatory time for emergency work; (h) codes for disciplinary action when necessary; and (i) explanation of the evaluation system used in the department. In addition, manuals may deal with specific regulations covering policies having to do with work performance, such as restrictions on the use of department cars, handling of funds, physical control of participants, staff dress codes, drinking, drug use, and the like.

Normally, such information or expectations should be made clear to the job candidate in hiring interviews, and during the orientation process, in part through the use of departmental manuals which provide full details of work schedules and assignments.

Apart from the formal expectations laid down by departments in staff manuals, what are working conditions like today for recreation employees? In general, they have become much more realistic and attractive. No longer should an individual have to take a position demanding that he or she might have to work at all hours of the day or night—with insufficient time for family needs or the employee's own recreation. Today, most enlightened department heads will expect a recreation professional to have a working schedule similar to that of other employees on comparable levels of authority. True, some of it will be evening work, or possibly weekend assignments.

However, this should be compensated for by free time elsewhere in the weekly schedule. The recreation professional may be called upon to participate in many meetings, to address civic groups, and to serve as a resource consultant or advisor for other agencies in the community. But, for the recreation leader or administrator who is interested in people, in promoting a sound philosophy of leisure, and in strengthening the influence of his or her own department, these represent opportunities rather than unwelcome chores.

In other types of agencies, such as corporate/employee, campus, or private leisure-service organizations, there is not likely to be a formal orientation process or agency manual. In large commercial recreation businesses, such as theme parks, however, there may be a carefully developed training program with a general introduction to the philosophy and personnel policies of the organization and specific training in the job area that each employee will be entering. Indeed, the Walt Disney organization has developed a complex training program known as Disney University, in which they have adapted the most modern training techniques used in industry to the task of preparing personnel for work in the theme park field.

In most governmental agencies, there is a set period of time (usually from one to three months) during which new employees are on probationary status. Following this, if their performance has been satisfactory, they become regular or permanent employees. In some situations, new employees may be hired provisionally, with the understanding that they must take an examination before being given permanent status. In most cases, however, the probationary period serves to test the individual's ability and commitment and—if these are satisfactory—he or she moves directly into permanent status. Other types of organizations are not as likely to have a formal probationary period and official transfer to permanent status as a normal personnel procedure. However, in most situations, a newly hired individual is obviously "on trial," in the sense that, if his or her performance is not acceptable in the early period of employment, the job will be terminated.

In-Service Education

Well-organized recreation and park organizations provide systematic programs of in-service education, to ensure that their staff members on all levels continue to upgrade their skills and professional knowledge. The most common forms of in-service training are:

1. Some departments provide courses, usually on a once-a-week basis, for several sessions for staff members on a community-wide or district basis. These courses may either deal with specific recreation skills in areas such as sports, music, or working with special groups, or may deal with problem areas, or even supervisory or administrative concerns.
2. Special institutes or workshops, which may range from a single afternoon or evening to several days, usually deal with single problems or programs, or with preparing personnel for a new season. Not infre-

quently, several small municipal departments pool their resources to sponsor such events cooperatively. (See Appendix, p. 286.)

3. Staff meetings frequently provide a setting for talks, skills demonstrations, or group problem-solving sessions.

4. Recreation and park agencies may also encourage professional growth by providing films, libraries, and other resources, tours of facilities or programs, and by enabling staff members (through released time or special grants) to attend nearby colleges, conferences, or even extended workshops.

It is essential that in-service training be assigned as a regular responsibility to one or more staff members, that all personnel have the opportunity to contribute to planning and evaluating it, and that it be carefully organized, scheduled, and staffed. While it provides an excellent contribution to staff development, if it is done haphazardly or carelessly, it will simply be a waste of time. Some departments or institutions *require* that personnel take specified in-service courses to be eligible for promotion. An example of in-service training on a national level may be found in the National Professional Training Plan of the Boys' Clubs of America.

Boys' Clubs of America–National Professional Training Plan

Section A: Formal Training Process—BCA Training Continuum

Phase 1: New Worker Briefing and Registration (beginning of full-time employment)

Phase 2: Orientation Seminars (first year of full-time employment)

Phase 3: Advanced Program Seminars (two to three years of full-time employment)

Phase 4: Management Training Programs (determined by position)

Phase 5: Executive Training Programs (determined by position)

Section B: Special Training Services Provided by Boys' Clubs of America and other Organizations

BCA Sponsored: Institutes, Symposiums, Administrative Conferences, Big Cities Conference, National Convention, Scholarship Programs

BCA-Developed Materials: Newsletters, Keynote, Program Packages, In-Service Training Packets, Tapes and Cassettes

Other Organizations: General Publications, Commercial Material, Inter-Agency Collaboration, College Continuing Programs, Specialized Training (AMA, Red Cross, National Training Laboratories, etc.)

Other national voluntary organizations sponsor extensive training programs and publish educational materials both for their professional staff and the large numbers of volunteers actually conducting programs.

For example, the Boy Scouts of America has given a strong thrust to programming for several categories of disabled youngsters, including physically disabled, mentally retarded, visually impaired, and deaf. To accomplish this, they have published a number of excellent manuals dealing with such programs, and provide other leadership experiences and training materials. The Special Olympics program, sponsored by the Joseph P. Kennedy, Jr. Foundation, is a leader in the field of physical fitness and sports competition for mentally retarded children and youth, and has also developed special training programs and manuals for coaches, officials, volunteer aides, and families of participants in its competitions.

Role of National or Regional Organizations.

Numerous other national or regional organizations, both governmental and voluntary, provide resources and programs to assist in the process of in-service or continuing education.

In the United States, the National Recreation and Park Association has strongly promoted continuing education, chiefly in the form of major conferences, workshops, publications and courses, symposiums, and other services geared to improve the work of professionals in various areas of leisure-service. Its Park Practice publication series, issued cooperatively with the National Park Service, has involved three publications, *Design, Trends,* and *Grist,* which have, for over a quarter of a century, provided valuable, practical assistance to such diverse professional groups as state or county park superintendents, playground supervisors, forest rangers, or campground owners.

In a recent year, NRPA sponsored a wide range of Park and Recreation Maintenance Management Schools and Workshops, Innovative Programming Forums, Workshops on Computers, Executive Development Programs, Forums on Community-Based Recreation Programming for Special Populations, Revenue Sources Management Schools, and other schools or workshops related to the arts, safety management, and sports. The National Therapeutic Recreation Society has sponsored outstanding Therapeutic Recreation Management Schools, and issued a number of important training publications in this field.

Training in Special Areas of Program Leadership.

Within specific activity areas, other professional or special-interest organizations have also sponsored important training and certification programs. In Canada, for example, a number of provinces have taken leadership training in the field of outdoor recreation. The Outdoor Recreation Section of the Alberta Recreation and Parks Department has established a unique training facility, the Blue Mountain Centre, which provides leadership training and certification programs in such areas as archery, backpacking, climbing and mountaineering, canoe and kayak, environmental programs, flyfishing, orienteering, pioneer outdoor pursuits, wilderness crafts, and outdoor living skills. By the early 1980s, over 12,000 persons had taken such courses.

In the area of youth sports, a number of major organizations, such as the Youth Sports Institute, provide research, publications, seminars, and specific coaching-skills programs in various sports areas. In Canada, there are outstanding national certification programs which address both physiological and psychological aspects of coaching, sponsored by the Coaching Association of Canada. Little League and other specific sports organizations provide similar training programs. Still other organizations, such as the American Camping Association, provide outstanding training programs at various levels of camping responsibility, leading to certification on professional levels.

In the area of commercial recreation, numerous associations and private corporations have moved into the field of management training, and have published magazines and sponsored conferences, exhibitions, and training workshops dealing with facilities design, management techniques, marketing systems, security and vandalism, personnel practices, and similar concerns.

Programs Offered by Colleges. A number of the major continuing education programs offered by NRPA or other professional societies are sponsored in collaboration with colleges and universities. Other recreation and park curricula obviously offer advanced specializations or curricula in various aspects of recreation leadership or management. In some cases, they also sponsor special workshops, such as special institutes or symposiums in travel and tourism, that individuals who are working in the field may take as part of degree programs, for credit, or simply on a one-shot basis.

Summing up, there are two basic approaches to providing in-service education for recreation professionals: (1) internally, through the use of courses, workshops, or meetings that are sponsored *within* the agency; and (2) externally, by making use of available resources sponsored by *other* organizations or educational institutions. To promote staff development and maximize productivity, many leisure-service agencies use both approaches.

In addition to introducing recreation personnel to new theories or techniques, an important value of much in-service training or continuing education is that it compels employees to evaluate their work and the problems facing their agencies. Often, it leads to improved communication processes and better teamwork in attacking problems facing the organization. Ideally then, in-service training not only facilitates growth on the part of employees, but pays dividends in terms of agency productivity and efficient operation.

Ongoing Supervision

The primary element in the overall staff development process consists of supervision. Within all agency structures, there is typically an organization chart or chain of command. This means that within a pyramidal-like structure, individuals at a particular level of responsibility supervise the work of subordinate employees and at the same time have their own work supervised by others above them in the structure.

For example, recreation center directors might supervise the work of leaders in their centers who work directly with groups, while at the same time, they must report to district supervisors who are a step above them in the chain of command.

From a program point of view, the key supervisory relationship is the one in which district or program supervisors work with leadership personnel to help them function effectively and make a maximum contribution to the department. It involves: (a) the supervisor regularly observing the leader at work, and assisting him or her by making specific suggestions of a technical or interpersonal nature; (b) the supervisor providing a two-way communications channel, by transmitting policy messages or other information from top administration to ''line'' personnel, and making the views, needs, and suggestions of leaders known to top administration; (c) the supervisor serving as a trainer and trouble-shooter, who spots problems as they develop, and intervenes to help solve them; and (d) the supervisor evaluating the work of subordinate employees, meeting with them regularly to discuss their progress, and making recommendations as to promotion, transfer, or other personnel actions.

Modern management theory suggests that the most effective supervisors are those who are democratic in approach, who use participatory techniques in involving lower-level employees in planning, problem solving, and designing work schedules, and who rely on establishing an atmosphere of trust, confidence, and favorable motivation, rather than threats, to keep production high.

At the same time, it must be recognized that supervisors are responsible for the work done by subordinate employees and, in effect, represent a middle-level form of management. This means that they may be required to recommend disciplinary action, and certainly to make other recommendations for promotions, task assignment, and possible demotion or transfer. Thus, although it is desirable to have a highly cooperative, sharing, and informal relationship between supervisors and leaders, it is also necessary to maintain some degree of separation, based on the professional responsibilities of both levels of personnel.

The actual task of personnel supervision may involve varied types of assistance or guidance. At the simplest level, the supervisor may *assign* leaders to carry out specific tasks or other responsibilities. They may also *instruct* them in the precise way in which these tasks are to be accomplished—assuming that a single correct technique may be identified.

At a somewhat more advanced level, supervisors may *coach* leaders in the way they carry out their responsibilities, giving suggestions or cues, or providing constructive assistance to them. Supervisors may also *counsel* leaders, when problems occur, or when leaders are experiencing other kinds of difficulties on the job.

Strengthening Motivation of Leaders.   A key task of supervisors is to enrich and strengthen the motivation of program leaders. There are a number of obvious ways in which this can be done: (1) through direct rewards, such as praise, favorable evaluations, or promotion; (2) through the assignment of a higher level of responsibility or more challenging assignments; or (3) by making the job situation more satisfying or rewarding in terms of the leader's personal needs and abilities.

A number of major theories of motivation have been developed, including Maslow's needs hierarchy, which emphasizes the importance of "self-actualization" opportunities, and Herzberg's two-factor theory of "satisfiers" and "dissatisfiers" in the job situation. While none of these provide completely satisfactory explanations of on-the-job motivation, they are helpful in considering the factors that may influence employees in their work.

Maslow's Hierarchy of Needs.   Abraham Maslow developed a theory of human needs which had important implications for understanding the behavior of recreation participants and also that of employees in various fields of work. He took the position that all human behavior is purposeful, and intended to satisfy certain felt needs. The needs themselves are identifiable and can be classified in a hierarchy in which the most basic and important needs are at the bottom, and the subsequent needs placed on higher levels (see Figure 13–2). Physiological needs related to basic survival come first, and must be satisfied before the individual seeks to satisfy the next levels of needs, such as the needs for security, social relationships, personal esteem, and self-actualization.

Edginton and Williams point out that Maslow's hierarchy theory had considerable impact on management approaches to improving motivation, since each of his levels could clearly be associated with aspects of the work situation:

> Physiological, or basic, needs can be associated with salary. Security needs can be associated with seniority, union subsidy, severance pay, and so on. Social or belonging needs can be associated with the formal and informal groups at work. Esteem needs can be associated with title, status symbols, and promotion. Finally, the highest level, self-actualization, is associated with employee achievement wherein the employee gets satisfaction out of the work itself.[1]

In a sense, this model is somewhat arbitrary, in that the needs may not always appear in the order indicated, and it is possible for individuals to seek need satisfaction on a number of levels at once. Edginton and Williams comment that one of its major contributions was the concept that people tend to reach for things they do not always have; thus, once a need is met or satisfied, it no longer serves as a motivator. This is the implication:

> . . . one must constantly be searching for ways to motivate employees by providing new challenges. The employer must try to be aware of what is likely to be the next need an employee will pursue, one that will excite her or him enough to do an outstanding piece of work.[2]

FIGURE 13–2   Maslow Hierarchy of Needs

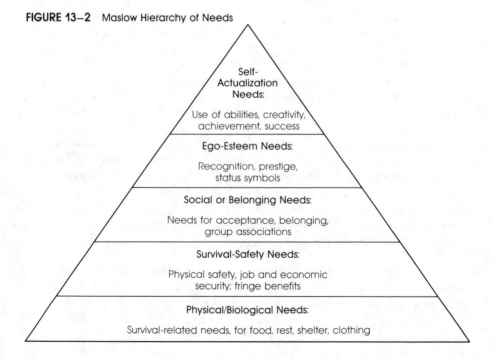

Self-
Actualization
Needs:

Use of abilities, creativity,
achievement, success

Ego-Esteem Needs:

Recognition, prestige,
status symbols

Social or Belonging Needs:

Needs for acceptance, belonging,
group associations

Survival-Safety Needs:

Physical safety, job and economic
security; fringe benefits

Physical/Biological Needs:

Survival-related needs, for food, rest, shelter, clothing

Herzberg's Two-Factor Model of Motivation.   An equally influential model of employee motivation was developed by Frederick Herzberg, who carried out research leading to a two-factor theory of on-the-job satisfaction and dissatisfaction. The two factors were identified as "hygiene" factors and "motivational" factors. Hygiene factors were concerned generally with working conditions, interpersonal relationships among employees and supervisors, and such work factors as salary, job status, and security. It was believed that such factors do not in themselves make employees happy or satisfied, but do prevent them from being unhappy and dissatisfied.

In contrast, motivational factors are directly concerned with the work process itself, in the sense that challenging or meaningful work, recognition for doing a good job, or increased responsibility were all seen as providing positive satisfactions and helping directly to improve motivation and work productivity. Herzberg's theory helped to shift the focus of management away from simply regarding higher wages or increased fringe benefits as the best way to improve employee motivation and performance. Instead, it emphasized the need to create work situations that will positively enhance the employee's interest in his or her work and upgrade productivity.

Actually, both types of factors are critical in maintaining a happy and productive work environment—hygiene factors to reduce job dissatisfaction and keep employees working at a steady level, and motivator factors to promote satisfaction and increase both the quality and the amount of work output.

McGregor's Theory X and Theory Y.   Both Maslow's and Herzberg's analyses must be viewed in relation to Douglas McGregor's model of employee attitudes and work performance. McGregor suggested two models or sets of assumptions which were influential in management theory and process: Theory X and Theory Y.[3]

Theory X is described as the traditional or conventional perception of employees' attitudes, including these convictions: (1) the average person dislikes work and will avoid it if possible; (2) people prefer to be directed, don't want responsibility, have little ambition, and desire security above all; and (3) for these reasons, the "carrot and stick" approach is necessary, with people having to be coerced, tightly supervised and controlled, and threatened with punishment to get them to put forth adequate on-the-job efforts.

Theory Y is a much more positive and contemporary view, which holds: (1) physical and mental efforts in work are as natural as rest and play; (2) external controls and the threat of punishment are essentially not as productive as supervisory approaches which help employees develop self-control and self-direction; (3) motivation can be improved by giving people more challenging and autonomous work assignments which require imagination, ingenuity, and creativity in solving problems, and by rewarding them for their achievements in practical and psychological ways; and (4) ultimately, people will not only accept but will seek greater responsibility, with the right managerial approaches.

McGregor's views were influential in promoting a number of newer approaches to personnel management—particularly those emphasizing shared-decision-making and goals setting, and other forms of participative management. They helped to create a climate in which Japanese management concepts were caught up by many

American management experts and business executives. The use of "quality circles," for example, became increasingly widespread. Henderson and Goode define the quality circle as:

> . . . a voluntary group of workers who have a shared area of responsibility. They meet on a regular basis to discuss, analyze, and propose solutions to quality problems. They are specifically taught group communication, decision-making strategies, and evaluation and problem-solving techniques.[4]

Quality circles have increasingly become helpful in many business concerns, in improving staff relationships, promoting employee understanding of company problems, and upgrading work output and quality. They represent a tool that more and more leisure-service agencies are likely to use as a helpful supervisory technique.

Other Approaches.   Numerous other theories have been developed with respect to the improvement of employee motivation. Gibson, Ivancevich, and Donnelly, for example, show how *path-goal theory* can be directly helpful in strengthening the motivation level of employees. They write:

> According to the path-goal theory leaders should increase the number and kinds of rewards available to subordinates. In addition, the leader should provide guidance and counsel to clarify the manner in which these rewards can be obtained. This means the leader should help subordinates clarify realistic expectancies and reduce the barriers to the accomplishment of valued goals. For example, counseling employees on their chances of receiving a promotion and helping them eliminate skill deficiencies so that a promotion becomes more of a reality are appropriate leadership behaviors. The leader works at making the path to goals for subordinates as clear as possible [considering] the *personal characteristics of subordinates* and the *environmental pressures and demands* with which [they] must cope in order to accomplish work goals and derive satisfaction.[5]

Evaluation

Finally, supervisors must *evaluate* subordinate employees, both to assist them in improving the quality of their performance and as part of the overall personnel process within the organization.

Too often, evaluation is thought of as something that happens at the end of a work period or program, or once a year, to meet Civil Service personnel codes or union job contracts. However, the leader's work should be *regularly* evaluated, both through informal observation and in day-by-day contacts with the supervisor, and through formal, periodic conferences. The purposes of such meetings is to give the individual employee helpful insights, and to improve his or her performance. It should also permit the leader to give the supervisor his or her perception of the job assignment, and to make suggestions for improving the program or overall agency performance. Thus, evaluation should be a *two-way, ongoing* process, rather than a *one-way, periodic* event.

Many public and voluntary leisure-service agencies make use of evaluation forms which rate employees on the basis of specific categories of personality and on-the-job performance (see Figure 13–3). Ideally, such forms should examine the individual's performance in depth, rather than consist of a brief listing of desirable traits or statements to be rated. They should also permit the identification of strengths and weaknesses, and areas of needed improvement or recommended projects or professional enrichment tasks to be undertaken during the rating period ahead.

Customarily, each employee should be evaluated on the basis of such rating forms at least once a year, with the report going into his or her personnel folder. The report is then used as part of the process of considering possible personnel actions for the individual employee within the agency structure.

Two-Way Evaluation.   Traditionally, personnel evaluation was usually approached as a one-way process, with administrators or supervisors making arbitrary, one-sided, and sometimes hidden judgments about their subordinates. Today, good personnel practices stress the two-way, open nature of the evaluation process. For example, in Long Beach, California, the Employee Appraisal System stresses evaluation which will encourage communication and mutual assistance in the department, give both supervisors and leaders "feedback" on their work, and provide a full record for job promotions, reassignments, dismissals, and references. Each employee is expected to develop a statement of his or her personal objectives at the beginning of each report period, and success in meeting these objectives is carefully reviewed in the "Employee Progress Report" which must be prepared at least once each year. The procedure follows:

> *Progress Report.* Employee and supervisor *each* fill out a copy independently, meet to discuss what they have written, and if major agreement is reached, the supervisor makes up and forwards to his supervisor (the reviewer) a final copy. The employee should note minor disagreements on the back of final copy. The employee should also be encouraged to take notes during the appraisal interview. If, however, the employee and supervisor cannot reach major agreement, either can request a meeting with the reviewer in which the three discuss the appraisal. If no agreement results from this meeting, employee should file objections on the back of the form and the reviewer will see that the form is reviewed by the Assistant Director for Program and Facilities. Major agreement is defined as when both parties are content to let the appraisal stand.[6]

As further evidence of the two-way nature of this appraisal process, at least once a year supervisors must be evaluated in written form by *their* subordinates. Throughout, staff development is seen as a continuing, dynamic process, in which evaluation helps to identify areas of strength and areas in which improvement is needed.

Ideally, then, personnel evaluation should be based on McGregor's Theory Y, which stresses an atmosphere of trust and open communication, in which the supervisor assumes that the recreation leader is highly motivated and wishes to improve his or her work, and the leader feels free to discuss his or her performance with the supervisor, without fear of reprisal. In reality, however, if the evaluation process must at some point end in the supervisor making an entry in the employee's personnel folder that may influence future decisions with respect to job promotion, transfer, or other personnel actions, it is difficult to achieve an atmosphere of trust and openness.

Indeed, Teague points out that formal employee evaluations often tend to yield unsatisfactory results, in part because of resistance from the supervisors who are

FIGURE 13–3 Evansville, Indiana, Recreation Supervisory Rating Record

Name of Employee_____	Rating Period from Unsatisfactory
Title_____	_____ to _____ Satisfactory
Date_____	Total score: Outstanding

How to Mark the Service Rating: After each of the traits below there is a line drawn with descriptive phrases placed along it and above the line a numerical rating. Each of the scores describes the degree to which the individual being rated possesses that trait. Place a check mark at the place on the line which you believe shows the degree to which the description applies: Poor Performance on the Left, and Strong Performance on the Right.

1. Attendance

0 10 20 30 40	50 60 70	80 90 100
Can't be depended on; absent	Moderate number of absences	Rarely absent

2. Appearance appropriate to job

0 10 20 30 40	50 60 70	80 90 100
Unsatisfactory and neglected	Sometimes dressed inappropriately	Dress always neat and appropriate

3. Leadership

0 10 20 30 40	50 60 70	80 90 100
Creates fear; drives instead of leads; creates antagonism	Fairly successful in direction of others	Outstanding leader; has respect of others and brings out their best efforts

4. Organizing ability

0 10 20 30 40	50 60 70	80 90 100
Unable to organize work; cannot adopt or adhere to a plan	Plans work fairly efficiently	Excellent organizer and planner; delegates authority successfully

5. Ability in instructing

0 10 20 30 40	50 60 70	80 90 100
Poor instructor; does not prepare material or communicate effectively	Fairly effective; sometimes has difficulty	Highly effective; teaches with clarity and enthusiasm

6. Control and discipline

0 10 20 30 40	50 60 70	80 90 100
Discipline weak; lacks effective and consistent control	Moderately successful in discipline	Highly effective; shows skill and courage in difficult situations

7. Judgment

0 10 20 30 40	50 60 70	80 90 100
Judgment poor or inconsistent	Usually uses good judgment	Exceptionally sound judgment

8. Initiative

0 10 20 30 40	50 60 70	80 90 100
Little initiative; lacks resourcefulness	Some initiative; fairly resourceful	Dynamic self-starter; highly resourceful and creative

9. Responsibility

0 10 20 30 40	50 60 70	80 90 100
Poor; cannot be counted on	Usually accepts responsibility; sometimes fails to carry out assignment	Eagerly welcomes responsibility and carries out tasks independently

expected to administer them. This may be attributed, he writes, to the following causes:

> (1) a normal dislike of criticizing a subordinate, and very possibly, having to argue about it; (2) lack of skill needed to effectively manage an appraisal interview; (3) mistrust of the validity of appraisal instruments; and (4) dislike in implementing a new procedure with its accompanying operational changes. Managers express real misgivings when they are put in the position of "playing God."[7]

In some cases, the problem is made even more severe by union contracts or Civil Service regulations which may call for a protest, grievance procedure, or other hearing, if any substantially negative comment is placed in the employee's folder. For this reason, both sides are often content to permit evaluation procedures to be routine and superficial—rather than dynamic and probing. The key point is that evaluation is often seen as threatening and critical. Ideally, if the ongoing process of evaluation can be linked with day-by-day supervision, and interwoven with coaching and counseling on the part of the supervisor, it becomes less threatening. The actual submission of an evaluation report may then be seen as a natural outgrowth of the overall performance of the employee and, since it is based on mutually shared understandings of supervisors and leaders, should not represent a severe shock or critical attack.

Personnel Evaluation Based on Performance Record

In many cases, personnel evaluation may be based not on the supervisor's judgment of the employee's personality or leadership style, or on any other element but actual on-the-job productivity. Efforts should be made to specify all elements of performance in terms of quantitative measures—of programs initiated, participants served, fees collected, or other program outcomes. This approach tends to reduce the element of personal judgment of the employee, and places the focus on job productivity.

An example of this approach may be found in an evaluation form used in U.S. Navy recreation programs, which focuses on task performance. It deals with possible reasons why work is not being satisfactorily accomplished, and suggests appropriate courses of action for dealing with specific situations (see Figure 13–4, p. 268). The implication is that personnel evaluation does more than simply ask whether a recreation leader is performing effectively. It also looks at the way he or she is being used, and examines the total program in a critical but constructive way.

Personnel Actions: Promotion, Transfer, Termination

Based on each employee's record of performance over a period of time, certain administrative actions may be taken.

If the record has been a good one, there should be opportunity for advancement to higher levels of responsibility and pay. Customarily, most civil service

FIGURE 13–4 To Improve Performance

Ask yourself:

1. Exactly what hasn't this person been doing that he/she needs to do?

_____

_____

2. How will he/she and I know when the task is done well enough?

_____

_____

3. Does this person *truly* need to do this task? (If NO, stop here.)

_____

_____

4. Does the task itself *truly* need to be done this way? (If NO, eliminate or change task.)

_____

_____

5. Do any other employees do the task well enough? If yes, what is different about this person from the people who do the task?

_____

_____

6. Has this person ever done this task before anywhere? If yes, what is different here and now from the way it was when the person last did the task?

_____

_____

7. Considering all of the above, what are the most likely reasons WHY this person hasn't been doing what he/she needs to do?

☐ Obstacle   ☐ No advantage   ☐ Doesn't know how

Explain: _____

_____

8. Use the chart below to decide what actions you should take.

If Employee Hasn't Been Doing This Because . . .	And . . .	Then You Should . . .
any reason at all	the task is not truly needed	Eliminate the task
he/she doesn't know why the task is important		Explain how the task fits in the overall picture
he/she doesn't have the tools or equipment		Provide them
the task is unreasonable or complicated		Change the task

If Employee Hasn't Been Doing This Because . . .	And . . .	Then You Should . . .
there isn't enough time to do everything and other tasks are more important		Reassign tasks, get more people, reassign priorities, examine consequences to make sure they reward the right things
he/she is "punished" for doing the task		Remove "punishment," arrange pleasant consequences for completion of the task if possible
he/she is ignored whether or not the task is done		Arrange pleasant consequences (if possible) for doing the task; create unpleasant ones for not doing it
he/she knows what to do but hasn't had enough practice yet to get it right all the time		Provide practice opportunities in off-the-job situations, then on the job with decreasing supervision and assistance
he/she could do it but doesn't know what to do or how well		Tell him/her what to do and how to tell when it's done well enough
he/she knows what to do but doesn't know when to do it		Tell him/her what the cues are that signal "time to begin"
he/she once knew but has forgotten how to do it	he/she will do it frequently	Provide review training
	he/she won't do it often	Provide a job aid to be used when necessary
he/she never knew how	he/she is going to have to do it soon	Provide training

Source: Naval Military Personnel Command, Recreational Service Training Unit, Patuxent River, MD (Courtesy of Pam Crespi, Naval Material Command, Washington, D.C.)

systems provide for automatic advancement—assuming favorable performance—through several steps or increments within a given job series. However, to move to a new and higher series, such as promotion from *leader* to *supervisor,* or *supervisor* to *division director,* normally would require the candidate to meet additional requirements—such as a graduate degree or minimum number of professional courses in recreation—or to take a promotional examination. In some situations, the appropriate personnel action may be transfer to a similar position in another district of the department, or in another division. In some cases, personnel action may be taken resulting in a demotion or suspension for cause, although this is not common. Unsatisfactory performance, retirement, or resignation because of serious illness or to take a position elsewhere may all result in job termination.

In large public and voluntary agencies, procedures for such personnel actions are usually carefully defined in personnel codes or Civil Service operational manuals; often they are defined also in union contracts. As a result, management must often be extremely cautious in taking disciplinary action or transferring individuals when such action may be the subject of a union grievance. Even in the grading of examinations and ranking of candidates, management may be subject to petitions, lawsuits, or other claims of unfair practices, including disagreements with the way examinations were composed or scored. There may be charges of favoritism, political influence, or discrimination. For all these reasons, personnel actions tend to be cumbersome and slow in such organizations, and it is often difficult to promote effective leaders swiftly, because of the rigid seniority system.

In contrast, other types of leisure-service agencies—such as private, commercial, or employee recreation departments—can be quite flexible in making personnel changes, and frequently do so based simply on the judgment of supervisors or other managerial personnel.

JOB ENRICHMENT

A final area of concern within many large public recreation and park departments, as well as in many large voluntary agencies or therapeutic recreation departments, has to do with job enrichment. Particularly when such organizations have a rigid or frozen bureaucratic structure, recreation leaders may tend to get locked into one position and job location over a period of time, with a minimum of change or challenge. This can be extremely detrimental to morale and job performance, particularly if program plans are developed centrally or at a high level in the department, and the recreation leader out in the field or therapist responsible for direct service delivery is simply expected to carry them out.

Many agency managers or supervisors therefore strive to enrich the job experience of employees, both to maintain their morale and motivation at a high level, and to help them contribute more fully to the success of the program. This is done in several ways: (a) every effort should be made to get all employees involved in policy discussions, program planning, and problem-solving, thus encouraging their creative participation; (b) in many cases, leaders may be rotated from job to job at different seasons of the year, or even during a given week or month, by having them work in more than one job setting; (c) the special skills of different leaders and supervisors should be used in in-service training programs, or on committees to plan and carry out district or community-wide special events; and (d) team or task-force approaches should be developed which encourage employees to take an active part in special projects, encouraging a high level of team cooperation and interaction.

In addition, other techniques should be used to maintain effective motivation and morale, and to enhance leader productivity. These techniques may range simply from "stroking," through positive verbal reinforcement, to more formal acts of recognition (employee award banquets or citations for outstanding performance) or rewards, through promotion or salary raises.

Summing up, this chapter describes the entire staff development process in terms of the step-by-step process of recruiting, selecting, orienting, training, supervising, and evaluating personnel. This process might also be looked at from another perspective—that of the young recreation leader himself or herself. The final chapter does this, by examining the professional-to-be's selection of the leisure-service field as a career choice, and exploring the ultimate question, "How does one become a better and more effective leader?"

NOTES

[1]Christopher R. Edginton and John G. Williams, *Productive Management of Leisure Service Organizations: A Behavioral Approach* (New York: John Wiley, 1978), p. 89.

[2]Edginton and Williams, pp. 89–90.

[3]See Douglas McGregor, *The Human Side of Enterprise* (New York: McGraw-Hill, 1960), pp. 33–48.

[4]Karla Henderson and Virginia Goode, "Employee Participation Through Quality Circles," *Parks and Recreation* (January 1984): 74.

[5]James L. Gibson, John M. Ivancevich, and James H. Donnelly, Jr., *Organizations: Behavior, Structure, Processes* (Plano, Tex.: Business Publications, Inc., 1982), p. 269.

[6]*Employee Appraisal System Manual* (Long Beach, Calif.: Recreation Department, 1974).

[7]Michael Teague, "Performance Appraisal: A Bold Plan," *Therapeutic Recreation Journal* (1st Q. 1980): 5.

STUDENT PROJECTS

1. Small groups of students visit leisure-service agencies, to examine their personnel procedures with respect to recruitment and hiring, orientation and in-service education, and similar processes. Report on these to the class, and compare their approaches.
2. Plan role-playing sessions based on the personnel evaluation process, with supervisors "meeting" with leaders and reviewing their past performances. In developing these sessions, which will then be presented to the class, show a diversity of approaches, including both positive and negative types of evaluation methods.
3. Examine the literature with respect to varied theories of employee motivation, and form a panel which reviews the major theories as they apply to work in leisure-service agencies. As a concluding statement, develop appropriate guidelines for staff development and personnel management in this field.

SUGGESTED READINGS

Edith L. Ball and Robert E. Cipriano, *Leisure Services Preparation* (Englewood Cliffs, N.J.: Prentice-Hall, 1978), Module 7.

Christopher R. Edginton and Charles A. Griffith, *The Recreation and Leisure Delivery System* (Philadelphia: W. B. Saunders, 1983), Chapters 6, 7, 9.

Richard Kraus, Gay Carpenter, and Barbara Bates, *Recreation Leadership and Supervision* (Philadelphia: W. B. Saunders, 1981), Chapters 10, 11, 12, 13.

E. William Niepoth, *Leisure Leadership* (Englewood Cliffs, N.J.: Prentice-Hall, 1983), Chapters 10, 11.

H. Douglas Sessoms and Jack L. Stevenson, *Leadership and Group Dynamics in Recreation Services* (Boston: Allyn and Bacon, 1981), Chapters 8, 9, 10.

CHAPTER 14

Building a
Career Foundation and
Becoming a Better Leader

The preceding chapters in this text have examined the basic concepts underlying recreation leadership, group dynamics as an aspect of leisure-service programming, and the roles and functions of recreation leaders. They have presented an overview of popular recreational activities and leadership methods, and have examined the processes of problem-solving and staff development as important agency responsibilities.

This concluding chapter shifts to the direct perspective of the professional-to-be and describes the process of beginning a career in the leisure service field. Finally, it asks, "How does one become a better and more effective leader?" and provides some helpful suggestions and answers to this question.

CHOOSING RECREATION AND PARKS AS A CAREER FIELD

How should the prospective recreation and parks professional explore whether or not this is an appropriate career field, in terms of his or her interests, skills, and ambitions? And what are the most appropriate strategies for actually getting into the field?

Obviously, the individual who has already completed a two- or four-year degree in recreation or one of its specializations—parks management, program supervision, or armed forces, employee, or therapeutic recreation—has already made a career choice. But the high school graduate or college freshman or sophomore who is considering entering this field should look into it thoroughly before making the decision to enter it. This involves both self-examination and a careful study of the field.

Self-Examination

The prospective recreation major should take a hard look at the following questions:

1. Have I shown, by my own involvement in varied types of recreation activities and programs, that I have a real interest in this field? Have I engaged in sports, games, social clubs, arts and crafts, camping, outdoor recreation, and similar activities? Am I really recreation-minded?
2. In groups in which I have been a member, have I played a leadership role? Do I enjoy taking responsibility for planning, organizing, and carrying out program responsibilities? Do I seem to be respected by others, and do they seem to trust me as a leader?
3. Have I taken on leadership roles in other settings? Have I shown interest in the field by doing volunteer work on playgrounds, in hospitals or nursing homes, in Boys' Clubs, or through service organizations? Have I had paid experience, on a part-time or summer basis, which would give me a realistic picture of how well I might function professionally in the recreation field?
4. How about my personality? Do I really enjoy being with people, and can I accept people of many different kinds? Am I patient with others, sensitive to their needs, and able to command their affection and respect? Do I *like* to take on group responsibility and to take the lead in social situations? Am I generally able to get started on projects and to carry through on them without prodding? Would I enjoy doing the kinds of work that a recreation professional does?

Study of the Field

A second important area of knowledge for the prospective professional is the field itself. How much does he or she really know about the kinds of positions that are available, the tasks that are required, the salaries and working conditions, and the availability of openings? While a beginning recreation major might not have *all* the answers to such questions, recognizing too that the field itself changes over a period of time, certainly he or she should have a reasonably accurate picture of career possibilities and options. This can be achieved in the following ways:

1. Personal experience on a volunteer or part-time basis is invaluable in getting a realistic picture of agencies and how they operate. As indicated, many young people have such experience *before* entering a major in recreation; others might get it at a very early point as a beginning field work experience or special class project.
2. It is helpful to talk to friends who work in the field, and get a fuller picture of it from them, or to actually visit a variety of agencies to learn how they operate, and what the leader's responsibilities are.

3. Reading about the field in professional magazines or textbooks provides a general picture of employment trends, programs, current issues, and problems that gives depth to the individual's understanding.
4. Attending professional conferences, meetings, or workshops on a national, regional, or local level will give greater familiarity with the field, and will also provide an opportunity to rub shoulders with practicing professionals.
5. Finally, if the student is already in college, he or she might take one or two courses in recreation as an introduction to the field, which should provide a fuller perspective as the basis for career choice.

AWARENESS OF NEW CAREER OPPORTUNITIES

The prospective professional should also be aware that recreation is an extremely dynamic and rapidly changing field, with many new opportunities opening up, as new forms of leisure involvement become popular. For example, Samuels describes the growth of theme parks which, beginning with the opening of Disneyland in California in 1955, have evolved from passive, entertainment-oriented programming to various other forms of attractions. These include multitheme approaches such as EPCOT Center, parks which rely heavily on thrill rides, participatory or recreation-oriented theme parks, and a number of other variations on these themes. These commercial recreation attractions represent a highly technological, systematized approach to leisure-services delivery, with advanced engineering techniques. At the same time, Samuels writes:

> As more and more leisure service professionals join theme park staffs and existing staffs realize the value of good programming, there has been more traditional recreation programming [such as] festivals and special events.[1]

He concludes that this is an excellent time for leisure service professionals to seek careers in theme parks and related enterprises, for the following reasons:

> . . . increased requirements for recreational programming, the need for humanistically oriented managers and creative thinkers, and the shift from a strictly entertainment/ passive to a participatory orientation in a growing segment of the industry. The best positions for recreators are in general management, personnel management (including employee recreation), and marketing, particularly promotional programming.[2]

Emergence of Leisure Entrepreneurs

As another example of a relatively new professional role, Kunstler describes the emergence of independent entrepreneurs in the field of therapeutic recreation service. In the past, recreation leaders typically were employed on a full-time basis in therapeutic recreation agencies, and most programs were internally generated. In many privately operated hospitals or nursing homes, the practice began to develop of bringing in activity specialists on a per-session basis, to conduct musical, dance, or arts and crafts activities, or perform other leadership tasks. Similarly, many nursing homes employed part-time consultants in recreation who helped them meet state health department certification requirements. Kunstler comments:

> The consultant was employed in order to help overcome the problems caused by understaffing, unqualified staff, lack of resources, low priorities given to the leisure needs of disabled individuals, and limited public awareness of the nature and benefits of therapeutic recreation.[3]

Today, a growing number of private entrepreneurs or companies in the field of therapeutic recreation are providing services ranging from staff-training programs to leisure counseling, program planning and supervision, and packaged activity leadership. Particularly as chains of nursing homes or other health-care facilities developed, the operators of these institutions have used program specialists in a number of different settings, rather than assign them to one location.

These illustrations suggest that young people entering the recreation field should carefully study present trends and, if possible, identify roles and functions that are new and on the upswing in terms of professional adoption—rather than career roles that may be declining throughout the field.

WAYS OF BUILDING A CAREER FOUNDATION

Assuming that the individual enters a degree program, it is extremely important that he or she continue to build personal strengths in the field. Today, not even those who graduate from reputable colleges with degrees in recreation and parks will necessarily find it easy to find a professional position quickly. Those who are well-qualified, capable, and determined will succeed, for a large number of job openings appear each year. However, the poorly qualified or lackadaisical candidate will have difficulty in landing a desirable first job. It is therefore essential to do the following:

1. *Build skills.* The student major in recreation should make every effort, while attending college, to build personal skills. This should not only be in areas of direct leadership, such as sports, games, music, or nature activities, but also in areas of supervisory or administrative functioning. Thus, the graduate who is highly skilled in public relations, and who can write an excellent press release, or prepare and deliver an inspiring slide talk, has a marketable skill. Other important abilities might relate to budget planning and auditing, carrying out surveys, design or maintenance of facilities, or program planning.

2. *Keep Working.* In addition to taking classes, the recreation major should attempt to hold down seasonal and part-time jobs in recreation agencies and programs. Apart from income, this provides additional knowledge about the field, important contacts with professionals that might lead to future job leads, and practical experience that helps to enrich academic courses. Finally, in terms of meeting civil service or other agency requirements that demand previous paid experience, such seasonal and part-time jobs can be extremely helpful.

3. *Be a Professional*. From the outset, the student major should join local, state or national recreation and park organizations. If possible, he or she should take on responsibility in student major clubs, or in joint faculty-student efforts. Such experiences will enrich his or her knowledge of the field, and promote a professional outlook.

4. *Identify Specialization*. Although many authorities feel that the undergraduate major experience should be a broad, nonspecialized one, and that students should only become specialized on the graduate level, there is much to be said in favor of identifying one's area of special interest at an early stage. The college freshman who decides that he or she is interested in working with aging persons can take a special block of courses in geriatrics and gerontology, can do volunteer work in senior centers or nursing homes, and can make this the subject of special course papers and projects. By graduation, he or she is well-equipped to seek a position in the field of recreation for the aging. Similarly, an individual interested in environmental programs, industrial recreation, youth services—or any other specialization—should seek to build this special area of competence as fully as possible.

Seeking the First Position

Assuming that the recreation graduate has looked realistically at himself or herself, and at the field itself, before selecting recreation as a career field, and that a solid career foundation has been built, he or she is ready for the moment of truth when graduation arrives. It should be understood that many graduates with majors in a specific degree program do not necessarily intend to go directly into that field. For example, few history majors today really intend to become historians or history teachers, just as few English majors expect to be writers or English teachers. By the same token, many recreation graduates have taken a degree chiefly to have a college major that was interesting and personally valuable (along with general liberal arts requirements), or because they are interested in the broad field of social service.

However, since recreation is a specialized professional field, it should be assumed that the majority of recreation graduates actually intend to find employment in this field. The following guidelines should be helpful in this effort.

Start Early. The process of looking for a job may take months of preparation—tracking down leads, getting out mailings, answering advertisements, preparing personal résumés, and holding interviews. Many candidates begin early, and have their job by the time graduation rolls around. Even if they have not succeeded in landing a position, they are well along the way in identifying leads, narrowing down choices, and getting their image across to prospective employers.

Prepare Personal Résumé. Many students get initial experience in preparing a personal résumé as part of required field work courses in college. Others do it for the first time when looking for a position after graduation. Résumés should be: (a) complete, covering all important matters, including complete names and addresses of references, dates of employment, institutions attended, etc.; (b) neatly and attractively presented, with professional typing; (c) selective, in that the candidate presents major background information, but not every minor experience or exposure he or she may have had; and (d) positive and upbeat in their presentation.

Identify Job Leads and Sources.   This may be done in several different ways. On the local level, the candidate should do the following: (a) identify all possible leads that appear in newspaper advertisements, professional journals or newsletters, or at conferences, and follow up immediately by sending a résumé and, if the position seems attractive enough, by making a telephone call requesting a personal interview; (b) fill out forms for the college placement office and follow up with applications to job openings that appear on their notices; (c) check regularly with college faculty members to learn whether they have heard of positions; and (d) review all past contacts, including field work and past part-time jobs, to determine if there are openings now or expected in the near future.

A recent doctoral study carried out at Temple University examined the practices of a large number of college and university recreation and leisure studies departments, with respect to placement assistance given to students. Dayton found that a high proportion of faculty members regard placement as an important area of departmental responsibility, and provide considerable assistance to students, by distributing job listings or directly recommending students for openings, by conducting workshops in job-application skills, and by vigorously soliciting job-opening notices from leisure service agencies in their regions.[4] Major students in recreation and parks should expect such forms of assistance from their department faculty members, and should make full use of them.

A second approach to job seeking on the local level is to develop a comprehensive list of appropriate agencies in the area, and to send them a résumé with a cover letter requesting an interview. In some cases, although there may not be an opening at present, this strategy may result in later notification of a job examination being held or an anticipated opening.

Sources of Information on the National Level.   The National Recreation and Park Association carries out regular personnel surveys of municipal, county, special district and state park agencies, and reports manpower findings in *Employ*, a newsletter published nine times each year. This is part of NRPA's employment service package, which many colleges subscribe to, and which also includes job bulletins listing nationwide recreation and park openings, as well as guidelines for the job search process. In a publication of the Society of Park and Recreation Educators, Austin provides useful guides for recreation and park graduates under several headings: Outdoor Recreation (Federal and State levels), Military Recreation, Therapeutic Recreation, and County Extension Service.[5] Several examples follow:

Outdoor Recreation

Federal Level. Federal Civil Service positions include: *Park Technicians* and *Technicians* who work with professional personnel. Technician positions (Grades GS-4 and GS-5) usually require a minimum of an AA degree in recreation, forestry, park management, or similar field.

Outdoor Recreation Planners, Park Managers, or *Park Rangers* usually
require a BS or MS (grades GS-5, GS-7, GS-9).
Foresters, Landscape Architects or similar positions usually require a BS
in a specific degree field (grades GS-5, GS-7, GS-9).

For further information on such positions, apply to the regional office of the
U.S. Forest Service, Soil Conservation Service, National Park Service, Fish and
Wildlife Service, Bureau of Land Management, or other appropriate agency. There are
also regional Federal Job Information Centers which provide job announcements,
publications, pamphlets, and information on how to apply for federal jobs.

For information on seasonal employment as Park Aides, Technicians, or
Rangers, apply to Seasonal Employment Unit, National Park Service, 18th and C
Streets, N.W., Washington, D.C. 20240, for Form 10–139.

State Level. State level positions in outdoor recreation include such titles as
State Park Administrator, or *District* or *Regional Administrators,* which
usually require an MS or BS, and *Park Administrators* at specific sites.
Foresters, Horticulturalists, Recreation Resource Specialists and *Planners,*
which usually require a BS. Other positions, such as Security Officers or
Park Aides, usually require a high school diploma or an AA degree. For
further information, applicants should write the State Department of Natural Resources, Conservation or Parks and Recreation in their home
states.

Military Recreation

For information about military recreation programs, including dependent
youth programs, applicants should write the Civilian Personnel Officer or Special
Services Officer at their local military base. National Offices which can provide
information include:

Department of Defense
Overseas Employment Program
Washington, D.C. 20301

Director, Special Services Div.
(PERS-72)
Chief, Bureau of Naval Personnel
Washington, D.C. 22201

Director
U.S. Army Recreation Services Directorate
HQDA (DAAG-RE)
Washington, D.C. 20314

Directorate for Morale, Welfare and
Recreation (DPMSOC)
Randolph Air Force Base
San Antonio, Texas 78148

Therapeutic Recreation

This covers a very wide range of job opportunities. Several specific examples
of major job categories follow.

Nursing Homes. Nursing homes in all states now employ activity directors.
Requirements vary from state to state and from home to home. Write
state level government agencies, usually State Department of Health, for
position information, or inquire at local nursing homes.

Mental Health and Mental Retardation. In all states, state psychiatric hospitals, schools or developmental centers, and community mental health centers employ therapeutic recreation personnel. Write State Department of Mental Health for information, or inquire at local facility.

Veterans Administration Hospitals. V.A. Hospitals have Recreation Therapy Departments with positions for *Therapeutic Recreation Specialists* and *Recreation Assistants.* For information, inquire at a local facility, or write:

> Chief, Recreation Therapy
> Rehabilitation Medicine Service
> Veterans Administration Central Office
> 810 Vermont Ave., N.W.
> Washington, D.C. 20420

Corrections. Recreation positions in penal and correctional institutions may be explored on the local or state level (State Department of Prisons, Corrections, or Social Services), or by writing:

> U.S. Bureau of Prisons
> Department of Justice
> HOLC Bldg., 101 Indiana Ave. N.W.
> Washington, D.C. 20001

Cooperative Extension Service

The Extension Service is the educational agency of the U.S. Department of Agriculture, and is associated with the land-grant university in each state. Positions available to recreation majors vary from state to state, but job titles include: *Assistant County Agent, Youth Agent* and *Community Development Agent,* which usually require a BS degree, and *Program Assistant,* which usually requires an AA degree. Information on these positions can be gotten through the county extension office, Director of the State Extension Service, or land-grant university in each state.

STRATEGIES FOR SUCCESS

Within each area of specialized career service, different strategies for successfully obtaining a good position apply. At a recent conference on recreation management in the armed forces sponsored by Temple University, it was made clear that there were essentially two tracks to employment—one by going through central channels and the other by applying directly for positions as openings occur at a particular base. Military personnel who were present described the frustrating process that many job applicants went through, because they were not familiar with the procedures, or did not know the key personnel involved.

Within *all* specialized career fields, recreation and park majors would be wise to begin their preprofessional involvement at an early point, by part-time or seasonal work (volunteer, if necessary), and by attending state or regional professional conferences and workshops. Probably the key element that gives one job candidate the edge in terms of applying for desirable openings is solid experience in a similar setting, and being knowledgeable about the job area and the people in it.

Thus, the college recreation major who intends to work in the field of employee recreation would do well to seek out available programs in his or her area, and to apply for part-time, seasonal, or other work with them. At the same time, it would be an excellent idea to join the National Employee Services and Recreation Association, receive its publications, and attend its workshops or conferences.

Similarly, students who hope to work in the field of campus recreation should become active in recreation and other student activities on their own campus, assuming leadership or other supervisory roles wherever possible. Depending on their own interest, they may wish to work in a housing or residential role connected to college dormitories, or scheduling campus concerts or other programs, or taking on an assignment in the college union. Linked to such experience, membership and involvement in the National Intramural Sports Association, College Union International, or similar appropriate organizations would be helpful.

In commercial recreation, which is an extremely broad and diverse field, there are a number of separate membership organizations which relate to special functions such as travel and tourism, the operation of private clubs and sports facilities, health spas, or similar businesses. Again, those planning to work within this field should seek internships or other early work experiences related to their professional goals, and should join appropriate organizations to promote and enrich their experience and employability.

THE MARKS OF A PROFESSIONAL

This chapter has reviewed the development of recreation and park professionals and has described professional qualifications and positions on various levels—along with strategies for entering the field and prospering in it.

At this point, it is appropriate to ask "What sort of person should the successful recreation professional be?" Howard Danford made an excellent statement a number of years ago; here, paraphrased, is part of his description:

1. He/she is motivated primarily by ideals of service rather than by money. He/she is in recreation because he/she loves it, and would not be in any other type of work even if it were available. He/she believes that people, not activities or facilities, are the most important thing in the field, and that the basic purpose of recreation is to enrich the lives of people.

2. He/she is an educated person who has undergone a period of specialized preparation for his/her work. He/she knows the values which should be sought through recreation in a democracy, and is deeply committed to promoting them.

3. He/she constantly seeks to improve himself/herself professionally, and voluntarily joins appropriate societies or associations, pays dues, attends meetings, and contributes both time and energy to furthering the work of the profession and elevating its standards.

4. He/she behaves at all times in such a manner as to enhance the prestige and dignity of the profession. He/she knows that people judge a field by the individuals who are in it, and that his/her professional life and conduct must be regulated by a code of behavior based on ethical and moral principles.

5. The professional man or woman seeks to exclude from the field those who are not qualified to enter it. He/she believes that the state or the profession, or both, should exercise some form of control over those who may enter into at least the most responsible recreation positions. He/she wants no quacks, frauds or unfit individuals in the profession.

6. He/she is a team player, not a prima donna, and prefers cooperation as a way of life. He/she works with all agencies and individuals in the community on matters of common concern. He/she is motivated primarily by the idea of public service and benefit for those who are served.

7. He/she insists on high standards of excellence, and is not satisfied with mediocrity, but is constantly working to upgrade his/her professional performance. He/she is motivated by a spark of divine discontent, seeking perfection although never quite achieving it.

8. And finally, the professional man or woman in recreation enjoys life. He/she has fun, and is no sourpuss, no stuffed shirt, no kill-joy. For how can one lead others in joyous living without living joyously oneself?[6]

When Danford first wrote this description, he referred only to the "professional man." Today, the situation is quite different. Although discrimination clearly existed against women in the past—particularly in high-level recreation and park positions or those that dealt with the administration of resource-based agencies—considerable progress has been made.

All government agencies today practice affirmative action hiring policies, and increasing numbers of women are moving up the ladder into key positions in the leisure-service field. It is apparent that, although subtle forms of discrimination may still exist, capable women today should not hesitate to work toward such goals.

All students who are preparing themselves for leadership roles and further career development in the field of recreation and parks should recognize the need to be *future-oriented*.

Without question, as our society goes through radical changes in terms of economic trends, social values, technological developments, and human life-styles, both leisure availability and the ways in which we provide recreational opportunities will continue to change radically. The key advice, then, to young professionals in this field would be to be open to innovation and change, and to respond to the immense opportunities that exist for them in new and exciting leisure-service agencies and roles.

WAYS OF BECOMING A BETTER LEADER

Finally, as this book draws to a close, it is appropriate to ask, "How does one become a better leader?" Both the young person who is entering or about to enter the field and the more experienced professional should be concerned with the continuing need to examine his or her own performance, and to learn more effective ways of functioning as a leader.

Obviously, there is no magical phrase or magic wand that will bring this desired result about easily. This text has presented numerous concepts, analysis of leadership functions and roles, and techniques for program development or working with participants or other staff members. It suggests appropriate leadership styles and participative management approaches, as well as problem-solving methods and case examples.

In the final analysis, however, the leader must ask himself or herself, ''How well am I doing? What are my strengths and weaknesses? How could I perform more effectively—both for the sake of building my own career and in order to provide better programs and services for others?''

While there are no easy answers to such questions, it is possible to suggest useful ways of approaching them.

1. *Conviction that the Job's Important.* Recreation leadership is a peculiar field in the sense that recreation, play, and leisure have often been disapproved of in past history. Even today, many people have a sense of guilt about spending their time in nonproductive activity, and there is often a limited awareness of the value of organized recreation service or the role played by professional leaders in this field.

For this reason, it is important for the leader to come to grips with his or her own attitude about recreation and leisure. Ideally, he or she should be a recreation enthusiast, in the sense of having a variety of absorbing interests or outlets that help to contribute to the quality and health of his or her own life.

Beyond this, the leader should strive to develop a conviction that the work he or she is carrying on is important and makes a vital contribution both to the lives of participants and to community or agency well-being. This conviction must be based in reality. If the job is not achieving significant outcomes, he or she must strive to make it so, by focusing on personal or community needs, and by initiating programs and services that *are* important.

2. *Using Personal Skills and Qualities to the Fullest.* The leader should take an honest look at himself or herself, and determine the extent to which his or her personal skills and qualities are being used. It is not enough to ''get by,'' using only 50 percent of one's abilities. Instead, the leader needs to feel that all of his or her personal resources and qualities are being challenged and used fully.

This does not mean that the leader must operate at such a frantic or pressured rate that stress and burnout result. It does mean that the job will be more rewarding if it demands the full creative efforts of the individual, and if it brings not only the rewards of monetary pay or security, but also the psychic payments that come from having done one's best and made a real difference in the lives of others.

3. *Recognizing Strengths and Weaknesses.* The previous chapter describes the formal process of personnel evaluation, in which supervisors review the work performance of leaders. Leaders also should seek to evaluate themselves honestly and fully. They should identify and explore their own strengths and weaknesses within various spheres of activity, such as working with others, on-the-job efficiency, direct activity leadership, carrying out administrative tasks, community relations, and similar areas of performance.

When strengths are recognized, it is important to maximize and build on them, in the sense of making them even better and using them fully. The leader who has a knack for enlisting volunteers, planning special events, or teaching a particular skill, should build on that strength and use it as effectively and fully as possible.

On the other hand, weaknesses must not be ignored! The leader should explore why he or she has a particular area of difficulty, and how it can be overcome. If necessary, he or she should seek help from supervisors or agency administrators, by asking, "How can I improve myself in this area of performance? What would you suggest?"

Sometimes simply recognizing a problem will help to suggest the answer; the supervisor may suggest new ways of operating, or strengthening the leader's performance. The leader may wish to set new goals and objectives, to develop new routines, or to take special training within a given area of job responsibility. If and when a weakness can be transformed into a strength, a major roadblock will have been overcome on the way to becoming an outstanding leisure-service professional.

4. *Using Self-Management Techniques.* Many otherwise capable individuals tend to handicap themselves by poor self-management techniques. They procrastinate, feel that they are excessively burdened with petty tasks, and that they are on a never-ending treadmill of deadlines and projects. Paperwork piles up and phone calls go unanswered; department reports are late in being submitted, and the individual feels increasingly unable to cope.

Often the answer to such problems is simply to develop a better system for managing one's time. At the outset, it helps to maintain a diary which shows how the work time is actually spent over a week or two. This may immediately reveal if time is being spent fruitlessly, with meaningless tasks or wasted effort.

Beyond this, it is important to develop a system for getting work done efficiently. This may involve keeping a visible record of specific tasks that are to be accomplished by set deadlines, and crossing them off as they get done. It may involve putting periods of time aside to accomplish certain jobs, such as preparing reports, correspondence, or requisitioning supplies. It may involve recognizing where time is being wasted, and cutting ruthlessly into such activities. Often, it means that the leader must decide not to procrastinate—but to get going immediately on certain tasks that may be viewed as difficult or distasteful.

Sometimes the leader must learn to say "no," rather than try to please everybody by undertaking every possible assignment. Some tasks may be delegated or shared. Job responsibilities may be placed in a priority order, and less important tasks may be postponed, if necessary. In large measure, the task of self-management is one of being orderly. Instead of having memos, schedules, notes, equipment, files, and similar materials in a hopeless jumble, if the individual can organize these aspects of the work environment so that they are easily accessible and in a well-organized state, this will help in the total job performance.[7]

5. *Effective Relations with Others.* Probably the key to the total functioning of the recreation leader involves his or her relationships with others. The leader who is outgoing, friendly, interested, and supportive is likely to find that others respond positively. The leader who is secretive, cautious, distant, and critical will often find that others behave toward that person in the same way. The leader who initiates or develops cliques that freeze out others may himself or herself be frozen out. The leader who manipulates or is dishonest about his or her motivations will usually find that others cannot be counted on.

Both common sense and research in social psychology suggest that the most effective supervisers are those who trust others, praise them, delegate responsibility, and are confident in the outcomes. Leaders should therefore avoid being overdefensive, and should not play games. Honesty and openness are key attributes, whether one is working with a group of children, co-workers, or a community recreation advisory group. Beyond this, enthusiasm, warmth, and energy will communicate themselves to others, and encourage similar behavior on their part.

6. *Being True to Oneself.* Some views of leadership see it as a charismatic, high-energy, dynamic kind of role. In their eyes, the most effective leaders are those who are "showy," outgoing, forceful, and intense—almost as one might think of a circus ringmaster or a high-pressure used-car salesperson. In contrast, others see effective leaders as being persons who are quiet, thoughtful, nondirective, and concerned with hearing others, being sensitive to their needs and feelings, and functioning chiefly as enablers, rather than managers or teachers.

Which approach is best? The answer is both and neither, or in the words of the television show, "Different strokes for different folks." While it is obvious that different job situations may place a premium on certain kinds of leadership skills or qualities, the reality is that people must be themselves and function in ways in which they feel comfortable. Obviously, recreation leaders are likely to be most effective if they are reasonably outgoing, personable, and warm as human beings. Beyond this, however, they should feel free to present themselves in the most honest and sincere way possible, and be confident that this will work.

Summing up, leaders are encouraged to strive constantly for self-improvement and—probably most important—to enjoy what they are doing. If they see their work as challenging, entertaining, and significant, and if they invest themselves fully in the process of program planning and group leadership, their participants and fellow employees will undoubtedly respond in the same way.

NOTES

[1]Jack B. Samuels, "Theme Parks: Program Variety and Employment Options," *Parks and Recreation* (November 1983): 61.

[2]Samuels: 62.

[3]Robin Kunstler, "Entrepreneurship in Therapeutic Recreation," *Parks and Recreation* (November 1983): 64.

[4]William Dayton, *A Study of Placement Practices in Four Year Recreation and Park Curricula* (Philadelphia: Temple University Doctoral Dissertation, 1983).

[5]David R. Austin, "Creating a Stronger Job Market," in Donald C. Weiskopf, ed., *Proceedings of the 1975 Society of Park and Recreation Educators Institute* (Arlington, Va.: Society of Park and Recreation Educators, 1975), pp. 29–32.

[6]Adapted from Howard G. Danford, "The Marks of a Professional Man in Recreation," *Journal of Health, Physical Education and Recreation* (November 1960): 31.

[7]See Stephen J. Virgilio and Paul S. Krebs, "Effective Time Management Techniques," *Journal of Physical Education, Recreation and Dance* (April 1984): 68, 73.

STUDENT PROJECTS

1. Each student is asked to review his or her own interest in the field of leisure service, along with his or her level of motivation, specialized career interests, and degree of past experience. These may then be shared with other students in small group discussion sessions, which examine students' uncertainties or areas of indecision, and suggest new ways of strengthening their career foundations.
2. As a class exercise, students may prepare a chart describing each of the eight types of recreation and park agencies presented in Chapter 4, including the kinds of professional opportunities offered and roles that leaders play in it. This breakdown is then discussed by the class, including the positive and negative elements surrounding employment in each type of sponsoring agency.
3. Students individually review their own professional involvement, including both past and present volunteer and paid experiences, and membership or other participation in professional societies or conferences. As in Project 1, they may then discuss their own situations and plans for the future with other students in small-group buzz sessions.

SUGGESTED READINGS

Reynold E. Carlson, Janet R. MacLean, Theodore R. Deppe, and James S. Peterson, *Recreation and Leisure: The Changing Scene* (Belmont, Calif.: Wadsworth, 1979), Chapters 14, 15, 16.

Richard Kraus, Gay Carpenter, and Barbara Bates, *Recreation Leadership and Supervision* (Philadelphia: W. B. Saunders, 1981), Chapters 1, 2.

H. Douglas Sessoms, *Leisure Services* (Englewood Cliffs, N.J.: Prentice-Hall, 1984), Chapters 10, 11.

Donald C. Weiskopf, *Recreation and Leisure: Improving the Quality of Life* (Boston: Allyn and Bacon, 1982), Chapters 7, 8.

Guides for Training Conference

In-service workshops, conferences, planning sessions, or study groups are essential to the improvement of recreation leadership. The following outline illustrates a typical three-day Playground Leader's Workshop, prior to the beginning of a Summer Recreation Program. It is attended by all regular staff members, but focuses on the preparation of temporary summer personnel. It is held in late June, in a large community center with an adjacent playfield.

First Day	*Introduction to Department*
9:00 A.M.–9:30 A.M.	Registration period.
9:30 A.M.–10:00 A.M.	Opening message by Director of Department. He outlines the Workshop schedule and introduces its staff.
10:00 A.M.–11:30 A.M.	Presentation of philosophy of department. Its role in the civic structure is examined, along with other municipal services. Basic procedures and regulations for recreation employees are presented, along with rules for clothing, behavior, public relations, legal responsibilities, and similar topics.
11:30 A.M.–NOON	Questions and discussion.
NOON–1:00 P.M.	Box lunch.
1:00 P.M.–2:30 P.M.	Departmental structure is presented, and key personnel are introduced: supervisors, specialists, maintenance personnel, etc. Each explains his or her role, and how he or she will work with summer leaders.

2:30 P.M.–3:00 P.M.	Presentation of color slides of previous summer's program, including highlights in different areas of city, tournaments, special events, and trip programs.
3:00 P.M.–4:00 P.M.	Program objectives and needs and interests of different age groups are analyzed. Then the actual schedule of activities followed in general by playground directors, is presented:

1. daily schedule, with typical time blocks
2. weekly schedule, with special themes and weekly programs
3. special events, trips, and culminating activities
4. use of citywide specialists

Second Day   *Program Activities*

9:30 A.M.–10:00 A.M.	Analysis of effective leadership methods and teaching techniques in the area of physical recreation activities.
10:00 A.M.–NOON	Mass demonstration and participation in games and sports: low organization and lead-up games, softball, track and field, volleyball, badminton, and other widely used activities.
NOON–1:00 P.M.	Box lunch.

Three one-hour workshop-demonstrations in special activities like:

1:00 P.M.–2:00 P.M.	nature programming, arts and crafts, dramatics
2:00 P.M.–3:00 P.M.	dance, trip programming, science exploration
3:00 P.M.–4:00 P.M.	special events, music, rainy day programs

In each one-hour session, a specialist introduces activities, and playground leaders participate in them. At each hour, they attend a different workshop.

Third Day   *Departmental Regulations and Procedures*

9:30 A.M.–11:00 A.M.	Accident prevention, safety, and first aid are presented. First aid procedures for minor injuries are demonstrated by a Red Cross specialist. Municipal attorney outlines procedures to be followed in case of more serious accidents. These include, according to the situation, calling the playground director, police, an ambulance, and the parents of the child.

Proper use of playground equipment, and necessary procedures for trip programs are presented.

11:00 A.M.–NOON	Examination of departmental forms: (a) attendance reports, and reports for special programs (b) supply requisition forms

(c) accident report forms

(d) damage or vandalism report forms

(e) payroll procedures and schedules

(f) insurance procedures and forms

NOON–1:00 P.M.   Box lunch.

1:00 P.M.–2:00 P.M.   Analysis of leadership role on playground:

1. maintaining discipline and control
2. providing guidance to children; working with "problem" youngsters
3. working with volunteer leaders or parents
4. community relations role of playground leader

2:00 P.M.–3:00 P.M.   Questions and discussion.

3:00 P.M.–4:00 P.M.   Issuance of materials and supplies.

Announcement of weekly training session, to be held on midweek evening for all playground leaders, in community center. Includes social hour, for *leaders'* recreation.

Closing remarks by Director—"looking forward to successful summer."

INDEX